Madams

BAWDS &
BROTHEL-KEEPERS
of LONDON

Madams

BAWDS &
BROTHEL-KEEPERS
of LONDON

FERGUS LINNANE

The
History
Press

First published in 2005
This edition first published in 2009

The History Press
The Mill, Brimscombe Port
Stroud, Gloucestershire, GL5 2QG
www.thehistorypress.co.uk

British Library Cataloguing in Publication Data.
A catalogue record for this book is available from the British Library.

ISBN 978 0 7509 3307 0

Typesetting and origination by The History Press
Printed in Malta

CONTENTS

ACKNOWLEDGEMENTS

I am grateful to Alex Warner of the Museum of London for permission to use extracts from his unpublished manuscript 'Immoral Earnings, Eighteenth-century Style'. Dr Sheila O'Connor of the British Museum was unfailingly helpful. My editors at Sutton, Christopher Feeney and Clare Jackson, showed grace under fire.

INTRODUCTION

Bawds are the impresarios of the sex industry. While courtesans and whores are the adored and spoilt darlings of the profession, the hard-working bawds stay in the background, setting the scene, choosing the cast, creating a fantasy that accords with the fantasies of men. They recruit and groom the star performers, the young women who are the industry's lifeblood. Over the centuries the great London bawds launched young beauties, often born poor and with looks their only obvious assets, on careers that ended in marriage with men of importance and social standing. The most obvious example is Elizabeth Armistead, who married the Whig leader Charles James Fox in 1795 after a long career on the town. Others, including Nancy Parsons and Harriet Powell, married into the aristocracy.

The trade has flourished in London since Roman times. Its heydays were the eighteenth and nineteenth centuries. For about two hundred years the sex industry was the biggest employer of women in London after domestic service. Estimates of the numbers of prostitutes at the end of the eighteenth century vary widely, but Patrick Colquhoun, founder of the Thames River Police, put the figure at 50,000 in 1796. So the industry was an economic powerhouse. 'In 1782 it was reckoned that the eight leading courtesans were spending at least £3,000 a year each' – £285,000 today (I.M. Davis, 1986). One of these women, Sophia Baddeley, got through money at a prodigious rate, and when her friend and biographer Mrs Steele suggested she should cut back and dress on £100 (£8,550 today) per annum, replied: 'Christ, that is not enough for millinery!' (K. Hickman, 2003). The more numerous women in the rank immediately below each spent almost as much. Dan Cruikshank has suggested that towards the end of the eighteenth century London's sex industry was worth around £10.4 million a year (BBC History website). At the same time the city's building trade was worth about £4.5 million. The money went on maintaining houses, servants, carriages, horses, clothes and jewellery, the finest food and drink. London's luxury trades depended on free-spending courtesans and the numerous kept women. The building trade itself would perhaps have slumped without the stimulus provided by bawds renting expensive new houses as brothels, particularly in the St James's area.

This is the story of how a group of forceful, intelligent and often ruthless businesswomen turned what had been a squalid and sometimes dangerous business into one that compared with the best that Paris had to offer. During periods in history when there were few opportunities for enterprising women they set up luxurious establishments providing the best food and drink and a background of perfumed sumptuousness. They attracted the highest in the land, including royalty. The great bawds, Mother Needham, Mother Wisebourne, Charlotte Hayes among others – until the middle of the eighteenth century bawds were sometimes known as Mother, although most would have made rather heartless parents – provided them with an unfailing supply of young beauties. Some they found in orphanages, some were bought from their parents. The vicious Mother Needham hung around the coaching inns to spot young girls arriving from the country in search of work. Mother Wisebourne specialised in curing her girls of the pox and re-virginising them. Charlotte Hayes, greatest of the late eighteenth-century bawds and friend of the future King George IV, remarked that 'a maidenhead is as easily made as a pudding'.

Of course, this being London, the veneer of taste and manners was thin, and the innate wildness of the city kept breaking through. At times of moral panic bribes could fail, and even the leading harlots and the great bawds were in danger of being thrown into the city's prisons for debt, riot and keeping disorderly houses. Mother Needham died after a spell in the pillory. Sally Salisbury, the first acknowledged Toast of the Town, died in prison after stabbing her lover in a jealous quarrel. There were other dangers: young Sophia Baddeley, so loved and famous that the audience at a London theatre stood to applaud her in her box one night in 1771, died broke and a drug addict less than twenty years later, her fabulous wealth squandered. Lucy Cooper, a Great Impure whose sexual and alcoholic exuberance were uncommon even for her time and profession, died in miserable poverty. Nevertheless, some bawds lived into prosperous old age and the best brothels in St James's and the *bagnios* around Covent Garden were usually safe from police raids because the Establishment used them. If the Church was the Tory Party at prayer, the luxury brothels were the Establishment *in flagrante*. With the upper classes 'more permissive than in any subsequent generation until the twentieth century', new money from what was at that time probably the strongest economy in the world poured into London's vice industry (I.M. Davis, 1986).

Harlots at the very top of their profession had all the allure of today's media celebrities, their fans able to keep up with their comings and goings in the papers in sections headed 'Cytherean Intelligence'. On 2 July 1784 the *Morning Post* reported: 'Kensington Gardens and the Park Promenades were yesterday exceedingly crowded. The latter particularly, in the evening, exhibited a very grand show of the Cyprian corps in the proper uniform.' The same fans could gawp as the fair Impures arrived at the theatres in the splendid carriages of their aristocratic keepers. To a pretty young street girl there was no greater incentive than to see one of her own kind and class dressed in rich silks and being treated like a lady; it was one of the complaints of the righteous against the eighteenth-century courtesan Kitty Fisher that more girls had been corrupted by her display of luxury than by all the rakes of the town. It was the age of 'Almighty Curtezan, that glorious insolent thing' in the words of the seventeenth-century playwright Aphra Behn.

Their sexual allure, so intangible, so mysterious, has not survived well in paintings or the printed word. Kitty Fisher looks commonplace in some of Reynolds's portraits, although a painting of 1765 by Nathaniel Hone does catch something of her beauty. Sophia Baddeley, who drove the town wild for a few years in the 1770s before her brief candle burned out, looks unappealing in the pictures I've seen. Yet the Duke of Ancaster told her that she was 'absolutely one of the wonders of the age . . . no man can gaze on you unwounded. You are in this respect like the Basilisk, whose eyes kill those whom they fix on.' Cora Pearl, one of the *grandes horizontales* of the nineteenth century, looks ugly and drab in photographs. Yet even those who agreed she was ugly testified to her extraordinary sexual allure. Elizabeth Armistead, who after a career on the town married the Whig leader Charles James Fox – a singularly happy marriage – looks stately rather than beautiful. Perhaps beauty alone was not enough: D. Shaw, author of *London in the Sixties*, said of Nelly Fowler, another mid-Victorian temptress: 'This beautiful girl had a natural perfume so delicate, so universally admitted, that love-sick swains paid large sums for the privilege of having their handkerchiefs placed under the Goddess's pillow, and sweet Nelly pervaded – in spirit if not in the flesh – half the clubs and drawing rooms of England.'

One evening in the 1760s the great womaniser Casanova was introduced to Kitty Fisher in a St James's brothel. She was waiting for a duke who was to conduct her to a ball, and was resplendent in diamonds worth 500,000 francs. In his *History of My Life* Casanova says he was told that pending the duke's arrival he might have her for 10 guineas. He claims he declined, but a probably more reliable version of the story has her snubbing him, Kitty making it clear that she never accepted less than £50. On another occasion she set her minimum rate at £100 (about £9,200 today). It was a good time to be a high-class whore in the capital.

This book is a history of almost a thousand years of bawdry, charting its rise and fall, for the joyless massage parlours and anonymous suburban brothels of today surely represent a nadir, having little to offer compared to the veritable temples of love of centuries past.

NOTE ON CURRENCIES

In 1720, £1 had the purchasing power of about £113 today, in 1820 about £55 and in 1920 about £24 – very roughly halving every hundred years.

ONE

MY BOUNCING LASSES

Jack Harris, arch manipulator of London's eighteenth-century sex industry, boasted: 'The whole amount of the Charge against me is that I am a Pimp . . . I grant it. I need not be ashamed of the Profession from its Antiquity. Nay!' It is unlikely that Harris, compiler of that rough guide to whoredom the *List of Covent Garden Ladies*, knew quite how immemorial the profession was, or that in 1161 when King Henry II guaranteed the Bishop of Winchester's right to exploit the eighteen brothels on Bankside in Southwark for the next 400 years it was said that the area had already been associated with brothels or stews 'since time out of mind'. Most of the Bankside brothels of the twelfth century were run by men, but by Harris's time it was unusual for them to play such a prominent role, and Harris was himself something of an anomaly. By then men were the exploited consumers and women were asserting themselves as the rightful proprietors of an industry peculiarly suited to their expertise.

Court records for the medieval period throw a fitful light on the business of selling sex. In 1438 a woman named Margaret was accused of procuring a young girl named Isobel Lane and forcing her to prostitute herself with Lombards and others in the brothels of Bankside and elsewhere. Margaret, clearly a procuress, perhaps in a big way of business, was also accused of taking a girl named Joan Makelyn to a house in the parish of St Colemanstreet for sex with a Lombard who paid her 12*d* (about £17), out of which Joan had to pay Margaret 4*d* for the introduction. Nor was Joan an innocent victim – she introduced Margaret to a 'very prodigal Venetian'. The report of the case says that 'both women for a long time taking no thought for the safety of their souls had carried on this base and detestable manner of life'. Not much later the poet John Skelton (*c*. 1460–1529), tutor to the future Henry VIII, mentions in *Hickescorner* a brothel called the Hartshorne whose resident whores Kate, Bess, Sybil and Jane were 'all full pretty and wanton . . . [they] will make you weary!'

There were regular attempts to confine prostitution to a few official red-light districts – as early as 1240 the aptly named Cock Lane in Smithfield became the first legal promenade for whores – but records also show that whoredom quickly burst any bounds set by the authorities. From Bankside and the old brothel areas of the City, particularly Gropecuntlane by Old Jury and Cock Lane, vice spread into the new suburbs. When Henry VIII closed the licensed brothels on Bankside in 1546 because syphilis was rampant, the girls were dispersed and harlotry spread far and wide. In 1640 the ballad 'The Merrie Man's Resolution' used the conceit of a young man bidding farewell to the city's women of pleasure to survey the whole of London's sex industry. He includes the new suburbs:

> Farewell to the Bankside
> Farewell to Blackman's Street
> Where with my bouncing lasses
> I oftentimes did meet . . .
> And all the smirking wenches
> That dwell in Redriff town . . .
> Now farewell to St Giles
> That standeth in the Fields
> And farewell to Turnbul Street
> For that no comfort yields.
> In Whitecross Street and Golden Lane
> Do strapping lasses dwell
> And so there do in every street
> Twixt that and Clerkenwell.
> At Cowcross and at Smithfield
> I have much pleasure found
> Where wenches like to fairies
> Did often trace the ground.
> Farewell! Luthner ladies, for they have got the Pox
> Farewell the Cherry garden – for evermore Adieu!

St Giles, later the location of the most notorious of all the rookeries or criminal ghettoes, was then far to the west of the City; in the nineteenth century it was partly demolished to make way for the building of New Oxford Street. Turnbull Street, another stronghold of whoredom, was in the Farringdon Road–Clerkenwell Green area. Redriff was Ratcliff: the Ratcliffe Highway was for many years the haunt of low seamen's women, the poorest and most drunken of all their kind. Lewkners (Luthner) Lane, now Macklin Street, was called Dirty Lane. In 1722, the historian Lord Macaulay wrote of 'country squires coming up to London and resorting to painted women, the refuse of Lewknor's Lane and Whetstone Park [who] pass themselves off as countesses!' Whetstone Park, at the northern end of Lincoln's Inn Fields, was described as a 'receptacle for wanton does'. It was there, years earlier, that the great seventeenth-century bawd, Mother Elizabeth Creswell, had a brothel. 'The Merrie Man's Resolution' also mentions the Cherry Garden near the present-day Trafalgar Square. Here the celebrated Mother Cunny had a brothel convenient for the gallants of the royal court. She too had an establishment in Whetstone Park.

The Merrie Man, who seems so companionable and well-informed, mentions Bankside first, and we can retrace his steps to meet its most famous bawd.

TWO

MOTHER HOLLAND
A DECEIVING BAWD

The medieval whores Margaret, Isobel and Joan could have plied their trade at any period: the basics don't change. What did change was the background for dalliance. The first brothels were spartan, judging by early illustrations. In the seventeenth century rising standards of bourgeois taste and comfort led clients to expect more than rough food and drink, a bed and a whore. Rooms became better furnished, and we can tell from early engravings that in high-class brothels music became more important. The girls were expected to be able to sing and play, and perhaps hold their own in conversation on the topics of the day. Some were prized for their mastery of foreign languages as there were foreign clients among the merchants and embassies. The food, drink and furnishings approximated to what rich clients were used to in their own homes and prices rose to reflect this.

The first luxury brothel we know of in detail is the Holland's Leaguer on Bankside. The bawd was Elizabeth Holland, who was born in about 1570. Like some noted bawds of a later era – Mother Cresswell, Mother Wisebourne – Holland came from a comfortable middle-class background. Her doting parents, who lived in the north of England, sent the headstrong child to the care of a wealthy family in London, where she was to be given a veneer of metropolitan sophistication. Instead, her earliest biographer says, she proved wild and ungovernable. She married very young and then misbehaved serially with her husband's wealthy friends. Soon she was the mistress of 'a rich and handsome young Italian merchant' who had little difficulty in persuading the willing youngster that she should be paid for what she had hitherto so enthusiastically given for free. Her uninhibited enjoyment quickly made Elizabeth a star of the sexual underworld and a wealthy woman, but seeing the high casualty rate among whores at a time when venereal diseases were more potent and ubiquitous than ever, she decided to get out while she still had her health and looks.

Even without the hazards of her profession, women lost their looks young – they were often referred to as worn out in their forties. In 1632 her anonymous biographer says she decided it was better to be 'no more a bewitching whore but a deceiving bawd . . . the sins of others shall maintain her sin' and duly opened her first establishment, in Duke Humphreys Rents by Puddle Dock in the City. The building seems to have been an old castle – in *Queen of the Bawds* Burford speculates that it was the former royal property Baynards Castle. She redecorated it, making it 'wonderous gaudie and handsome'. She then set about recruiting the 'living furniture', not least important among whom was a suitable bruiser to act as doorman, in this case a man she had somehow 'saved from the gallows'; with a nice classical touch she called him her Cerberus. Her Hades, however, needed a large staff – of women, maids, waitresses, laundresses and so on, strong young women who although not of the most attractive would not shame the house if called upon in an emergency to take their clothes off and satisfy a client. Finally there were the indispensables, 'petulant, paynted and halfe-gilded'. Her chronicler says that these women she 'brought up whole sale from the country. There needed not much search: sinne is found in every corner.' There were several good reasons for providing fresh goods. Jaded roués liked new faces, and the girls' inexperience was to some extent an insurance against venereal disease. On the other hand, they would need careful training before they were ready to receive clients.

During her apprenticeship Elizabeth had seen the best the vice industry had to offer, and knew she could do better. The customers would be fleeced to the very skin, but with taste and style. Above all, they would be sent away happy. She knew that the combination of drink and sexual frustration could be lethal. Her girls were taught crisis management – the skill of disengaging before the client reached for his dagger and began to break the furniture. The girls were also taught how to get the clients to buy expensive food and drink, and to wheedle a generous 'present' out of them.

Word spread quickly about this new sexual Elysium and it was soon 'crammed like Hell itself where wicked creatures lay bathing themselves in Lust'. The food was particularly good, and 'the visitants came flocking so fast that her kitchen was ever flaming'. But success brought problems. Other long-established brothels were suffering as their clients deserted them to favour her, girls dismissed from her establishment complained that she had treated them badly, and she was rapacious. Worse, the Puritans of the City were alerted by the sounds of people enjoying themselves. After she had opened another establishment in Finsbury the Lord Mayor and the aldermen were persuaded to act, and in November 1597 one Elizabeth Holland was arrested 'for evil and loose turpitude' and keeping a brothel. The sentence was the 'carting' that had been the penalty for whores and bawds for hundreds of years, although she seems to have been spared the lashing at 'the cart's arse' which was usually part of the punishment.

> It is adjudged by the court that she shall be put into a cart at Newgate and be carted with a paper on her head showing her offence from thence to Smithfield from thence to her house from thence to Cornhill from thence to the Standard in Cheap from thence to Bridewell and all the way basins to be rung before her, at Bridewell to be punished. From thence to be brought to Newgate there to remain until she have paid a fine of £40 [£4,100 today] or put in sureties for the same and to be bound to her good behaviour . . .

So Elizabeth soon found herself in another kind of hell, Newgate Prison, which stood on the site of the present Old Bailey. It was a pestilential death-trap, and good citizens crossed the road as they passed it, such was the ghastly stench that pervaded the area. In 1719, nearly two hundred years later, Captain Alexander Smith would write: 'Newgate is a dismal prison . . . a place of calamity . . . a habitation of misery, a confused chaos . . . a bottomless pit of violence, a Tower of Babel where all are speakers and no hearers.' Jail fever was rife, and about thirty of the inmates died each year. In 1750 two prisoners with typhus were taken from the prison to court at the Old Bailey where they proceeded to infect everyone in the courtroom – among those who died

were the judge, all the trial lawyers, all the jurymen and many spectators. Because of the dangers physicians refused to enter the jail. Yet
for those inmates with hard cash – known as rhino – almost anything
might be bought, including sex. Drink brewed inside the prison was
freely available; mainly gin, it was known among other names as 'Kill-
Grief', 'Comfort' and 'Meat and Drink'.

Prisoners without money starved: young girls traded their bodies for a
crust while older women facing the death sentence gave sex free, in the
hope of getting pregnant and so being able to 'plead their bellies' – pregnant women were not hanged. The playwright and magistrate Henry
Fielding called Newgate 'a prototype of hell'.

Elizabeth's wealth protected her from Newgate's worst abuses, and
before her trial she escaped with the help of friends in high places who
no doubt had been among her customers. The corrupt old Keeper was
bribed and Elizabeth slipped into the monastery of the Grey Friars,
which stood next to the prison and where the monks were happy to
grant sanctuary to so beautiful and rich a young woman. Within days she
had left the monastery, and the City's jurisdiction. We can deduce from
the lack of any record of further proceedings against her that she got off
with a large fine. It was time to start earning again.

Elizabeth had learned a valuable lesson. If her friends were powerful so were her enemies, and she was not safe in the City. She had
spent a large part of her fortune on her escape and in negotiating a
laissez passer with the authorities. It had become necessary to move
her operations beyond the reach of the law. 'She will no more trust
old ruins, or religious neighbours. The one will endure no batterie;
the other will abide no bad dealing.' Its freedom from vexatious City
regulations drew her to Bankside, across the river in the unregulated
badlands of Southwark, where she was advised that the Paris Gardens
Manor House, then a deserted ruin, might suit her.

At length she is informed of a place . . . being wonderous commodious
planted for all accommodations. It was out of the City yet in view of the
City, divided only by a delicate river; there were many handsome buildings
and many hearty neighbours . . . yet at first foundation it was renowned for

nothing so much as the memory of that famous Amazon, Longa Margarita, who had for many years kept a famous infamous house of open hospitality.

(*Holland's Leaguer*, 1632)

This is a reference to Long Megg of Westminster, an almost legendary bawd reputed to have been nearly 7 feet tall and with the physique of a prize-fighter. The customers quailed before her wrath. Burford (1973) says she is referred to by the religious writer William Vaughan in his tract *The Golden Grove*:

Some bawds have a dozen damsels, some less, yet of every man they take largely, as 20 shillings a week or ten pound a month. It is said that Long Megg of Westminster kept always twenty courtesans in her house, who by their pictures she sold to all comers . . .

A 2d chapbook which appeared in 1582, *Long Meg of Westminster*, undermines the myth somewhat. It has Megg wandering the streets of London by night in men's clothing, taking on men and beating them in fair fight. However, she marries a soldier and vows to be a submissive wife. 'It behoveth me to be Obedient to you, and, never shall be said, though I cudgel a Knave, that Long Meg shall be her Husband's Master.' Not sentiments that would have appealed to Elizabeth Holland.

Long Megg, who was reputedly buried in Westminster Abbey, was by now long dead, but the provenance of the ruined mansion was no doubt a spur to Elizabeth's ambitions. She wanted to be rich and independent, and she also wanted to be Queen of the Bawds, an important figure in her own right. So, sometime between 1599 and 1602 – the lease document is missing – she went to see the ruin, known then as the Paris Gardens Manor House. Later it would be known as the Holland's Leaguer after it was besieged – beleaguered – by officers of the law.

A fort citadel or mansion house so fortified and environed about with all manner fortifications that ere any foe could approach it he must march more than a musket shot on a narrow bank where three could not march abreast:

betwixt two dangerous ditches . . . and behind, a drawbridge . . . then a world
of other bulwarks rivers ditches trenches and outworks which hemmed in the
orchards . . . making one capable of . . . every fight to go on for many hours to
play with an army.

This moated mansion with gatehouse, drawbridge and other out-
buildings was proof against surprise raids by the authorities, and from
Elizabeth's point of view it was in an ideal neighbourhood – the centre
of London's entertainments industry. The Globe and Swan theatres
were nearby, there were bear- and bull-baiting rings, taverns and brothels. Elizabeth didn't fear competition: she planned to attract customers
away from longer-established houses. And many of her best customers
lived just a short distance away across the river in the City. She leased
the mansion from the Queen's cousin Lord Hunsdon, which must have
assured her of a measure of immunity. Hunsdon, incidentally, ran a male
brothel, 'a house of beasts', in Hoxton-next-Shoreditch.

Elizabeth, by now known as Mother Holland, duly acquired the mansion
and turned the gardens into a pleasant backdrop for dalliance. There were
walks with trees and shrubberies, prefiguring the pleasure gardens at
Vauxhall and Ranelagh. Above all it could be defended, for Elizabeth had
already decided that if she was raided again she was going to put up a fight.

During her time as a fugitive Elizabeth had pondered her mistakes.
She had made and spent a fortune, and she now realised that she could
have made more. The secret was to provide an incomparable service, and
to admit only the richest clients. Her biographer says:

> Her wine, though more in measure, yet shall be drunk in lesser glasses: her
> music shall speak sharply and just as sweetly, but not so loud: her wenches shall
> be fair and handsome, yet but few in number . . . for when supplies are want-
> ing she knows how to fetch them from places of fair reputation: her ordinary
> servants shall be comely and industrious . . . and when extremity come upon
> her, she shall have disguises to make them appear half-angels . . .

In other words, she would have a small core of fine whores, and when
demand outstripped supply the 'comely' servants could double as whores.

Her customers, among whom were King James I and his favourite, George Villiers, Duke of Buckingham, all agreed with her catchphrase 'This Chastitie is clean out of date, a mere obsolete thing'. A Roxburghe ballad, 'The Kinde Beleevynge Hostesse', compares a rival brothel to Holland's Leaguer. In it the bawd extols her girls Bess and Dolly, 'brave wenches stout and jollye . . .' and the ballad continues:

If you on sport be eager
and that you will not swagger
Kind Gentleman
you need not then
go unto Holland's Leaguer.
For Wenches she can get yee
and of all sorts, can fit yee;
most bravely cladde
as may be hadde
if leisure but permit yee
A girl attired in Sattin
can speke both French and Latin.
If you have gold
you may be bold
and have a fine room to chatte in.
A country Lass that's pritty
or one fetched from the Cittie
or, for your sport
one tall one short –
a handsome lasse that's witty.

London probably never produced a more rapacious bawd than Elizabeth Holland. She fleeced her customers more expertly and completely than a modern clip joint, but with style. A rueful customer recalled a visit to her brothel in what is virtually a tribute to Mrs Holland's expertise:

At Holland's Leaguer there I fought
But there the service proved too hot!

MADAMS: BAWDS & BROTHEL-KEEPERS of LONDON

Then from the Leaguer returned I
Naked, cold, hungry and dry.

(In Burford, *Orrible Synne*)

It is unlikely that the gallant was really left hungry and dry. The Leaguer employed a large and expert staff – cooks, wine waiters or 'apple squires' who would see that the customer's glass was always full, scullions, laundresses – and, of course, whores. Mrs Holland's four resident girls were acknowledged to be of the very best. Apart from their expertise they were chosen to be very different from one another, and intended to suit different moods. Beta Brestonia, 'impudent above all measure and insolent beyond comparison' was a fiery giant and clearly a bit of a challenge. However, for those who could stand the pace she had the reputation of giving very good value for money. Next was Eliza Caunce: 'By chance her father begot her; by chance he forsook her; by chance she turned whore; and by chance Mrs Holland (the best bawd in all England) had lighted upon her.' This tiny young thing was a complete contrast in every way to Beta, except that she too was 'a wondrous wanton' – Mrs Holland's biographer suggests that Eliza was a nymphomaniac. The third woman, Longa Maria, was a tall blonde, cultured and softly spoken, a fine musician who played the viol and could sing well. 'She was not so rampant nor so rude.' Just the kind of girl a tired businessman would like to spend a few relaxing if expensive hours with after a hard day's work across the water in the City. Finally there was a live-wire named Maria Pettit, 'a small handful of a woman yet pleasant with all motion and action . . . nothing was more irksome to her than sleep and silence'.

This quartet, which could satisfy at least all the conventional desires, formed the heart of the business. Other girls were on call from 'places of fair reputation': their pictures and descriptions adorned the rooms and the customers could ask for them to be summoned. Guest whores of renown might also drop in if business was slack across the river. Almost as important was the resident doctor, whose job it was to stop the clients catching the Great Pox, or syphilis, and the Little Pox, or gonorrhoea.

If a girl was unfortunate enough to catch a disease which could not be easily cured she would be expelled unceremoniously, a seemingly heartless practice but one that was really vital to the reputation of a brothel, and remained the accepted rule for centuries.

Mother Holland would greet each guest in person, and discreetly quiz him to ascertain his financial status and special wishes. There was no credit: anyone temporarily embarrassed financially would not be admitted, however exalted. Nor would she tolerate rowdy or violent behaviour, such as ill-treating the girls. The girls paid for room and board, and handed over a percentage of their earnings. However, Mother Holland probably made a large part of her income from the sale of food and drink.

For thirty years at the beginning of the seventeenth century the Leaguer was the most famous brothel in London. Its exclusiveness, efficiency, the quality of its whores and food and drink and its formidable owner – described as a small woman, still beautiful – ensured its success. But the moral climate was changing, the Puritans becoming more powerful. Mother Holland had many enemies, and when James I died and was succeeded by Charles I, who ordered the suppression of brothels, they saw their chance. Discipline also seems to have been breaking down at the Leaguer. The parties grew noisier and rowdier, the girls less genteel and ladylike. The pamphleteer Daniel Lupton expressed some of this concern when he wrote of the Paris Gardens in about 1630:

> this may be better tearmed a foule Denne than a Faire Garden . . . heeratte foule beasts come to itt and as badde and worse keepe it; they are fitter for a Wildernesse than a Cittee: idle base persons . . . the Swaggering Roarer, the Cunning Cheater, the Rotten Bawd, the Swearing Drunkard and the Bloudy Butcher have their Rendezvous here.

Mrs Holland had already been in trouble with the authorities. The playwright Shakerley Marmion, a contemporary of Shakespeare and himself a customer of the brothel, wrote a play called *Holland's Leaguer*. In it he has Mrs Holland say:

MRS HOLLAND:

Pox on the Marshall and his Constable!
There cannot be a mystery in this trade
but they must peep into it! Merciless Varlets
that know how many fall by our occupation
and yet would have *their* venery for nothing ...
But we must give them good words!
Show them a Room.

She was not prepared to be so welcoming when in December 1631 a
troop of soldiers was sent to close down the Leaguer. The story goes
that Madam Holland, who was now about sixty but as fiery as ever, first
enticed them on to the drawbridge, then suddenly dropped it down-
wards so that the men were plunged into the stinking moat. As they
floundered about in the slime her jeering whores pelted them with mis-
siles and poured the contents of their chamber pots on their heads. The
soldiers regrouped several times but were repulsed and eventually with-
drew in disarray.

A larger force was later sent but it too was driven off several times,
while Mrs Holland 'derided [them] beyond sufferance'. The whores'
victory was short-lived, however; by the following year the Leaguer was
successfully closed down. About thirty years spent running the most
expensive brothel in London – what the court wit Sir John Harington
called making 'sweete gaynes of stynkynge wares' – had left Mrs Holland
very wealthy. Her last stand with her whores before slipping away was
probably motivated by her strong sense of mischief rather than fear of
losing her livelihood. That is the last we hear of Madam Holland and
her girls, but the house kept the name. On a map of 1746 it is called
Holland Leger. Today Hopton Street runs through the site. A tribute to
the sumptuousness of the interior was the local nickname for the water-
girt mansion, which was still known as 'the Nobs' Island' fifty years later.

The march of whoredom went on. In *The Merrie Ballad of Nashe his Dildo*
the playwright Thomas Nashe describes a visit to a brothel in about

1600. He performed so badly that his expensive whore had recourse to a new-fangled importation from France – a dildo. Incidentally, Nashe mentions brothels full of sixpenny whores which operated next door to magistrates' houses and unsurprisingly surmises that the magistrates had been bribed. 'Dishonest styrumpettes . . . were clustered night and day at the entrances to brothels as freely as if they were entrances to taverns . . . and every one of them claimed to be a gentlewoman.' The going rate for whores a few rungs up the ladder was a stiff half a crown ($£15$) and Nashe described the city suburbs as 'licensed stews'.

The spread of whoredom at the beginning of the seventeenth century can be traced in the registers of the Middlesex Sessions. Anne Robinson of Aldgate is a 'notorious common whore' who sits by her door until eleven or twelve at night 'to entertain lewd persons that resort to her'. John Burgoyne of Cripplegate accepted customers with the 'Frenche Poxe' and even with the plague. Joan Woodshore of Clerkenwell was a 'noted whore' who tried to stab two sailors with 'a spit or rapier'. Cow Cross is frequently mentioned. Anne Morrow had a brothel there and admitted 'bringing half a dozen whores to bed': clearly hers was a large establishment. Many lewd persons in Turnmill Street, we are informed, 'keep common brothel houses and harbour divers impudent Queens'. King James I, whose own sexual preferences were otherwise, issued an ordinance in 1622, *Touching Upon the Disorderly Houses in Saffron Hill*: 'To restrain the shameless women . . . bawds who entertained and lured men into divers houses for base and filthy lucre . . . by sitting outside the doors and beckoning in the clients' (Burford and Wotten, 1995).

In 1630, the poet John Taylor wrote what amounted to an instruction manual for bawds. Burford speculates that Taylor's *The Virtuous Bawd* is based on the life of Elizabeth Holland of Holland's Leaguer fame. Taylor, known as the Water Poet, was a licensed ferryman and would have known the great bawds and their customers, many of whom he would have rowed to their tipsy assignations. His intention is partly ironic as he compares the 'virtues' of bawds with the standards of tradesmen, those other sellers of services. He points out the arduous training a young whore undergoes to become a bawd before her attractions fade in her late twenties. By assiduous study of her trade she learns the rigours of the laws, the penances and whippings and all the other hazards of the profession, including the handling of the justices' clerks – even, when necessary, of the justices themselves. She becomes a bawd 'as the proper right for her long services to Society'. By then she will have learned how to sell a maidenhead three or four hundred times and have mastered the language of love and commerce and even science, since having spent so much time 'on her back performing all sorts of planetary movements' she will have acquired a thorough knowledge of the stars. There is some nonsense about her mastery of music, the 'pricksong', and playing the 'sackbut', not the musical instrument but the wine barrels which will be a source of profit in her brothels. Finally she shows her knowledge of art in her choice of erotic pictures to arouse her customers. Taylor takes an optimistic view of bawdry as a business: it is 'not some upstart, newfangled *bauble* or *toy* . . . but a real solid lasting thing'. If her luck holds, he says, the bawd will 'extract from sin and wickedness, good money, good clothes and almost anything good except good conscience – and that is but a poor beggarly virtue!!' Taylor considered that 'a bawd is only a loathsome figure to a satiated lover'.

Some thirty years later, the author Richard Head gives a vivid description of a visit to a brothel in his *The English Rogue* (1665), an establishment which Burford (1990) identifies as Mother Cunny's, perhaps her house in Whetstone Park north of Lincoln's Inn Fields. Head chose a girl from pictures the bawd showed him, and when the young beauty appeared she made Head a startling proposition. He must deposit ten gold pieces and every time he had intercourse with her he could take one back; her fee would be what remained of the £10 in the morning. If he managed sex ten times the night would be free, and he could depart next day 'with a great deal of applause, without expending a penny, but what you shall be pleased to distribute voluntarily among the servants'. We are not told what would have happened if he had managed sex more than ten times.

Head was 'stark mad to be at it', and found next morning that he had saved £8, or so he claimed. 'But I deserved to have had my money trebled: however for the present I thought forty shillings was never better spent, nor eight [gold pieces] husbanded with so much recreation and delight.' Moreover, he realised that his companion of the night was not a prostitute but a gentlewoman seeking sexual thrills. Some other women in the brothel too were 'persons of no mean quality, which came hither to satisfy (what was impossible) their insatiate lusts'. They would study the customer through a spy hole, and if they didn't fancy him, or he was someone of their acquaintance, they would pass him on to one of Mother Cunny's regular girls.

Mother Cunny is mentioned, too, in John Garfield's guide to London harlotry *The Wand'ring Whore* (1660–3) which suggests this veteran was still in business in the early 1660s. In 1660, while serving a spell in Newgate Prison, Garfield wrote another guide with the subtitle *The Unparalled Practices of Mrs Fotheringham*. Priss Fotheringham was one of the great bawds of the age, and Garfield also provides a list of what he claimed were the other most famous contemporary bawds: Mrs Cresswell, Betty Lawrence, Mrs Curtis, Mrs Smith, Mrs Bagley and Mrs Russell. There is no mention of Mrs Holland of Holland's Leaguer, who must have been long dead.

Priscilla or Priss Carsewell was probably born about 1612. She is first heard of at the Middlesex Sessions in July 1658 when she was charged with theft. Sentenced to be hanged, she was granted a conditional pardon by the new Lord Protector, Richard Cromwell. She married into the brothel-keeping family of the Fotheringhams. Her husband Edmund was her pimp and at least ten years her junior.

Priss had been afflicted with smallpox, and the effects were worsened by the treatment she got from a quack, but as we shall see it was not her face that was her fortune. Her husband was a bully who gave her a venereal disease and beat her – he 'befrenched her and pockified her bones soundly'. She ran away with a sword cutter, taking her husband's money. When it was gone the sword cutter deserted her, and she went back to her husband, who had her tried for theft. She spent about a year in Newgate where she met the bawds Damaris Page and Mrs Cresswell. She also met there her biographer, Garfield.

Priss specialised in a particularly successful money-spinner known as 'chucking'. One of her early chroniclers described it: 'Priss stood on her head with naked Breech and Belly while four Cully-Rumpers chucked in sixteen half-crowns into her *Commoditie.*' She performed this feat several times a day to acclaim from a crowd of enthusiastic fans. So popular did her brothel, the Six Windmills in Chiswell Street, Cripplegate Without, become that it drew customers from far and wide. In Newgate Prison it was proposed that she link the fortunes of her 'Chuck Office' with the business of the Last and Lion in East Smithfield, whose speciality was fellatio (its popular name was 'the Prick Office'). It was run by a man named Hammond, and before a woman was taken on she had to 'buss the end of his trapstick as he [lay] naked upon his bed with his *tarse* standing upwards'. Priss seems to have decided to pass up this somewhat unorthodox opportunity and to stick to what she did best.

Garfield recounts several anecdotes of the goings-on at Priss's brothel, including one about a Mrs Cupid, one of Priss's whores and an expert at the chuck-game. This tells how 'one evening French Dollars, Spanish Pistoles and English Half-Crowns were chuck'd in as plentifully pour'd in was the Rhenish Wine . . . the Half-Crowns chuckt into her *Commoditie* doing lesser harme than the Wine . . . for its smarting and searing quality'. When Priss performed she would allow only the best sack wine to be used because it smarted less. Since a half-crown was a considerable sum at the time, Garfield was led to exclaim: 'A Cunny is the dearest piece of flesh in the World!'

By then a wealthy woman, Priss died in about 1668, probably in her mid-fifties. Although she must have been a fit, even an athletic, woman to have performed the 'chuck ceremony' several times a day when younger, she was later much afflicted by disease. Garfield wrote in 1663 that she was 'now overgrown with age and overworn with her former all-too-frequent embraces'. Her husband was dying, 'rotten with syphilis'. It was said of her that 'in the practice and proficiency of her profession' Priss had 'outdone and outstripped the oldest beldam in men's memory'.

The next great bawd of the era, also mentioned by Garfield, was probably a gentlewoman. Like Elizabeth Holland, Mother Elizabeth Cresswell, who was born in about 1625, combined a keen business sense with considerable knowledge of male psychology: 'If Privy Councillors, Judges, Aldermen, Doctors, Dukes, Lords, Colonels, Knights and Squires may be made into beasts by stupid *jades*, how thinkest thou such Cullies [fools or dupes] can be handled by women of *Sense* and *Understanding?*' 'A man will pay for a *Duchess*, yet all the while he embraces in Reality a common Strumpet.' Like Holland before her, she knew men would pay high prices for pleasure in the right surroundings: 'Costly clothes and rich furnishings advance the profit and advantage . . . the price of the vendibles notably increases when dispensed in a splendid magnificent shop.' She was long remembered for her cry of 'no money, no cunny'.

Cresswell was born into a well-connected family, possibly in the village of Knockholt in Kent. By July 1658 she was a bawd 'considered without rival in her wickedness'. A constable testified against her: 'Elizabeth Cresswell living in Bartholomew Close was found with divers Gentlemen and Women in her House at divers times: some of these women were sent to Bridewell.' She had tried to bribe the constable to hush up the case.

The following October she was again in trouble for running a very disorderly house. By now she had moved to St Leonard's, Shoreditch. Westminster court heard of the lively goings-on at her new premises 'by Day as by Night'. A large number of angry neighbours accused her of entertaining 'divers loose Persons, Men and Women suspected to have committed bawdry . . . the said Elizabeth having lately taken a House . . . whereunto many Persons well-habited have resorted. . . . [They] continued Drinking, Ranting, Dancing, Revelling, Swearing . . . demeaning themselves as well on the Lord's Day and Fast Days.' Witnesses told of seeing men and women going into rooms, 'the Woman having stript to her Bodice and Petticoat going into a room where they have shut the Casement and locked the Door . . . on the Lord's Day at noon some Company drunk about a Dozen bottles of Wine and further that divers Women suspected of Lightness have . . . declined the way to the House at the fore-gate when Neighbours looked on . . . and did surreptitiously slip in at a back gate whereby much infamy is brought upon the Place'.

As the party warmed up the behaviour became more outrageous. One of the whores 'in the habit of a Gentlewoman began to propose a Health to the Privy Member of a Gentleman . . . and afterwards drank a Toast to her own Private Parts'. The court was told that some of the neighbours were ready to move away because 'their Daughters and maidservants were often taken for Whores by the Men who frequent that House'. Cresswell was sentenced to hard labour in the House of Correction, provided she was well enough – she suffered from a 'hacking cough'.

By the time of the Restoration in 1660, when Charles II came to the throne, Mother Cresswell was considered to be at the head of her profession. She had a gift for advertising, boasting of her 'Beauties of all Complexions, from the cole-black clyng-fast to the golden lock'd insatiate, from the sleepy ey'd Slug to the lewd Fricatrix'. To find these beauties she spread her net far and wide, corresponding with procurers and scouring the capital. No doubt London's slums provided her with many of the girls she needed. Appreciating that personal hygeine and good behaviour made her business more attractive, she set her girls high standards of cleanliness and manners. The greatest offence was to catch the pox. They had to douche with a concoction of wine and vinegar after each bout and consult the resident physician if in doubt about a customer's state of health. Mother Cresswell was known to insist on her girls being sober, elegant, well-spoken and, above all, fragrant.

Over the years she ran many brothels, one of the principal ones being in Whetstone Park by Lincoln's Inn Fields, where she sold 'Strong Waters and fresh-fac'd Wenches to all who had Guineas to buy them with', although this was not her main place of business. That was in Back Alley off Moor Lane in Cripplegate – Moorgate Underground station stands on the site. This substantial building was described by the conman and wencher Richard Head in *The English Rogue* (1665) where he relates how he and a companion went to Mother Cresswell's, 'formerly famous for the good Citizens' Wives that frequented her house'. She 'still rode Admiral over all the rest [of the bawds] about the Town'. Head obviously had a good time. 'The truth of it is, of all the bawds I know, she merits most, having a house fit for the accommodation of the best.' They were led into a large handsome room, and a servant brought them French wine and meats. Head observes that this seemed to be the custom of the house, and it was an expensive one. Presently Mother Cresswell, described by Head as the 'old matron' although she was in her forties, came in, greeting them by chucking them under the chin. After some banter she left and sent in a young girl, 'very proportionable'. But the girl was impudent and Head decided that though 'at the beginning the needle of my microcosm was touched by love's lodestone . . . if I might have had a hundred pounds I could not have meddled with her'. Another girl was sent in, 'one of Venus her chief darlings'. He offered her a crown, which she indignantly refused. The girl asked for a guinea, and they settled on half a guinea.

Five years later Cresswell received the highest accolade. According to the Chevalier Phileas de Charles, 'His Majesty Charles II personally honoured her with his Presence and deigned to inspect her house . . .'. She also ran a kind of branch office in Millbank, according to Burford (1990), with a couple of 'secretaries' to supply whores to noblemen from the nearby court. Her other properties included a mansion in Clerkenwell, and in the City she had a 'house of assignation' where randy City wives and their daughters could meet their lovers. She acted as agent for fallen gentlewomen, many of them from Cavalier families ruined in the Civil War. These women, known as 'Countesses of the Exchange' or 'side-pillows' operated from the alleys round Gresham's Royal Exchange. It was said of them: 'They master your *Britches* and take all your Riches.' Because of their gentle birth they would sell themselves only to gentlemen. Cresswell's sales pitch suggested that part of their earnings would be sent to their fathers 'so they could spend their days quietly hunting'.

In 1668 thousands of London apprentices attacked and pulled down brothels in what came to be known as the Bawdy House Riots. The outbreak lasted five days and one of the brothels the apprentices destroyed was owned by Cresswell. Apprentices traditionally attacked bawdy houses in an excess of moral zeal on Shrove Tuesday, their holiday. The rioters viewed the brothels as symbols of Charles II's 'flagrantly debauched' court, Pepys writing that 'these idle fellows' regretted only that they had destroyed small bawdy houses and not 'the great bawdy house at Whitehall'. Large bodies of troops were called out, and Pepys said their commander acted like a madman. Alarms were sounded, 'as though the French were coming to town'. The law also temporarily lost its head, and four apprentices were hanged, drawn and quartered for high treason. Charles II pertinently enquired why the apprentices frequented the bawdy-houses if they wanted to pull them down.

The burning of the brothels made many whores homeless. Mother Cresswell was one of the sponsors, along with Damaris Page and other madams, of the seditious pamphlet *The Poor Whores' Petition to Lady Castlemaine*, a sly blow aimed at the King's vicious and greedy mistress Barbara Villiers, Countess of Castlemaine and Duchess of Cleveland. The pamphlet, thought to have been written by the diarist John Evelyn, who detested Castlemaine, is ostensibly an appeal on behalf of the whores 'in Dog and Bitch Yard, Lukener's Lane, Saffron Hill, Moorfields, Chiswell Street, Rosemary Lane, Nightingale Lane, Ratcliffe Highway, Well Close, Church Lane, East Smithfield &c' affected by the riots. It implores Castlemaine, because of her great experience in whoring, to help her poorer sisters.

However, the greatest crisis in Cresswell's career was caused by her private life. Cresswell was the lover of Sir Thomas Player, the City Chamberlain, a man of turbulent political inclinations, and she stood by him in adversity. This rabble-rousing anti-Catholic frequently visited Mrs Cresswell's country house in Camberwell and gave lavish parties for political associates 'which turned into sexual orgies' (Burford, 1990). Mother Cresswell is said to have provided some three hundred girls for one of these parties, a considerable feat of organisation even given the profligacy of the times. This particular party is described in the ballad 'Oates' Boarding School in Camberwell'. It concerns a fund-raising function for the anti-Catholic perjurer Titus Oates, the man who concocted the Popish Plot.

> There shall all Provision be made
> to entertain the Best.
> Old Mother Cresswell of our Trade
> For to rub-down our Guest.
> Three hundred of the briskest Dames
> in Park or Fields e'er fell
> Whose am'rous Eyes shall charm the Flames
> of the Saints at Camberwell.

Sir Thomas supported the succession to the throne of the Protestant Duke of Monmouth, bastard son of Charles II, which infuriated the

Catholic heir, James, Duke of York. Sir Thomas's support for Titus Oates was eventually to ruin him, and in the meantime he was borrowing large sums of money from Mother Cresswell for the cause. She tried to distance herself from these political intrigues, and remained a power in the underworld and among certain courtiers. A regular visitor to her brothels was the King's confidant Sir Anthony Ashley-Cooper, later Lord Shaftesbury, whose tastes oscillated between whores and homo-sexuals. When the King declared James, Duke of York his successor, there were riots in the City of London and Sir Thomas attacked the Duke, saying the City would 'raise no more Money to pay for the Whores at Whitehall . . . and not for arbitrary government . . . the Crown is at the disposal of the Commons, not the King'. The authorities struck at Mother Cresswell, Player's financial backer, the *Imperial Protestant Mercury* reporting in November 1681:'The famous Madam Cresswell was on trial . . . at Westminster convicted after above thirty years practice of Bawdry . . . some of her Does most unkindly testifying against her.' Mother Cresswell later claimed that 'a malignant jury' had dispossessed her of her 'lovely habitation . . . which I have many years kept in Moorfields to the joy and comfort of the whole Amorous Republic'. But her court appearance was little more than an inconvenience, for she was soon back in business.

Sir Thomas Player died in 1686 and Mother Cresswell was asked to honour a £300 bond she had guaranteed for him. For some reason she does not appear to have paid, although her will showed her to be still wealthy. For her non-compliance she was sent to the Bridewell, where she died. Mother Cresswell left substantial legacies to relatives and others, and two of her girls were given three years to pay off the debts they owed her estate. She asked to be buried in the parish church at Knockholt, and left 20s to the poor of the parish. George Shell dedicated his book *The Whore's Rhetorick* to her 'because of her recent misfortunes'. Subtitled *Mrs Cresswell's Last Legacy*, it is a satirical manual for the instruction of whores. The fictional Mother Cresswell it depicts is described as livid in appearance, with hoary eyebrows, yellow gummy eyes, sagging breasts and a beard. It contains this passage satirising her instructions to young whores:

You must not forget to use the natural accents of dying persons. . . . You must add to these ejaculations, aspirations, sighs, intermissions of words, and such like gallantries, whereby you may give your Mate to believe that you are melted, dissolved and wholly consumed in pleasure, though Ladies of large business are generally no more moved by an embrace, than if they were made of Wood or stone.

By the time she died Clerkenwell had become respectable, populated by immigrant Huguenots, and the high-class brothels had moved westwards to Covent Garden and its environs. There other madams would maintain the high traditions associated with Mother Cresswell.

Apart from the luxurious brothels around Covent Garden there were houses at the opposite end of the scale, places where the poorest could solace their lives for a few pence. *The Wand'ring Whore* mentions Damaris Page, known to Pepys as 'The Great Bawd of the Seamen'. Born in Stepney in about 1620, she became a teenage prostitute. Early in her career she was charged over the death of a pregnant woman named Eleanor Pooley on whom she was accused of carrying out a crude abortion by thrusting a fork 'about four and a half inches' into her belly. She was sentenced to be hanged for manslaughter but because she was pregnant the sentence was deferred. She appealed to Cromwell's son Richard, the Lord Protector, and in January 1659 was granted a conditional pardon. From then on her business flourished. Operating partly at the lowest end of the market in the Ratcliffe area, an ancient haunt of vice, where her customers were mainly sailors newly in port and ready to spend their money on a buxom companion, however rough and ready, Page also imported and exported whores, the former including Venetian women who were among the most expensive and expert in Europe. They were beyond the means of ordinary seamen, and they went to her brothels at the luxury end of the trade nearer the court or were hired out to other madams.

After her death at her house in the Ratcliffe Highway in 1669 her will showed that she had made a fortune from vice. She had commended her soul to God, 'who hath in his great mercy blest and endowed me . . . with a considerable temporal estate withal'. Page was remembered for the phrase, 'money and cunny are best commodities'.

By the late 1660s the best brothels were to be found around the Strand and Covent Garden. Mother Elizabeth Bewley ran a fine house in Durham Yard in the Strand, where she specialised in entertaining foreign noblemen who were visiting London. She once famously sued the Archbishop of Rheims, Charles Maurice Tellier, after he bilked her over the hire of some young ladies he had asked her to lay on for his entourage when he came to London on a diplomatic mission. She was well enough known to be mentioned in the playwright Elkanah Settle's *The Empress of Morocco* (1674):

> A Helthe! a Helthe! to Betty Bewley
> Though she began the Trade but newly;
> Of country squires there's not a few lie.

Clearly most of her customers paid up, unlike the Archbishop. She died in 1677, leaving directions that 'all her plate, jewels, goods and chattels' should be sold and the proceeds held in trust for her young son (Burford and Wotton, 1995).

For those who fancied that surely rarest of all sexual sensations, a 'royal fuck', there was Graydons in St James's Street, where Lady Mary Tudor plied her trade. According to Burford, she was the nymphomaniac daughter of Charles II by his mistress Moll Davis (Burford and Wotton, 1995). The Earl of Newburgh, however, wanted a change, asking for 'some fine thing; I am tired of fucking quality'.

A little further east, 'Old Bess' Blundell kept three brothels in Dog and Bitch Yard off the Strand; Pepys visited the yard in July 1644 and found it 'full of loathsome people and houses'. There were whorehouses at all points of the compass and John Garfield's *Wand'ring Whore* mentions some of them: Mrs Kirby had two, the Red Robin and the Little John in Holborn; Mother Daniel also had two, the Gridiron and the Horseshoe in Beech Lane; Mrs Pope was the proprietor of a house in Petty France, while Susan Lemmon and Mrs Orange had houses respectively in Moorfields and Bunhill Fields. There was even a floating brothel, the *Folly*, with an enclosed deck with curtained booths and moored at Cuper's Stairs near the Savoy. Pepys visited it in April 1668 and the Swiss Baron von Offenbach described it in 1707 as 'a low tavern and bawdy-house' – and recorded his amazement at the 'prodigious' prices. It gradually became more disreputable and was, aptly enough, renowned for 'folly, madness and debauchery'.

The early years of the seventeenth century could be called the first golden age of bawdry. Women such as Holland and Cresswell raised standards and made the business of selling sex safer for clients and whores alike. Their achievements were, however, threatened by the rise of the Puritans.

THREE

THE RISE OF
COVENT GARDEN

The Commonwealth (1649–60) brought hard times for bawds and
their whores. In a determined attempt to alter what they perceived
as the climate of immorality, the victorious Puritans proscribed both
brothels and prostitution, also theatres, gambling houses and racecourses.
The death penalty was decreed for a second offence of adultery and one
woman, Ursula Powell, was hanged.

> Fines and corporal punishment shut out, even from children, games, danc-
> ing, bell-ringing, rejoicings, junketings, wrestling, the chase, all exercises and
> amusements which might profane the Sabbath. . . . It seemed as though a
> black cloud had weighed down the life of man, drowning all light, wiping out
> all beauty, extinguishing all joy, pierced here and there by the glitter of the
> sword and by the flickering of torches, beneath which one might perceive the
> indistinct forms of gloomy despots, of bilious sectarians, of silent victims.

A blight descended on the country: maypoles were cut down, the bears
used in the popular sport of bear-baiting were shot. The whores' favourite haunts, including alehouses and taverns, were strictly controlled. A
contemporary observer wrote:

> If you step aside into Covent Garden, Long Acre and Drury Lane, where
> these *Doves of Venus*, those Birds of Youth and Beauty – the Wanton Ladies
> – doe build their *Nestes*, you shall find them in such a Dump of Amazement
> to see the Hopes of their tradeinge frustrate . . . [before Puritan times] Ten or
> Twentie Pound Suppers were but Trifles to them . . . they are now forc'd to

make doe on a diet of Cheese and Onions . . . the ruination of Whoreinge was why the London Bawds hated 1641 like an old Cavalier.

This ruination was, however, relative. Court records suggest brothels continued to operate, if more discreetly. At Jane Foxe's house 'many men and women were discovered in lewd postures' while at Elizabeth Dunbar's two pimps were arrested and she was discovered in 'a very uncivil posture'. Some brothels, such as Oxford Kate's in Bow Street, continued to prosper, probably because their owners had powerful and influential customers. The politician Sir Ralph Verney ate at Oxford Kate's despite its reputation because the food was so good. From 1652 the ever-resourceful whores found a new outlet: coffee houses became meeting places for them and their clients.

The Restoration of 1660 changed the moral climate and brought better times for the sex industry. In that year John Garfield issued the first version of his *The Wand'ring Whore*, which listed the best-known women of the town, including the Queen of Morocco, Peg the Seaman's Wife, Long-Haired Mrs Spencer of Spitalfields, Mrs Osbridge's Scolding Daughter and Mrs Osbridge herself, said to have practised within Bedlam (sex was also sold in prison). Other well-known whores of the time were Jenny Middleton, Sue Willis, Doll Chamberlain and Moll Hinton. (Hinton seems to have given the poet and courtier the Earl of Dorset a dose of the clap. He wrote to her ruefully: 'A little Advice and a great deal of Physick may in time restore you to that health I wish you had enjoyed a Sunday night instead of — your humble suffering servant.') Displaying what seems an encyclopaedic knowledge of his subject, Garfield mentions the veteran whore Fair Rosamund Sugarcunt, of whom Burford says she operated around the Law Courts. London fairly pullulated with brothels: in some areas tents were set up and the customers queued outside. In 1691 appeared *A Catalogue of Jilts, Cracks & Prostitutes, Nightwalkers, Whores, She-friends, Kind Women and others of the Linnen-lifting Tribe*, a list of twenty-one women who could be found in the cloisters of St Bartholomew's Church during the riotous Bartholomew Fair in Smithfield. Like Harris's guide, it listed the women's physical attributes: 'Mary Holland, tall graceful and comely, shy of her favours but may be mollified at a cost of £20. Elizabeth Holland [her sister] indifferent to Money but a Supper and Two Guineas will tempt her.' Dorothy Roberts could be had for a bottle of wine; Posture Moll, a flagellant, wanted only half a crown; Mrs Whitby, who had obviously come down in the world, had previously charged more than 5 guineas but would now accept 10s from 'any ordinary fellow'. There are two black women on the list: 'Bridget Williams, a pretty little Negress ... not yet mistress of her profession so can be offered half-a-crown ... and bullied out of her money again' and Mrs Sarah Heath, 'a Negress ... her fee is higher ... will make no concession about fee'.

Every sexual whim was catered for. There were 'posture molls' or flagellants who did a kind of striptease in taverns to excite their customers, homosexual brothels called 'mollies' houses' and taverns with rooms full of prostitutes. When customers asked for the company of a woman these whores were sent out one at a time. Taverns which kept these women, known as 'tavern players', included Bob Derry's School of Venus in Maiden Lane and the Golden Lion in the Strand. Casanova encountered this interesting practice at the Star Tavern in Pall Mall in June 1763. The landlord told him that if he rejected a girl he had to give her a shilling. He rejected several and later complained of his pecuniary losses to his profligate new friend Henry Herbert, Earl of Pembroke, an expert in the ways of vice in London. Pembroke told Casanova that he should have made it clear from the outset that he was prepared to pay 4, 8, or even 12 guineas for a high-class whore. Garfield gives us an example of what a night in a high-class brothel would have cost.

For broaching a belly unwemmed and unbored [a virgin]	£1 0s 0d
The Magdalena's fee	10s 0d
The Hector's [pimp's] fee	2s 6d
For providing a fine Hollands smock	10s 0d
For dressing, perfuming and painting	5s 0d
For bottles of wine	£1 0s 0d
For pickled oysters, anchovies, olives	10s 0d
For sweetmeats, sugar cakes, peaches, walnuts	10s 0d
For music	£1 0s 0d

The bill totals £5 7s 6d. It is interesting that music costs a steep £1, and that the customer is expected to give the whore an expensive present – the Hollands smock. There is a generous allowance, too, for food and wine so it is likely the punter was paying for a whole night's entertainment rather than what would later be termed a 'flying leap'.

An area Casanova knew well was Covent Garden. It looms as large in the annals of eighteenth-century London debauchery as the Bankside had done in the Middle Ages, and St James's was to do later. The blind magistrate Sir John Fielding called it 'the great square of Venus'. Developed in the seventeenth century as an area 'fit for the habitations of *gentlemen* and men of ability', this upper-class enclave quickly went downhill, partly because some of the aristocratic tenants were Royalists ruined by the Civil War. By the eighteenth century many of the fine façades hid brothels. The *Tatler* said that every building was inhabited from cellar to garret 'by nymphs of different orders so that persons of every rank can be accommodated'. Windows opening on to the Piazza were lined with whores from seven at night until four or five in the morning, 'who in the most impudent manner invited the passengers from the theatres into houses where they were accommodated with suppers and lodgings, frequently at the expense of all they possessed'.

Just around the corner in Drury Lane was the establishment run by Mother Elizabeth Wisebourne, the greatest bawd of Queen Anne's time. To these 'considerable premises' came many of the great and the not-so-good. Two of King Charles II's bastard sons, the Dukes of Richmond and St Albans, were welcome guests and friends; the Bishop of Bath and Wells, Dr William Beveridge, enjoyed being thrashed by her strong young whores; and Dr Richard Meade, physician to the Queen and leader of his profession, liked to dally 'with two wantons at the same time'. He was an expert on venereal diseases, an area in which Mother Wisebourne was regarded as having some expertise herself, and they had useful exchanges of information. Meade was an agreeable companion: Dr Johnson said of him that 'he lived more in the broad sunshine of life than almost any other man'.

Elizabeth Wisebourne was born in the City of London in 1652. Her father was an Anglican clergyman and all her life she maintained at least a superficial air of piety. She carried a large brass-bound prayer book about with her, there was an open Bible on the hall table in her brothel and her girls were provided with devotional works so that 'for every minute they sinned they might repent an hour'. She had a house chaplain who read prayers twice a day and claimed that she had 'a parcel of honest religious girls about her . . . and as many Scripture texts at command as any Presbyterian parson'. There is no record of what the girls thought of this absurd regime.

In her early teens Wisebourne had been sent to Italy to finish her education. In his *Life of the Late Celebrated Elizabeth Wisebourn* (1721), her pseudonymous biographer, Dr Anodyne Tanner, tells how she went off the rails, developed a taste for luxury and elegance, was seduced and became interested in the Italian sex industry: 'She made some study of the customs obtaining in the best Italian seraglios.' Burford claims she was a protégée of Mother Cresswell and that she learned the trade from her, and this may be so, but she certainly picked up the rudiments in Italy. She also acquired there some knowledge of medicine and would-be cures for venereal diseases. Thus prepared for her future career she returned to London, where in 1677 she married a man named Edward Brook. Nothing more is heard of him, and she was known as Mrs Wisebourne (or Wiseborne, Wiseburn or Whyburn). By 1679 she was well established in the London sex industry, operating her 'discreet business' from premises near the theatre in Drury Lane. She used to visit prisons, clutching her Bible, to buy the freedom of likely girls, and also looked for recruits among children whose parents rented them out to beggars for the day. The children who were offered for sale outside the Church of St Martin-in-the-Fields provided another source of recruits for her brothel. Those she chose would be 'drest with Paint and Patches . . . and let out at extravagant Prices . . . she was always calling them young milliners or Parsons' daughters'. She specialised in restoring their virginity after selling their maidenheads to the highest bidder and taught them other tricks, such as touting for customers in church, as one of her girls recalled:

> We'd take all opportunities, as we came down stairs from the galleries, or as we past over the kennels [gutters] in the streets, to lift up our coats so high, that we might show our handsome legs and feet, with a good fine worsted or

silk pair of stockings on; by which means the gallants would be sure either to dog us themselves, or else to send their footmen to see where we liv'd; and then they would afterwards come to us themselves; and by that means have we got many a good customer.

Wisebourne's establishment boasted the services of some of the most celebrated courtesans of the day, among them the wild and doomed Sally Salisbury, the first working-class Toast of the Town. The relationship between bawds and these great courtesans was complicated. When she was between rich lovers, or keepers as they were called, a courtesan would require an income, but would need at all costs to avoid the loss of status involved in too obviously seeking out paramours. She could, however, appear at a distinguished brothel as the friend or guest of the proprietor, so discreetly indicating to the wealthy that she was again available. The advantage to the brothel owner of having such beauties on her premises is equally clear: although she would get no part of the money paid directly to the courtesan, the latter would act as a magnet to men who would spend freely, and the mere presence of these noted beauties was a free advertisement. So courtesans used the best brothels as men did their clubs – as somewhere to relax and gossip, particularly about wealthy men who were tiring of their partners and were looking for a change. Some men were known to be particularly flighty, acquiring trophy mistresses because of their cachet and dropping them as soon as something better became available. In this war of the sexes intelligence was all.

Wisebourne also found lovers for frustrated wives, as the chapbook *Crazy Tales* makes clear. It describes Wisebourne addressing a wealthy young man she spots strolling in Covent Garden:

> My Name is Wisebourne, from all parts repair
> To my famed roof the discontented Fair.
> Rich City Wives, and some not far from Court
> Who loathe their Husbands and who love the Sport:
> Brides matched with Impotence that wants an Heir:
> Numbers of these I succour every Day
> Who keep their Stallions well in Pay.

Normally Wisebourne was little troubled by the law, but in 1713 a drunken Sally Salisbury caused a riot at her brothel, the constables were called and Wisebourne was charged with disorderly conduct. She had to pay a large bribe to stay in business. It was at this time that the poet Matthew Prior called her 'the antiquated She Captain of Satan', implying that she had an evil reputation. There were, however, those who spoke up for the pious old bawd, pointing out that 'although she did a world of mischief . . . no beggars were turned away from her house without some help'. However, that she could also be a foul-mouthed harridan is suggested in a contemporary anecdote which tells how one night Wisebourne's coach was held up by the notorious criminal Joseph Blueskin Blake. Wisebourne had just been to Hampstead to sell the virginity of one of her young girls for 20 guineas. When Blake demanded her purse she said she recognised him, and would see him hanged. To which Blueskin is said to have coolly replied:

> You double-poxed salivating bitch, you deserve hanging more than I, for ruining both body and soul of many a poor man and woman, whom you procure to work iniquity for your own profit; there is nobody your friends, but the beadle and justice clerks who for a bribe may work your peace with [their] masters. Come, no dallying, deliver your money, or else your life must be a sacrifice to my fury.

Mother Wisebourne paid up with such bad grace, swearing at Blueskin 'a thousand names', that he stripped her naked and unceremoniously left her (Anon., *The History of the Remarkable Lives and Action of Jonathan Wild . . .*, 1725). She died in November 1719 and was buried in St Martin-in-the-Fields. One tribute runs:

> Muse, stop awhile, for thou hast cause to mourn
> And shed a tear o'er pious Wisebourne's urn
> Within thy walls the rich were ever pleased:
> From thy gates no lazar [beggar] went unfed.
> South Sea directors might have learned from thee
> How to pay debts, and wear an honest heart.

Mother Wisebourne, generous warm-hearted protector of vulnerable young girls or She Captain of Satan, died very rich.

She was the lover of the impresario John Jacob Heidegger, a Swiss so unattractive that he was nicknamed 'Count Ugli'. Early in the eighteenth century he produced Italian operas at the Haymarket Theatre, but soon became much better known for his obscene masquerades. The Church railed against what it called 'this grand Enemy to Liberal Sciences' and Heidegger replied in verse:

My Lord,
Your sermon, preached at Bow
Came to my hands some weeks ago.
By which I find you seem afraid
That harmless Pastime, MASQUERADE,
may spoil the Reformation Trade.
Tis prudence to supply with Art
Where Nature fails to do her Part:
When Borrow'd Looks give less Offence
To use one's own is Impudence.

Although they were popular, Heidegger's masquerades were eventually suppressed.

One of Wisebourne's successors was Sarah Lodge, a cheerful little soul known as Sally. She began her career as a prostitute at the age of four-teen in the 1790s, and soon had a high-class brothel near the Strand. Burford attributes to Alexander Pope a verse written about her around 1720 (Burford and Wotton, 1995):

My little Lodge, tease me no more
With promise of the finest whore
That cundum was e'er stuck in.
Give younger men the beauteous dame;
Alas! I'm passed the am'rous flame
and must give over fucking.

Sally's subsequent career shows that however successful, a bawd still needed a measure of luck to avoid the many pitfalls that awaited a working-class woman who had fought her way to the top. After being swindled by a conman she fell on hard times, emigrated, became the mistress of a rich planter, was left destitute when he died, returned and became a barmaid in a Wapping tavern, serving rum to sailors and to herself. Her love of a tipple made her fat, and she died of dropsy in 1735 aged about fifty, forgotten by the Quality who had once crowded her bordello, but 'well-known throughout the British fleet'. John Gay penned an epitaph on the all-too-predictable course of her career:

> Servant, Prentice, Whore, Mistress, Thief, Deserter
> Dupe, Derelict, Emigrant, Nabobess – final Failure.

By 1719 brothels and other disorderly houses had multiplied to such an extent that the Westminster magistrates complained to King George I that they could no longer police the 'Night Houses and Houses of Ill-fame . . . in which liquor was served'. Later that year they complained of gambling dens guarded by spiked doors and soldiers. In February 1721 there were mass raids on disorderly houses throughout the Hundreds of Drury and Covent Garden. *Mist's Weekly Journal* of October 1725 has an amusing account of a raid on a Drury Lane brothel:

> On Monday last several Bailiffs were busily employed in besieging some Nymphs of Drury in their Castle in Colson's Court, who defied them for some hours from their Windows, with a great deal of sharp Raillery and good Humour, but were, at last, basely betrayed by a next-door Neighbour, who, 'tis supposed, owed a spite to some of the poor Defendants, and therefore privately let two of the Officers through her House, and so getting over a Party wall, stormed the Castle backwards and got in, bringing all the Ladies down, who still kept up their good Humour, for they sung and danced all along Drury Lane to the Spunging House.

Among those arrested in the 1721 raids were the veteran vice-mongers Elizabeth Hayward and her husband Richard 'who kept the King's Head Tavern in Russell Street'. They were sentenced to three months' imprisonment and a spell in the pillory. After their pillorying they had to give sureties for their good behaviour for seven years, because of 'the length and extent of their evil activities'. Undaunted by their punishment they were soon back in business, this time in nearby Charles Street, with such success that in 1736 *The Rake of Taste* praised the excellence of their establishment. Two years later *The Paphian Grove* included Elizabeth Hayward among the 'Hags of Hell' who gathered at the nearby Moll King's coffee house, a celebrated venue in Covent Garden. Elizabeth must have been greasing many palms, as the authorities seem to have taken little further interest, even though Paul Whitehead in a satire against houses with pretensions to respectability stated starkly in 1739: 'Hayward's [is] a brothel.' In December 1743 The *Gentlemen's Magazine* reported that 'Mother Hayward, who for many years kept the *Bagnio* in Charles Street, Covent Garden, a lady well known to the Polite part of the World, is said to have died worth Ten Thousand Pounds' – a sum in excess of £1 million in today's terms.

While this seems an improbably large fortune, the career of the brothel-keepers Richard and Elizabeth Haddock suggests there was a great deal of money to be made. Richard Haddock, known as the Whoremaster General of Covent Garden, kept a chain of brothels and bagnios there from the 1720s into the 1740s. In 1740 the *London Journal* referred to one of his houses, the Blue Posts in Exeter Street: 'A café as they call it . . . constantly graced by three or four painted harlots'. He and his wife disguised their activities behind a façade of respectability. As early as 1721 Richard had a string of small shops, ostensibly selling coffee or chocolate or millinery, each with three or four young women who posed as waitresses. Most of what the girls earned in the back rooms he took, besides charging them rent and hiring them rickety furniture 'not worth in all above ten pounds . . . against a note of hand for forty pounds'. He had a fearsome reputation as a greedy rackrenting landlord. If a girl defaulted or displeased him or his wife he would have her thrown into the debtors' prison until she somehow found the money, usually by borrowing or by selling herself to other inmates. Haddock was a regular at Moll King's famous coffee house in the Garden, but Moll, who had once been one of the 'unchaste fair' herself, despised him for his heartless way with the girls. A pamphlet about King tells of their acrimonious relationship: 'One

H——K [Haddock] a noted Bagnio-Keeper, was never so well match'd as when attack'd by this Virago [Moll King], She was well acquainted with his Tricks, and told . . . of all the Slaveries he imposed on unhappy Women, by taking Coffee-Houses, and putting into them Mistresses. . . .' Haddock's brothels were usually run by women managers, who acted as a buffer between him and the law. Chief among them was Sophia Lemoy, who would have to take the blame when there was a raid by the constables. She eventually inherited the Haddock vice empire.

Richard Haddock died in 1748, and his wife ran the business until her death four years later. The 1752 probate inventory listing the contents of Mrs Haddock's various establishments shows her to have been very wealthy by any standards. By then she had just two bagnios, one at Charing Cross known as the Turk's Head, and the other in Covent Garden called Haddock's Bagnio. The historian Alex Werner has carried out extensive research on the inventory, and in the process has revealed, probably for the first time, just how impressive were the wages of sin in the eighteenth century ('Immoral Earnings, Eighteenth-century Style', unpublished manuscript). The inventory lists and describes the contents of her two bagnios, and also her large property at Worton in Isleworth, to the west of London. Werner's analysis of the inventory shows not only the scale of the business but the relative profusion, and sometimes sumptuousness, of the fixtures and fittings. The Covent Garden bagnio had thirty-two beds and fourteen dining tables, making it more like a hotel. The contents of the wine cellar were valued at £165 8s 5d, roughly £12,000 today. The silverware was worth twice as much.

Plate 5 of Hogarth's *Marriage à La Mode* shows a bedroom at the Turk's Head bagnio where one of the protagonists of the series, the countess, has repaired with her lover. The fact that the floor is carpetless can be misleading: only the principal rooms of even important houses would have been carpeted at this time. This bedroom is expensively furnished, as would be expected by the countess and her lover, who is seen climbing out of the window after stabbing the countess's husband.

The Haddocks' property at Worton consisted of two houses which were even more lavishly furnished. Elizabeth had an enormous assortment of china – she must have been a collector – which she kept in 'a neat mahogany Beaufett for China in the Chinese taste with folding glass doors'. Werner sees a connection between this description and a piece of furniture in Chippendale's design books. His famous *Gentleman and Cabinet Maker's Director* wasn't published until two years after her death, but his shop was near Covent Garden and she was wealthy enough to be a customer.

Finally, at the end of the inventory there is a list of debtors running to more than three hundred names. This form of 'deferred' payment must have been a feature of several businesses – interestingly, when the bawd Mrs Leeson got religion and retired she hoped to live on the many IOUs she had collected.

A bawd whose career drew together many of the strands of pleasure-seeking in that wild time and place was Elizabeth Dennison. As a young girl she had been seduced by the heartless rake the Honourable John Spencer, favourite grandchild of that *grande dame* Sarah, Duchess of Marlborough. (He was later the first to seduce Fanny Murray, one of the most famous of all courtesans, when she was barely into her teens.) Elizabeth went on to become the mistress of Sir Francis Dashwood, founder of the Hell Fire Club at Medmenham, and of Philip Dormer Stanhope, later Earl of Chesterfield, in acknowledgement of which liaisons she became known as 'Hellfire Stanhope'. In about 1730 she opened a brothel in Covent Garden with her husband Richard Dennison. As her friend Dashwood – rumoured to have had a share in the brothel – was a crony of the Prince of Wales, known as 'Poor Fred', the charges and the social pretensions of her customers were high. The soubriquet Hellfire was misleading for Elizabeth was described as having pleasant manners and wit, never drinking too much or being abusive or vulgar, rare traits in brothel-keepers at the time. She boasted that she provided her guests with only 'the very best pieces', excluding 'any Harlot whom she judged to be Improper for a Select Company'.

In June 1731, exasperated by the growing numbers of harlots and their rowdy customers who made the nights hideous, respectable householders and shopkeepers in the Covent Garden area presented a petition to the Middlesex Quarter Sessions asking for action. They complained that 'Several Persons of most notorious Character and Infamous Wicked lives . . . have taken up residence . . . in several streets and little alleys and courts such as Russell Street, Drury Lane . . . mainly in the neighbour-hood of Drury Lane which is infected with such Vile People that there are frequent Outcries in the Night, Fighting, Robberies and all sorts of Debauchings.' The authorities acted with unaccustomed speed. On 14 July, forty-six warrants were issued and among those arrested were 'Elizabeth Bird, *alias* Trent *alias* Needham' and Richard and 'Elizabeth Dennison *alias* Stanhope'. The Dennisons shrugged off this setback: it was only the pressure from citizens that had brought such action. Normally judicious bribes kept the police away. Elizabeth Dennison retired wealthy in 1760.

The 'Elizabeth Bird, *alias* Trent *alias* Needham' who was arrested at the same time as the Dennisons was Mother Elizabeth Needham, a famously heartless bawd whose brothel was in Park Place, St James's, the centre of high-class bawdry, much patronised by the court. She had been in trouble before: in July 1724 the newspapers reported that the 'celebrated Mother Needham' had been committed to Newgate after her brothel was raided by constables, who 'disengaged' a great number of 'Gentlemen and Ladies' there and took them off to the Round House, a kind of prison. The *Daily Journal* said it was the first time Mother Needham had received 'public correction', and speculated that it meant 'the ruin of her household'. Her ill-luck continued – in September her house in Conduit Street was destroyed in a fire, and a French half-pay officer named Captain Barbute perished, although quite what his rela-tion was to the 'notorious lewd prostitute and procuress' Needham is unclear (the *Daily Journal* speculated that he had been 'drawn in to spend his fortune and to keep her and her strumpets company'). Then the fol-lowing April, 'Mother Needham, alias Bird, alias Howard, alias Blewitt' was arrested for keeping a disorderly house in Union Street. The *Weekly Journal* reported rumours that she had 'peached' on 'several lewd women who keep private disorderly houses'. The paper said she had for many years 'escaped the lash of the law', relative immunity from prosecution it is possible she bought by being an informer.

Even in middle age Needham was considered striking, the painter William Hogarth describing her as 'the handsome old Procuress . . . well-dressed in silk and simpering beneath the patches on her face'. She is the bawd propositioning a pretty country girl newly come to town on a wagon in Plate 1 of Hogarth's print series *A Harlot's Progress*. The essayist Richard Steele wrote in *The Spectator* in January 1712 about a visit he had made to the Bell Inn in Cheapside where he had encountered Needham as she sought new recruits for her brothels: 'But who should I see there but the most artful Procuress in the Town examining a most beautiful Country girl who had just come up in the same Wagon as my Things . . .'. The girls would have been impressed by this handsome and well-dressed woman and her promises; only later would they experience her temper and vicious tongue, and her hard-heartedness. She also scoured the slums looking for likely young things, made compliant by hunger. Some girls she found sleeping at night on the 'bulks', the stalls which projected from shopfronts. She also, apparently, bought girls at auctions. The *Rambler* magazine carried this advertisement: 'TO BE SOLD by Inch of Candle at Mrs Kelly's Rooms several Orphan Girls under sixteen imported from the Countrey & never shewn before. Gentlemen of sixty-five and over are invited.' It is likely that she also bought young girls from various other sources — there was a widespread belief that London was ringed by female boarding schools, some of them run by bawds, which supplied West End brothels with helpless victims. On 17 June 1788 there were letters and articles on the subject in *The Times* which paint a lurid picture of the enslavement and ruin of these girls (Henderson, 1999). The brothel-keeper and her clients tire of a girl, 'she is turned into the streets to catch at the casual glance of an evening, where, in a short time, she takes to gin-drinking, and at an age when the virtuous part of her sex are just entering into life, she pines out a diseased existence in some garret, or cellar'. But this melodramatic representation of the girls' plight shows a misunderstanding of the value of young girls to the trade, and suggests the flimsy basis of the whole scandal. There are also premonitions here of the stories of girls being kidnapped into white slavery which would so horrify and fascinate the Victorians.

However, once Needham had young girls in her clutches it was difficult for them to escape. She was a tyrant, who treated them little better than slaves. They were forced to hire their clothes from her at outrageous rates, which kept them perpetually in debt, and she harried them to improve their work rates. If they still weren't earning enough or displeased her in some other way they would be bundled off to the debtors' prison and left there to rot until they agreed to her terms. When they were too old or diseased she threw them out, although it has to be said that this was the fate of girls in other brothels too.

Needham's brothel was patronised by the nobility, particularly the Duke of Wharton and his cousin, the extravagantly vicious and debauched Colonel Francis Charteris. For about twenty years she procured Charteris the kind of fresh strong country wenches he liked. But they fell out when he rejected a girl she took to his house in Bond Street, saying that the seventeen-year-old was 'too young for his rough usage'.

> Mother Needham fell into a passion, violently protesting that he was using her ill because she had been at great pains and expense . . . should she be obliged to offer the girl elsewhere it would blow her market, since few gentlemen would choose what the colonel had rejected, and the girl might be on her hands for a long while or have to be disposed of to some player or even a barrister or else she had to make her into a hackney-harlot in a week.

It is very unlikely that the girl's age was the reason Charteris rejected her; perhaps he felt she was not as fresh as Needham claimed.

Needham is believed to have arranged for a servant girl named Anne Bond to become Charteris's servant. Charteris raped her, and this may have led to Needham's arrest in March 1731 by the magistrate Sir John Gonson, a well-known scourge of prostitutes and procuresses. Fog's *Weekly Journal* reported: 'The noted Mother Needham convicted for keeping a disorderly house in Park Place, St James's, was fined 1s., to stand twice in the Pillory – viz. once in St James's Street over against the end of Park Place, and once in New Palace Yard, Westminster, and to find sureties for her good behaviour for three years.' Perhaps because she had friends in high places, Needham was allowed to lie face down and so protect her face. The *Daily Advertiser* stated: 'notwithstanding which evasion of the Law and the diligence of the Beadles and a number of Persons who had been paid to protect her she was so severely pelted by the Mob that her life was despaired of . . .'. Another newspaper, the *Daily*

Courant, reported that 'at first she received little Resentment from the Populace, by reason of the great Guard of Constables that surrounded her; but near the latter End of her Time she was pelted in an unmerciful Manner'. The *Grub Street Journal* observed ironically that the crowd had acted ungratefully, 'considering how much she had done to oblige them'. There is some confusion about her death with several papers claiming that she died soon after being taken down from the pillory, but subsequently the *Grub Street Journal* reported that 'Elizabeth Needham alias Bird alias Trent' was one of a number of brothel-keepers tried on 14 July and was committed to Newgate. She seems to have died shortly afterwards, for in September a broadsheet entitled *Mother Needham's Elegy & Epitaph* commented:

> Ye Ladies of Drury, now weep
> Your Voices in howling now raise
> For Old Mother Needham's laid deep
> And bitter will be all your Days.
> She who dressed you in satins so fine
> Who trained you up for the Game
> Who Bail on occasion would find
> And keep you from Dolly and Shame
> Now is laid low in her grave.

Five years earlier a wit had anticipated her fate with some accuracy, and published the following elegy:

> Here lies Dame Needham in this grave,
> The Lord have mercy on her,
> When living, she was kind and brave
> But as she's dead, he is a knave
> That tumbles down upon her.
> Her dealings were amongst the fair,
> At Lewkner's and Drury,
> But putting off some broken ware
> She slipped her foot in fatal snare

And felt the rabble's fury.
Raised on a precipice of wood
With woeful arms extending,
An hour the pious matron stood
The force of dogs and cats and mud,
Sound eggs and rotten, blending.
This broke her heart to see her love
To mankind so requited;
She died and made her last remove
Her body's here, her soul above
Or underneath benighted.

Wills and bequests are among the rare documents we have about bawds. In Needham's case we have the prologue to the elegy quoted above. It says she left her estate to the Duke of Wharton, with some exceptions, and these are interesting: her library went to Ned C———, a picture of Sodom and Gomorrah to D———n, 'a receipt to cure a Clap to little Quibus' and an ounce of *Mercuris Dulcis* to a Beau C———e of St Martin's Lane. Although the will is purely speculative, the writer must have known enough about Needham to be certain that she had a library. This suggests that she was educated.

Altogether different from Needham was the pious brothel-keeper Jane Douglas, celebrated by the playwright John Gay as 'that inimitable courtesan'. The satirical *Nocturnal Revels* (Anon., 1779) says that Mother Douglas attracted the nobility 'and she fleeced them in proportion to their dignity'. She seems to have been born about 1700 in Edinburgh, and by the age of seventeen was a harlot living in a house in St James's, Piccadilly. In later years drink would ruin her elegant good looks, but at this time she was described as ' a tall straight genteel woman with a clear complexion and a dignified comportment'. Clearly brothel-keeping rather than prostitution was her true métier and in the house in St James's 'she entertained Princes, Peers and Men of the highest Rank . . . and also Women of the highest Rank . . . who came incognito . . . the utmost secrecy being preserved'. Her girls were noted for their 'elegance, sweetness of disposition and sexual expertise'. The house was furnished with taste and the food was good. Among her lovers at this time was John Williams, later Earl of Fitzwilliam, by whom she had a child.

In 1735 she moved to a house in the Little Piazza in Covent Garden. There, the *Revels* says, poorly paid actresses from the nearby theatres joined her full-time whores to eke out their miserable wages. It mentions Campioni and the famous Peg Woffington as having 'often sacrificed at the altar of Venus in this chapel'. The seasoned man of pleasure could thus enjoy a celebrated actress's performance on the stage and anticipate enjoying her in the flesh later at Mother Douglas's. Before that later performance a uniformed footman would present the client with a condom tied with ribbons. Douglas was solicitous of the health of her clients, and sold these 'cundums' which she bought wholesale from J. Jacobs, 'Salvator and Cundum-maker' in Oliver's Alley in the Strand. 'Cundums', as they were then called, were prophylactic sheaths made from animal gut. They were reusable and secured with a silk ribbon. The writer James Boswell wrote of using them, however, with but 'dull satisfaction'. The original purpose was to prevent disease, not conception. Douglas also supplied aphrodisiacs.

A few years later in 1741 Douglas moved into the bigger King's Head premises under the Piazza. Betsy Carless, the Toast known as Careless, had run it as a brothel for a short time but had no head for business. Douglas furnished it with her usual taste: there was even a privy with running water, a rarity indeed. There were putative Old Master paintings – London had a flourishing trade in such optimistic wares – good carpets and dinner services. One of the regular clients, Prince William, Duke of Cumberland, whom she addressed as 'Great Sir', presented her with a massive silver service which she had displayed on a sideboard and referred to as 'Billy's Bread Baskets' (Burford, 1986). More important to her fame were the artists and writers who frequented her house. Hogarth must have watched the girls there carefully for it is difficult to believe that the lively young nymphs in the marvellous Plate III of his *Rake's Progress* are pure invention. He depicted Mother Douglas, most memorably as the pious bawd praying at a window in *The March to Finchley*, and also probably in *Enthusiasm Delineated* of 1761. Another customer, or so Douglas claimed, was Dr Richard Meade, he who had given Mother Wisebourne tips about prophylaxis so long ago. She said 'his great Delight was to have a number of wretched women dance naked before him'. Since he would have been in his seventies it is not so surprising that he no longer wished to frolic with 'two wantons', as he had of yore.

In the uncertain social and political climate of the eighteenth century no bawd's progress was altogether smooth. In Covent Garden they were constantly at risk because of the riotous behaviour of the young noblemen who patronised them. Among the worst were the Honourable John Spencer, Lord George Graham, brother of the Duke of Montrose, and the Honourable James Stewart. One evening the latter, reeling out from Douglas's establishment, assaulted a number of girls. The ensuing riot was broken up by the constables, the girls were locked up and the gentlemen went on their way. This incident cost Mother Douglas, a rather kindly and decent woman who went out of her way to avoid trouble, some large bribes in order to avoid prison. She was also in trouble from time to time with the magistrate Sir John Gonson, and had to spend short spells in prison. An altogether more serious affair occurred in 1759. She and Jack Harris, writer of the *List of Covent Garden Ladies*, a directory of prostitutes, were charged by Mr Justice Saunders Welch with 'procuring a young girl for a Gentleman . . . and taking poundage from her'. Harris went to prison, but her chronicler says 'the Veteran Abbess of the Piazza, by finding Bail, preserved her liberty'. Apart from these scrapes she also had her critics: Horace Walpole's correspondent Sir Charles Hanbury Williams called her house 'a Cattery, of which the Principal Figure is a noted fat Covent Garden lady, Mother Douglas . . . a great flabby stinking swearing hollowing ranting Billingsgate Bawd, very well known to most Men of Quality and Distinction in these Kingdoms, Bawd to all the World in general and Whore to Lord Fitzwilliam in particular'. Shortly before her death the playwright Charles Johnson met her and recorded: 'Her Face presents the remains of a most pleasing sweetness and beauty . . . her Body much bloated by Drink and Debauch . . . her Legs swelled out of shape . . . a nice cheerful old woman although suffering great discomfort.' About this time 'Covent Garden', a ballad attributed to Thomas Legg, records:

Dear Douglas still maintains her ground
Empress o'er all the Bawds around;
(Where innocence is often sold
For Hard Cash! for shining sordid gold)
By craft she draws th'unwary in
And keeps a public house of sin!

Mother Douglas died in 1761, 'thanking God for a successful life' which had included the invention of the mobcap, a once-popular garment now seen only in eighteenth-century engravings. She was one of the most genuinely liked and popular of all bawds. Her many aristocratic clients could enjoy poignant reminders of the joys of being fleeced by her when her 'fine Old Masters, rich Furniture and costly properties' were sold by auction. The auctioneer was her old friend Abraham Langford, who apparently made 'many witty remarks' as he knocked down the lots. Her funeral was impressive. Commodore Edward Thompson's *Meretriciad* comments:

Then big in Flesh see Mother Eastsmith stride
With Gould and Goadby by her side:
To bear their Trains, behind, three Pages creep . . .

Last but not least, Mrs Gould was another important madam, whose brothel in Russell Street was, according to the *Nocturnal Revels*, second only to Douglas's in reputation. Mrs Goadby was a great innovator, and it was she together with Mrs Gould and Charlotte Hayes, perhaps the most important eighteenth-century bawd, who took their profession to new heights of luxury and finesse.

FOUR

A CHOICE STOCK
OF VIRGINS

The later years of the eighteenth century witnessed a revolution in taste and style that altered the way the middle and upper classes lived. Dark-panelled interiors with their patina of smoke and grime were replaced by the brighter decorative schemes of the Adam brothers and others. The dignified, solid style of early mahogany was discarded in favour of the lighter, more elegant styles of Hepplewhite, Sheraton and the later Chippendale. Wedgwood and lesser potters provided affordable tableware. Bawds, as ever, were at the forefront of these innovations. There is a print dated 1784 in the British Museum of 'A St James's Beauty' showing a fashionably dressed young harlot sitting by a window in a St James's brothel. Through the window can be seen part of the façade of St James's Palace. Behind her stands a fine mahogany bookcase with sets of leather-bound volumes; she sits on a silk-covered chaise and on the floor is a fine carpet, probably Wilton. The drapes are sumptuous and the striped green wallpaper is *à la mode*. The mahogany tripod table cannot have been more than a few years old at this date. The woman is waiting for her client in what could be the library of a particularly well-to-do professional or minor aristocrat.

All this was made possible by the growing wealth of the nation. In the last decades of the eighteenth century the British economy enjoyed particularly strong growth, and much of this new money was pouring into the London sex industry. What the Haddock inventory suggests is something more than solid bourgeois comfort, but not quite the princely luxury that the best Paris brothels had to offer. This changed in about 1750, when Jane Goadby visited Paris and saw sumptuous brothels used exclusively by the aristocracy and the gentlemen of the *ton*. After she returned the newspapers rhapsodised about her new establishment in Marlborough Street. The *Covent Garden Magazine* twittered: 'Mrs Goadby, that celebrated Lady Abbess, having fitted up an elegant nunnery in Marlborough Street, is now laying in a choice stock of Virgins for the ensuing season. She has disposed her Nunnery in such an uncommon taste, and prepared such an extraordinary accommodation for gentlemen of all ages, tastes and caprices, as it is judged will far surpass every seminary of the kind yet known in Europe.' She engaged only the most beautiful and refined girls, and a physician was hired to carry out weekly medicals. Her cook was *au fait* with the best in French cuisine. In elegant surroundings similar to those of the best French salons the girls, dressed in the finest Paris fashions, down to their underwear, played music, sang or embroidered. The regime of fragrance extended to their breath: alcohol was forbidden, except a little with the guests, and the girls were encouraged to drink milk. Evenings in this chandeliered, mirrored, brocaded splendour might have seemed sedate, even dull, but of course Mrs Goadby was in the business of selling sex. After the theatres closed the carriages began to pull up outside. Admission was costly and, just as in a modern clip joint, the girls encouraged the clients to drink expensive wine while drinking little themselves. The man made his choice, and his fancy was usually offered a silk handkerchief; if she accepted she was his for the night. There was dancing, usually followed by an exquisite supper in a private room. Any present the man might give to the girl, and he lost face if he was not generous, had to be passed on to Mrs Goadby, and although it is not known what cut the girls got, it won't have been generous. The rate for a virgin was 50 guineas, the equivalent of the annual stipend of a curate (see Appendix 3 for prostitutes' prices).

One of Mrs Goadby's girls was Elizabeth Armistead, who, after passing through the arms and beds of the aristocracy right up to the Prince of Wales, became the wife of Charles James Fox. Goadby could also invite the Great Impures to grace her salon, if purely for the prestige and pulling power their presence brought. She was also always on the lookout for new faces: in 1779 the *Nocturnal Revels* reported that Goadby was still 'laying in good stocks of clean goods warranted proof for the races and watering places during the coming summer'. A pioneer in her working practices whose high standards were soon copied by other 'abbesses', she retired soon afterwards with a large fortune and a fine country house.

About this time the terminology of bawdry changed, too. Terms such as 'bawd' and 'mother' are used less often, particularly in newspapers, instead 'Lady Abbess' and 'Madam' come to refer to this new class of businesswoman, their girls are 'nuns' and their houses are 'nunneries' and 'seminaries'. Most of the more ambitious bawds aspired to an establishment for the aristocracy, if possible in that enclave of elite brothels situated in St James's around or in King's Place. But there were many wealthy men, particularly Jews and businessmen from the expanding middle class, who would not be welcomed by or feel comfortable rubbing shoulders with the aristocratic snobs who patronised some of these brothels. Mrs Elizabeth Gould saw an opening in the market. By the 1760s Covent Garden was in decline as the centre of gravity of the sex industry moved westwards and, going against the trend, Mother Gould opened a luxury brothel in premises on the corner of Russell Street and the Little Piazza – a house, incidentally, once occupied by Jane Douglas. She provided everything the jaded City businessman required after a hard day in the office, the best food and drink, safe sex with clean young girls, decorum and, above all, discretion. The *Nocturnal Revels* had this to say: 'This lady plumed herself much upon being the gentlewoman; she despised every woman who swore or talked indecently, nor would she suffer drunken females.' The *Revels* claimed she had the financial backing of a wealthy Jewish notary public, whom Burford identifies as Moses Moravia (Burford, 1986), a shipowner and broker, for whom, the *Revels* asserts, she had a great passion 'on account of his *uncommon parts* and *great abilities*'. In 1752 he was jailed for a year and pilloried for an insurance fraud; after his release he resumed the life of a free-spending man of pleasure.

Mother Gould insisted that her girls be frugal, save their money and never talk about their work or their customers, an insistence on a low profile that protected her from the attentions of puritans such as the magistrate Sir John Gonson. Keeping out bilkers was more difficult, if a story in *Memoirs of the Bedford Coffee House* (1763) is to be believed. According to this yarn, the actor-manager and playwright Sam Foote, a well-known character in the small bohemian world of the Garden whom Gould would have known or heard of, sponged off her outrageously. Perhaps she was out of town in 1762 when Foote arrived with a 'lady' and enjoyed the ambience of her establishment so much that, according to the *Memoirs*, he stayed for almost three weeks. He then tried to borrow money from Mrs Gould, who presented him with a hefty bill and ordered him out, whereupon Foote, a wily veteran of the hand-to-mouth existence, accused her of having 'the conscience to charge me near Forty Pounds ... which I shall not pay. If you arrest me I shall lay an information against you for keeping a public brothel.' The wise old bawd realised there would be trouble if she made a fuss. She wrote off the debt, even signing the bill as though it had been paid, and banished Foote for ever. Her charges were so exorbitant that she could afford to regard the incident as a business expense. No doubt that night other clients found their bills weighted to make up for it. The *Memoirs of the Bedford Coffee House* remarks, apropos of a charge of £5 14s for a night with one of its nymphs, that canny Mother Gould 'would have charged double ... [and] discovered some necessary articles such as a *Birch* to light your Fire with, a dozen or two of *Jellies*, White Gloves and Cold Creams ... and a string of etceteras.' Foote, incidentally, was a close friend of the bawd Charlotte Hayes. In 1766 he obtained through the Duke of York a patent for a theatre in Westminster in compensation for becoming the victim of a practical joke at a party which had cost him a leg (*Concise Dictionary of National Biography*).

In March 1769 much of the Little Piazza went up in flames. Mrs Gould's building was destroyed, and with it the colonnade, never to be rebuilt, where the perambulating harlotry had been so dense that the magistrate Sir John Fielding speculated all the whores in the country gathered there. Mother Gould moved to Bow Street, where she had kept her first brothel many years before. She died in 1784, having retired about five years earlier 'with a handsome fortune' (Anon, *Nocturnal Revels*, 1779). She was buried, like some other Covent Garden bawds, at St Martin-in-the-Fields. Where are their bones now?

The most important bawd of the later eighteenth century was Charlotte Hayes, who achieved wealth, fame and an unusual measure of social acceptance. That her husband owned the wonder horse Eclipse, and that members of the royal family and many aristocrats were among her customers, no doubt contributed to her success, as did her panache and flair for dramatic self-advertisement. Nevertheless she experienced wild fluctuations of fortune that saw her serve spells in prison for debt.

Charlotte was born in about 1725 in a Covent Garden slum, and was on the game almost from childhood. She started out in the company of two other young working-class beauties, Lucy Cooper and Nancy Jones. Lucy became one of the Great Impures only to lose everything through excessive alcoholic and sexual exuberance and died in wretched poverty. Nancy had no luck at all, dying at the age of twenty-two from the effects of smallpox and syphilis. Charlotte's first customers were mainly from the theatrical set who met at the Bedford Arms in Covent Garden and the nearby and dangerous Derry's Cider Cellar in Maiden Lane. She was one of the many loose young women whose beauty was acclaimed in Thompson's *Meretriciad*, where she was described as 'fair as ten years past, with little paint'. For a while she was kept by a rising young barrister, Robert 'Beau' Tracey, who was as generous with his money as she was with her favours – to others as well as Tracey. He was the ideal easy-going keeper for a wild and impetuous young woman who had no intention, for the moment, of being monogamous.

However, in 1756 he died suddenly and broke, to everyone's surprise. Charlotte found herself in prison for debt. Perhaps she had already decided, like Elizabeth Holland long before her, to get out before her health and looks were ruined, and took the same path to wealth. While in prison she met an Irish conman named Dennis O'Kelly. He had arrived in a hurry from Dublin in 1748 and worked for a time as a chairman, ferrying the wealthy through the streets, an occupation that brought him into the sort of close contact with well-born women not otherwise possible for a man of his station, and his charm soon had him in trouble with several husbands. He had become the lover and employee of a countess who lived in Hanover Square, so it is likely that the spell in prison saved him from a beating, at the least.

His partnership with Charlotte was surprisingly long-lasting, spectacularly successful and seems to have been marked by affection and mutual respect. Charlotte had a good business sense, O'Kelly was handsome and charming, and through his friendship with a 'lady of quality' he had contacts in the world of horse-racing. Losing no time, Charlotte set up a brothel while still in prison and used the proceeds to launch O'Kelly on a career which would see him become a wealthy colonel of militia and owner of what remained of the Duke of Chandos's estate, Canons, at Edgware.

But first she had to get them both out of prison. To this end she got her friend Sam Foote to have a word with the magistrate Sir John Fielding, founder with his brother Henry of the Bow Street Runners. Meanwhile, she 'fed [O'Kelly] and cloathed him and made him a Gentleman . . . in the Fleet [prison] . . . when he was in wretched tatters scarcely covering his nakedness'. She bribed the Keeper to let O'Kelly leave the prison during the day to gamble on horse-racing, of which he had a remarkable knowledge. They were released in 1760 under the terms of an Insolvency Act following the death of George II. The next year Charlotte opened a brothel in Great Marlborough Street for which the mischievous *Town and Country Magazine* declared O'Kelly supplied the finance, and Charlotte the 'nuns', although that seems hardly likely since it was Hayes who had provided the finance that enabled O'Kelly to become a successful professional gambler.

Soon they were both growing rich, and by 1769 'their gains in their different pursuits kept pace with each other . . . [they have] between them £40,000'. Since that sum is the equivalent of more than £3,800,000 today, it was certainly a wild exaggeration. Much of the money had been spent in Charlotte's brothel by O'Kelly's aristocratic racing friends who included the Dukes of Richmond and Chandos, the Earls of Egremont and Grosvenor and many of the lesser nobility, all of them noted for gambling and wenching. That year, too, O'Kelly had the great good fortune to buy a half-share in the racehorse Eclipse, once owned by the Duke of Cumberland. This marvellous animal never lost a race – the Eclipse Stakes are named after it. The following year he bought out the other half-share, and built another fortune. His high profile among the country's racing fraternity gave him an entrée to the highest, if not the most respectable, levels of society and friendship with the Prince of Wales, later George IV. Dennis bought a colonelcy in the Middlesex Militia, but failed to get elected to the Jockey Club – he was, after all, low-born and the partner of a bawd and former prostitute. Interestingly, Charlotte charged clients 50 guineas – now more than £4,000 – for a night with one of her girls, the same amount as Eclipse's stud fees.

Charlotte acquired a brothel in King's Place, St James's, epicentre of high-class vice, a seemingly insignificant alley near the royal palace where almost all the houses were brothels. By the Pall Mall entrance to the Place was Almack's palatial gaming house, opened in 1763. Nearby was White's. Thus the twin obsessions of the eighteenth-century man of pleasure, gambling and sex, were cheek by jowl. This profusion of pleasures drew wealthy men from all over the capital, Jews, stockbrokers, aldermen and merchants from the City, aristocrats, prosperous tradesmen and diplomats from the West End, politicians from Parliament, nobles from the court. The most ambitious of the city's young tarts naturally hoped to find a place in a brothel there. In *A Picture of England* (1789) the German traveller Baron J.W. von Archenholz described what the successful candidates could expect to find:

> The Noted Houses situated in a little street in St James, called King's Place, in which great numbers of nuns are kept for People of Fashion, living under the direction of several rich Abbesses. . . . You may see them superbly clothed at public places, even those of the most expensive kind. Each of these Convents has a Carriage and liveried servants, since these ladies never deign to walk anywhere except in St James Park.

The baron writes that prices in the King's Place nunneries were so exorbitant 'as to exclude the Mob entirely'.

In keeping with the new nomenclature Charlotte called her brothel a 'cloister', herself the 'mother abbess' and the girls her 'nuns'. The papers naturally had some fun with this conceit, the *Town and Country Magazine* in 1769 referring to her establishment as her Protestant Nunnery, 'which however administers Absolution in the most desperate Cases without Confession'. Sam Foote had dubbed her 'Santa Carlotta' and *Town and Country* called her 'a living saint', saying she should be canonised because she could 'make old Dotards believe themselves gay vigorous young fellows, and turn vigorous young men into old Dotards'.

Jews, whose community was centred on Bevis Marks synagogue in Bishopsgate, were now an important element in the commercial life of the city. It comes as no surprise, then, that Charlotte had some important

Jewish clients, among the most notable of whom were Sampson Gideon (1699–1762), a banker and one of the founders of the Stock Exchange, and the financier Isaac Mendes. She remarked that rich Jews were proud of their sexual prowess, and she liked them because they were polite and kind to her girls, 'usually rewarding them with Golden Guineas'. She herself, however, was not so generous, keeping the girls in a kind of benign servitude. Like other bawds of the day, she charged them so much for jewellery, rich clothes, food and lodging that they always owed her money. Their best hope was to find a wealthy protector who would buy them out and set them up with their own house and carriage. These would be men Hayes couldn't afford to displease. However, if a girl tried to break away without a powerful lover to back her Hayes 'made out such enormous demands as compelled the poor girl to stay or retire into a prison'. Nevertheless, brothels gave girls like these the only chance they would ever have of meeting and captivating members of the aristocracy, unless they went on the stage or became independent operators.

Nymphs who succeeded in graduating from Hayes's brothels to become famous independent courtesans included Kitty Fredericks, the 'veritable *Thais* amongst the *haut ton*, the veritable *Flora* of all London' and long-time mistress of the Duke of Queensberry, and Frances Barton, who turned into the actress Frances Abington, equally famous for 'so often exposing her lovely naked bosom to the gaze of lascivious leering gentlemen' as for her rich and varied love life. Another of her girls was Emily Warren, friend of the memoirist and man-about-town William Hickey (see Note on Sources). He wrote of visiting 'that experienced old Matron Charlotte Hayes in her *House of Celebrity* in King's Place'. Charlotte would have been about fifty at the time, but, as Ronald Pearsall says in *Worm in the Bud*, although speaking of a later generation, 'the leaves of autumn fell early then'. Hickey saw Hayes grooming the young beauty until she was fit for the company of her aristocratic clients, a process at which Hayes was noted for being most successful, particularly when applied to young girls from the slums whom she intended for service in her brothels. Of the exquisite Harriet Powell, another of Hayes's 'nuns', it was said that her conversation and society were so enchanting that men happily paid for the privilege of just talking or playing cards with her. This daughter of an apothecary later climbed higher in society than almost any other courtesan, marrying the Earl of Seaforth.

Even the freshest young things became stale after much use. Charlotte specialised in revirginising her 'nuns' – a maidenhead, she observed, was 'as easily made as a pudding'. So accomplished was she that men flattered themselves they had the first use of these girls, despite all the evidence to the contrary, and Burford claims that some had been made virgins again a hundred times – 'rearranging the crumpled blossoms of the rose' was the contemporary euphemism for this process (Burford and Wotton, 1995). A Miss Shirley 'had gone through twenty-three editions of virginity in one week . . . being a Bond Street bookseller's daughter she knew the value of repeated First Editions' – which tells us something about the numbers of clients the girls had.

One of the girls constantly 'refreshed' in this way was Harriet Lamb. She had been seduced by an aristocrat and abandoned at Hayes's brothel, where she became a great favourite. Commodore Edward Thompson wrote of her in his usual rough verse in *The Courtezan* (1770):

Hail, Harriet Lamb, who makes her daily food
The Lamb, the Maid, from different causes feel,
From different Feelings, licks the Butcher's steel:
Kind Charlotte Hayes, who entertains the Ram
With such delicious, tender, nice House-lamb!

The girls' health was a constant concern. Venereal diseases were rife among men of pleasure, and the girls had to be checked daily for signs of illness; losing a girl, however popular, was better than losing a valued client who might put it about that he had been clapped or poxed at Charlotte Hayes's. Her personal physician, a Dr Chidwick, examined the girls regularly. If they were found to have one of the lesser venereal diseases they were rested and treated until better, but there was no cure for syphilis until the discovery of Salvarsan early in the twentieth century, and girls with obvious signs of the disease would be sent away, to take their chances on the streets.

While there was no cure, there was prevention. Charlotte Hayes tried to protect her customers by supplying them with 'Mrs Phillips' famed new

Engines' – condoms – supplies of which she bought from Theresa Phillips's sex-aids shop in Half Moon Street, now Bedford Street in Covent Garden. Best known for her 'Implements of Safety for gentlemen of intrigue', Mrs Phillips also sold dildoes. She herself practised sexual autonomy to an extreme degree, as her biography makes clear. Mistress of the Earl of Chesterfield when she was only twelve, she had run through a legion of lovers before opening her shop in 1738. There she sold three different sizes of condom, and had an international clientele, or so she claimed, in 1776 maintaining that she 'hath lately had several orders for France, Spain, Portugal, Italy and other foreign places'. Part of her sales pitch went: 'Captains of ships and gentlemen going abroad' could procure 'any quantity of the best goods on the shortest notice'. She also had a catchy little jingle: 'To guard yourself from shame or fear/Votaries of Venus, hasten here;/None in wares e'er found a flaw/Self-preservation's nature's law.' Her main rival was a Mrs Perkins, against whom she conducted a 'handbill war'. Later the shop was run by a woman named Perkins, perhaps the same woman, who may have been Mrs Phillips's niece and advertised 'all sorts of fine machines called cundums'. The Earl of Chesterfield, author of the famous *Letters* to his natural son Philip, offered Theresa Phillips £200 to leave him out of her lively memoirs, *An Apologia for the Conduct of Mrs Theresa Constantia Phillips*. She countered with a demand for £500, he refused and she published. The *Apologia* contains details of her love affairs, many marriages and trial for bigamy. She settled in Kingston, Jamaica, where she was elected Mistress of the Revels at carnival time.

With their health in mind Hayes took her young girls for walks in the parks. It was customary for bawds to exercise their charges in this way, and when the Season ended they might take them further afield, traipsing around the spas and seaside resorts such as Bath and Brighton where there were wealthy clients seeking a cure. In July 1773 the *Covent Garden Magazine* reported that some Abbesses took coachloads of their girls to the Encaenia festivities at Oxford. 'M—tch—ll's family amused themselves one afternoon upon the Isis with some bons vivants, and made the banks echo with the chorus of "Lord have mercy, my bubbies" and "Lord have mercy, my bum"' – Mother Mitchell was one of Hayes's competitors. When business was slack in town Hayes also took her girls to Dashwood's Hellfire

Club at Medmenham, on the Thames between Henley and Marlow, where the members sometimes tired of debauching their fellow aristocrats. The courtesan Fanny Murray was another demi-mondaine who entertained some of the most powerful men in the country there, including the Earl of Bute, later Prime Minister, and the Earl of Sandwich, later First Lord of the Admiralty. Wilkes, Laurence Sterne, Horace Walpole and Lord March – the future Duke of Queensberry – were among those who watched or took part. Aristocratic ladies who were said – with varying degrees of probability – to have attended included Lady Mary Wortley Montagu, Lady Betty Germain and Dashwood's half-sister, Mary Walcott.

The prices at Charlotte Hayes's brothel have been described as astronomical. Her large four-storey house, newly built, was expensive to run, and she had to make most of her money during the Season, when her aristocratic clients were in town. Some idea of what she charged for her 'choice merchandise' can be had from what purports to be a price-list for her King's Place brothel. Although the style is facetious, the prices are believed to be accurate. Some of the customers' names are aliases.

Sunday the 9th January [1769]

A maid for Alderman Drybones. Nell Blossom, about nineteen, has not been in company these four days and was prepared for a state of vestalship last night . . . 20 guineas

A Bona Roba for Lord Spasm – if the first-rate at St Clement's should not easily be found, Black Moll from Hedge Lane if out of the Lock [VD hospital] and in good health, or bargearse Wilson, from Rupert Street . . . 5 guineas

Sir Harry Flagellum, exactly at nine. Nell Handy from Bow Street, or Bet Flourish from Berners Street or Miss Birch herself from Chapel Street . . . 10 guineas

Colonel Tearall, a modest woman. Mrs Mitchell's cook-maid, just come from the country and a new face; or the Countess of La Fleur, from the Seven Dials – N.B. her Flash-Man, La Fleur, must dress her to the best advantage . . . paper at least [a banknote]

Dr Frettext, after church is over, delicate, with a very white, soft hand, pliant and affable. Poll Nimblewrist from Oxford Market, or Jenny Speedyhand from Mayfair . . . 2 guineas

Lady Loveit, just come from Bath, much disappointed in her amour with Lord ATALL, desires to go upon sure ground and be well mounted this evening before she goes to the Duchess of Basto's rout. Capt. O'Thunder or Sawney Rawbone . . . 50 guineas

His Excellency Count Alto, a woman of fashion for a bagatelle only, for about an hour. Mrs O'Smirk just come from Dunkirk Square, or Miss Graceful from Paddington . . . 10 guineas

Lord Pyebald, to play a party at piquet, *patter les tetons* and the like, without coming to an extremity but that of politeness and etiquette . . . Mrs Tredrille from Chelsea . . . 5 guineas

It is interesting that prices for the simple services enjoyed by Dr Frettext and Lord Pyebald are low, those for a putative virgin high. The highest price of all is demanded for Lady Loveit. Henriques says that in a well-run brothel husband and wife could pursue their separate pleasures with no danger of an embarrassing confrontation (Henriques, 1962–8, Vol. 3). But there was no equality of the sexes: the wife had to pay at least five times as much as her husband. Nor do these prices include the many extras, food and drink, a gift for the girl (or man) and so on. In his *Royal St James's* (1988) Burford identifies some of these clients. Lady Loveit is the Lady Sarah Lennox, whom he describes as a nymphomaniac, and her lover Lord Atall is Lord William Gordon, whose baby she had. She ran away with him but the affair was short-lived, and she was ostracised. Alderman Drybones is Robert Alsop, Lord Mayor of London in 1752. Lord Pybald, so decrepit that he can only fondle girls' breasts, is Hugh, Viscount Falmouth.

Although the money was pouring in, the year of the price-list, 1769, brought troubles. Charlotte was buying a mansion at Clay Hill, near Epsom racecourse, and the couple had a financial setback when Dennis lost heavily at gambling. Later, in a drunken frolic at York Races, he tried to seduce a girl at his hotel. Befuddled with drink, he had entered the wrong bedroom and found a Miss Swinbourne in what he thought was his bed. 'Regardless of all restraint,' says his biographer, 'he commenced upon violent hostilities.' The girl woke to find that she was on the point of being raped, and screamed. Soon the room was full of servants. The girl insisted on prosecuting O'Kelly, and only the intervention of friends and a £500 donation to charity saved him from prison. Hayes complained that he had flung away 'more than she cleared by honest industry in a month'.

About this time Sam Derrick, an early lover, died. This perennially impecunious hack had taken over the editing of Jack Harris's *List of Covent Garden Ladies*. He left Charlotte 'my new system of Brothels, my apology for Whoredom and my *Treatise Upon Fornication*, not yet published'. It would be fascinating to know if any of these has survived. He also left 'the profits from the first edition [of the new *Covent Garden Ladies*] . . . for my old friend and mistress Charlotte Hayes . . . for her great services to the fair'. Derrick had been a close friend and drinking companion of Lucy Cooper, his benefactor when she was in funds.

In 1770 Charlotte married Dennis. There were rumours that he was already married, that he had run away from Dublin with his bride's fortune, but they were never proved. The following year Charlotte took over 5 King's Place, leaving No. 2 in the charge of a manageress. No. 5 became, if anything, even more celebrated among gentlemen of pleasure. Although Charlotte was never received in polite society, she climbed high in its louche version centred on the Prince of Wales. The Prince and the Duke of Cumberland would often dine at her Clay Hill mansion during the racing season, as would the Prince's friend the duc d'Orléans.

In 1770 the latest edition of Thompson's *Meretriciad* (see Note on Sources) saluted Charlotte's supremacy:

So great a saint is heavenly Charlotte grown
She's the first Lady Abbess of the town;
In a snug entry leading out of Pell Mell
(which by the urine a bad nose can smell)
Between the hotel and Tom Almack's house

The Nunnery stands for each religious use:
There, there repair, you'll find some wretched wight
Upon his knees both morning, noon and night!

To maintain market dominance Charlotte kept her name in the public eye by getting as much press coverage as she could – the *Town and Country Magazine* was always good for a paragraph or two: the issue of February 1769 contains a description of her King's Place brothels. And she would advertise the charms of her *mignons* in person, parading them in nearby St James's Park directly under the gaze of rich idlers. When the Pantheon, a vast pleasure complex, was opened in Oxford Street in 1772 the proprietors were determined to keep out the courtesans and prostitutes who frequented Mrs Cornelys's rival Carlisle House in Soho Square and other resorts of pleasure. One of the most celebrated courtesans of the time, Sophia Baddeley, was specifically barred because of her reputation and the fact that she was an actress. When she turned up and the bruisers hired to keep her and her like out barred the way, her escort, Sir William Hanger, and a large group of her aristocratic admirers who were waiting for just such an opportunity drew their swords and made it clear they would use them if she was not admitted. The guards stood back and Sophia entered. In her wake sailed Charlotte and Mrs Mitchell and their young beauties. Already inside were reigning Toasts Betsy Coxe and Kitty Fredericks, both graduates of Charlotte's nunneries. The Master of Ceremonies refused to allow Betsy to dance with her escort, Captain Scott of the Guards, whereupon Scott told the manager that 'if you turn away every woman who is no better than she should be, your company will soon be reduced to a handful'. One person present later reported: 'The Company were an *olio* of all sorts, Peers and Peeresses, Hons and Right Hons, Jew-brokers and Demi-reps, Lottery-insurers and Quack-doctors.'

Charlotte's greatest stroke of self-advertising was her 'Tahitian Feast of Venus', a nonsense concocted from the recent discovery of Tahiti by Captain Cook. He had reported that the natives copulated in public, and Charlotte, who wanted to counter the attractions of the new Pantheon, cashed in on the exotic fantasies raised among armchair travellers. She invited her best clients to the feast, at which she promised 'twelve beautiful spotless nymphs all virgins will act out the Feast of Venus as it is celebrated in Oteite' under her direction, and that Madame Hayes 'will play the part of Queen Oberea herself'. She also hinted that some of the maidens would be as young as eleven years old. 'Twenty-three Gentlemen of the highest Breeding, including five Members of Parliament' gathered in her drawing room to watch as twelve athletic young men faced the aforesaid twelve maidens, who were certainly beautiful if neither young teenagers nor virgins. After the youths had presented the girls with strange dildo-shaped objects the couples copulated with 'passion and dexterity'. After observing this performance with growing excitement for some time, the audience joined in. Eventually they fell back exhausted and then adjourned to supper. All agreed the evening had been well worth the astronomical outlay.

This was the apogee of Charlotte's career. She was thinking of retiring, although she still recruited new girls for her brothels, an important source of fresh talent being the newly created register offices for domestic servants. Charlotte would view the rows of country girls paraded like cattle and choose those who, from her long experience, she thought suitable material. The girls would then be invited to audition: after being wined and dined and made tipsy, they would find themselves in bed with one of Charlotte's customers.

The year 1776 saw Charlotte back in prison for debt in an affair never properly explained. We know that the creditors of a bankrupt Russell Street tailor had sued her for money she owed for her girls' costumes. Charlotte admitted the debt, but inexplicably chose to go to prison rather than pay up. Eventually Dennis, who had been away, paid to have her freed. By then he certainly can't have been short of money, as in 1785 he bought Canons Park. He died two years later at the age of sixty-seven leaving Charlotte an annuity of £400 (some £34,000 a year in today's terms), 'silver, jewellery and the she-parrot called Polly'. The *Gentlemen's Magazine* reported that Polly 'talks and sings correctly a variety of items and corrects itself if it makes a mistake in a bar ... and ... is reputed to be able to recite the 104th Psalm ...'. Alas, this remarkable bird died in October 1802 of 'a purgeing and bloody Flux'. Charlotte herself died in 1813 aged about eighty-seven, a life which spanned the heydays of whoredom from which she was said to have benefited to the tune of £20,000. Her husband's nephew and heir, Andrew Dennis O'Kelly, was elected to membership of the Jockey Club, an honour coveted but always denied O'Kelly himself.

For many years Charlotte Hayes's main competitor in King's Place was Mrs Sarah Prendergast. Sarah had married into the Prendergast family of brothel-keepers to become one of the most successful and wealthy of all bawds. However, at least among the Quality and the writers of interesting snippets for the gutter press, her fame owed almost as much to her embroilment in an absurd scandal involving one of her most important customers, the Earl of Harrington, known because of his sexual preferences as Lord Fumble and as a one-time and perhaps unsuccessful admirer of Sophia Baddeley. He and his wife were noted for their lechery, she for her lesbian affairs and for frequenting brothels and he for behaviour that got him referred to by the *Westminster Magazine* as 'a Person of the most exceptional immorality' and in 1773 as having 'sacrificed all appearance of Decency . . . for the lowest amusements at the lowest Brothels . . .'. The *Town and Country Magazine* said he was 'as lecherous as a Monkey'. That magazine listed some of his lovers, starting with the corpulent and greedy opera singer Signora Caterina Galli, whose demands almost ruined several lovers. The Jewish financier, poet and wit Moses Mendez, who may have been the Mendez who importuned Sophia Baddeley, allegedly almost lost his Stock Exchange business through her extravagance, and retired to die on his estate in Norfolk. She was followed in Harrington's affections by Kitty Brown, who had 'a fair complexion, brilliant blue eyes . . . with small, pouting Bubbies'; then he had a brief fling with the courtesan Kitty Fisher. Fisher was succeeded by an actress, Mrs Houghton. Seemingly insatiable, when the Duke of Dorset died the Earl took on his mistress, Jane Courteville, only to see her fall for 'the corpulent charms' of the bawd Mrs Rushton of King Street. At one stage he had a harem in his mansion, 'which comprised a Negress in a feather'd Turban, a young girl in pseudo-classical dress, another [dressed] as a Country-wench, as well as a Mandolin-player . . .'. After his affair with Mrs Lisle, the widow of a military hero, who had become a whore, the *Town and Country Magazine* said of the Earl and his wife: 'His Lordship is an impotent Debauchee and his Lady a professional *Messalina* [the cruel and debauched wife of the Roman emperor Claudius] who has little cause to be jealous – she would rather be inclined to laughter at this *liaison*.'

Lady Harrington, whose reputation was such that she was known as the 'Stable Yard Messalina', had a weakness for both sexes. When her lesbian lover Elizabeth Ashe deserted her for a diplomat she was 'quite devastated . . . her character had been demolished by this desertion'. Ashe, one of the many actress-whores of the time, was twice married and had many lovers. She claimed she was the daughter of Princess Amelia and Admiral Lord Rodney, and that she had been brought up at court. She was certainly accepted in court circles, although it was known she was a courtesan. She was described as 'a pretty creature, between a fairy and a woman'. After she died at the age of eighty-four Horace Walpole observed that she had had 'a large collection of amours'. Lady Harrington was an enthusiastic bisexual, although David Kerr Cameron's story of Casanova seducing her in her carriage cannot be true (Cameron, 2001). The Italian had been to the pleasure gardens at Ranelagh and, when he was ready to leave, after midnight, he found his hired carriage had gone. A beautiful woman gave him a lift in her private carriage, and during the journey back to his lodgings he seduced her. He asked her name but she demurred, saying they would meet again. Indeed they did, some days later in Lady Betty Germaine's anteroom. The lady sat reading a newspaper. Casanova approached and reminded her of their encounter; the lady coolly denied that they had ever met. Casanova asked if it was possible that she had forgotten him. To which the lady replied: 'I remember you perfectly, but a piece of folly is not a title of acquaintance' – and returned to her newspaper. If the incident ever happened, his prey cannot have been Lady Harrington, to whom Casanova had already been introduced.

The Harringtons were rich enough to be almost above criticism, except by the popular press, but the scandal which engulfed the Earl in 1778 was exceptional. Like other brothel-keepers Mrs Prendergast kept fewer than half a dozen resident whores, sending out for others when business was brisk. One of hers was Amelia Cozens, who later became a King's Place bawd herself, and another was a Jewish girl named Nancy Ambrose. One night in November 1778 none of her girls appealed to the jaded Earl, and Mrs Prendergast sent out to Mother Butler of Westminster for fresh supplies. Mother Butler sent her Elizabeth Cummings, known as Country Bet, and a girl known as Black Susan. The *Nocturnal Revels* says that having ordered them to undress the Earl 'began his manual operations, which were succeeded by theirs'. After an hour 'his Lordship *fancied* he had been highly gratified . . . they thought they had earned their present with great labour and much difficulty to bring his Lordship to the zest of his amorous passion'. However, the Earl paid them only 3 guineas, which was much less than they expected for their exertions.

When they got back to Mother Butler's she asked for her cut of 25 per cent, which Bet refused. Butler seized her clothes, Bet called the police and Butler was charged with theft. Things now got out of hand. With the aid of a vindictive magistrate Mrs Butler was charged with keeping a house of ill-fame and with ordering Bet 'to go in company with another woman of the lowest order to meet the Earl of Harrington at the house of Mrs Prendergast, who keeps a seraglio in King's Place'. Bet accused Mrs Butler's husband, a Sergeant Spencer Smith of the Grenadier Guards, of abetting his wife by transporting girls by coach to the King's Place brothels. Her deposition added that the Earl visited Mrs Prendergast's establishment on Sundays, Mondays, Wednesdays and Fridays and had two girls on each occasion.

The story had everything that appealed to popular publications such as the *Westminster Magazine*, the *Morning Post* and the *Morning Herald* – sex, aristocracy and money – and they milked it in a way now all too familiar. Harrington had been made to look ridiculous, and he was furious. He 'flew into a great passion, stuttering and swearing and . . . waving his Cane and shouting: "Why! I'll not be able to show my Face at Court"'. Mrs Prendergast too was alarmed, as Harrington had only just become a customer and she didn't want to lose him. He demanded that she buy up all the copies of the papers she could find, and she sent six people out to do so. They also went to clubs and coffee shops where papers were displayed for members and customers to read, and stole them. Prendergast promised Harrington that the girls would be ostracised by any brothel he was likely to patronise. She paid Bet 5 guineas to drop the prosecution and sent assurances to all her clients that nothing like the embarrassing episode would happen again. Her sympathetic handling of the crisis placated the Earl, but Mrs Prendergast felt something quite out of the ordinary was needed to restore confidence in the discretion of the brothels and their girls.

Her answer was a *Grand Bal d'Amour*, in 1779, at which 'the finest women in all Europe would appear in *puris naturalibus*'. She elicited subscriptions by sending out a list of these famous beauties. The Earl himself contributed 50 guineas and collected 700 guineas in subscriptions from friends. Money poured in, Mrs Prendergast eventually showing a profit of more than £1,000 (£84,000). Many Toasts of the Town graced the occasion, including the Hon. Charlotte Spencer, whose minimum rate was £50 a night; Gertrude Mahon, daughter of a minor aristocrat and known as the Bird of Paradise because of her liking for gaudy clothes; the rope dancer Isabella Wilkinson, who specialised in the diplomatic corps; the courtesan Harriet Powell, at one time mistress of Lord Melbourne, and Lady Henrietta Grosvenor – 'of moderate Beauty, no Understanding and excessive vanity' – who had been involved in a great divorce scandal concerning the Duke of Cumberland. The ball was a triumph. Apart from the professionals, aristocratic ladies flocked to dance nude for hours while an orchestra played facing the wall so as not to embarrass them. Afterwards the masked dancers repaired to 'sophas, to realize those rites which had been celebrated only in theory. The fervency of the devotion, upon this occasion, could scarcely be paralleled; and it is somewhat extraordinary that Lord Grosvenor and Lord L——r enjoyed their own wives without knowing it; and strange to tell! pronounced their imaginary Lais's most excellent pieces'. The *Revels* claims that when they realised that they had unwittingly given each other so much gratification the Grosvenors were reconciled. Lady L——r, however, gave her husband 'a Neapolitan complaint', not for the first time. It was 'a favour which she had received a few days before from a Foreign Minister, much esteemed among the ladies for his uncommon parts and amorous abilities'. After the orgy there was a banquet. When the carriages were called, Ladies Grosvenor and Lucan and the Bird of Paradise 'disclaimed their attendance-fee', donating the money to the servants. The ordinary whores who attended were each given 3 guineas and their chair-hire.

Lord Fumble continued 'as long as he could crawl to Mrs Prendergast's four times a week to indulge his whims with a Brace of New Faces'. He died not long after the famous ball, although he was only sixty. Despite this 'great affliction' Sarah Prendergast went on entertaining the Quality until her retirement in 1788, after thirty years 'unmolested by the Law or Reforming Busybodies'.

Another of Charlotte Hayes's competitors was Elizabeth Mitchell, who later took over her brothel in King's Place. Mitchell's first establishment was in Berkeley Street. For a hefty settlement she would find aristocratic husbands for her well-bred girls. One of them, the 'proud and haughty' Emily Colhurst, was the daughter of a successful Piccadilly haberdasher. She had been seduced by the Earl of Loudon after he spotted her serving in the shop. He set her up in a fine house with a carriage and the promise of £500 a year, but dropped her after six months. The seventeen-year-old became one of Mrs Mitchell's beauties. Emily would 'often refuse a £20 note if she did not fancy the presenter ... she would have no commerce with the Sons of Circumcision [Jews]'. Mrs Mitchell's other main girl was Lucy Palmer, daughter of Alderman Palmer, 'a gracious, well-bred and well-spoken' girl. Hayes's other competitors included the innovative Jane Goadby, who was to retire a few years later. Edward Thompson's *The Courtezan* praises Charlotte, but adds: 'This morning, when I'm fond of all things new, I go to Goadby's.'

In 1775 Catherine Matthews became the proprietor of Charlotte Hayes's brothel at 5 King's Place after that great bawd went into semi-retirement. She was one of several brothel-keepers who acted as panders to the Duke of Queensberry, the lecher of the age, and it was she who introduced him to Kitty Fredericks, the woman he probably came closest to marrying. Mrs Matthews could call upon the services of several other great Toasts on a part-time basis. One of these was Margaret

Cuyler, whose mother had been a lady-in-waiting to the Queen and who had been brought up in St James's Palace. William Hickey called her 'a great Jack-whore, with no pretentions to manners or beauty' and he had an even lower opinion of her acting ability when from necessity she appeared on the stage. A friend of his named Metcalf was her keeper at the time, and Hickey wrote: 'He at that time was the professed keeper of Mrs Cuyler, a woman without pretention to manners or beauty of face or person, and only an under-strapper upon the stage of one of the London theatres.' However, she must have had some attractions: at the age of fifteen she became the mistress of Colonel Cornelius Cuyler, who made truly lavish provision for her, including a settlement of £300 a year and a house and servants. She was naturally flighty and extravagant, and when the Colonel was abroad on campaign she gave frequent 'wild and often pornographic' parties with her friends Grace Dalrymple Eliot (Dally the Tall) and Gertrude Mahon (the Bird of Paradise). She soon ran through her allowance and to maintain her lifestyle would appear at Mrs Matthews's brothel, but whatever she earned there was not enough to stop her debts mounting. When Cuyler returned from service in the American War of Independence he settled the debts, but when she took up with the manager of the Covent Garden Theatre he cut her off, because she was 'being defiled by persons of a lower class'. A tolerant man, he had simply been pushed too far.

Another of Matthews's well-bred ladies, Elizabeth Hesketh, the daughter of a baronet, was a real beauty, but silly and over-conscious of her exalted birth, 'of shallow understanding and much given to boasting'. She had married a Revd Bone, who discovered she was having an affair with Colonel Egerton, the son of the Earl of Bridgewater. The Revd Bone advertised the fact that he would not be responsible for her debts, and she became a regular at Mrs Matthews's, where the other girls found her stand-offish and ridiculous. She was rescued from these straits by Colonel Egerton, who set her up in a house in Suffolk Street, the same in which Moll Davis, a mistress of Charles II, had once lived. Mrs Bone was visited there by Philip Stanhope, Earl of Chesterfield, and the fabulously wealthy Duke of Bedford, who built Russell and Tavistock Squares and was known as 'the Bloomsbury Squirrel'.

Little more is known about Matthews other than that her house was taken over by Mrs Dubery in 1786.

James Boswell was told of a brothel staffed entirely by black women, but the only coloured bawd to have an establishment in King's Place was Black Harriott, a native of Guinea. She had been shipped as a slave to Jamaica, where she was bought by a plantation owner named Captain William Lewis. He became the beautiful young girl's lover, taught her to read and write, fathered two children on her and took her to London to show her off in about 1766. Marriage to Harriott would have brought social oblivion for Lewis, but some wealthy men had black mistresses and women were often over-fond of their black servants. So Harriott was accepted as a mistress, and moved effortlessly in Lewis's moneyed and polite circles. Then Lewis died of smallpox, and some time afterwards Harriott was in the King's Bench debtors' prison. She was rescued from this 'mansion of misery' by some of Lewis's friends, and turned her house in Little Stanhope Street, Piccadilly, into a brothel. While there is no way of knowing how she did this – had she perhaps known something of the sex industry in Jamaica? – what is clear is that she had some flair. She is believed to have been advised by her neighbour Sarah Dubery, a successful bawd with considerable family ties in the business. No doubt her exotic background also helped make the venture a success, with a clientele of 'more than a score of peers and rich men'. Among them was John Montague, Earl of Sandwich, one of the inner circle of debauchees from the Hellfire Club. With Montague came some of the most dissolute men – and women – in London.

Harriott had already achieved a measure of success above the average for an outsider in the sex trade, when in 1774 she moved into a house in King's Place, buying the furniture and fittings from the previous owner. For a time she prospered, then business began to drop off: Burford says she had fallen in love with a client, an officer in the Guards, and neglected the day-to-day running of the brothel. Matters came to a head in 1778 when she was in Brighton with some of her girls, in pursuit of wealthy clients who were visiting the resort newly popularised by the Prince of Wales. In her absence the servants stripped her King's Place premises and ran up bills in her name. Black Harriott was sent back to the King's Bench prison, where she died.

Her erstwhile neighbour Sarah Dubery eventually took over Charlotte Hayes's former establishment in King's Place. She spoke Italian and French, and her brothel was favoured by foreign ambassadors and well-known actresses and divas. It was said she confined her clientele 'to foreign diplomats and English Peers . . . her Accommodations are most worthy of the Diplomatic body' while at her old address her brothel had been noted for the quality of the beauties it attracted, both amateur and professional, among the latter being Betty 'Little Infamy' Davis, a star of Harris's *List*. Such was the drawing power of Dubery's King's Place seraglio that the premier Toasts liked to drop in to see which men of power and wealth were there for the evening. Gertrude Mahon met the Portuguese ambassador, Count Louis Pinto de Balsamo, there and they had a fling. He was afterwards known as 'Mahon's pintle', an archaic word for penis. Another visitor was the outrageously avaricious opera singer Elizabeth Gambarini, whose demands made even the richest lovers retire from the fray. Isabella Wilkinson, the famous rope dancer or 'equilibrist' who performed at Sadlers Wells and Covent Garden, was an enthusiastic amateur. She was the mistress of the Swedish ambassador, Count Gustav von Nollekens. One night Mrs Dubery promised to introduce the Count to a 'new nun'. The Count, however, was furious to find that the 'nun' was his Isabella, 'whom he supposed was waiting for him at home as chaste as Penelope . . .' (Burford, 1995). Mrs Dubery restored peace by finding the couple a brace of lovers. Isabella was fond of drink and put on weight, which may account for her eventually breaking her leg. The *Nocturnal Revels*, which does not explain whether she was performing on the rope or in the boudoir at the time of the accident, says that while convalescing she 'rusticated' at the coffee houses and bagnios in Covent Garden, where her pick-ups included members of the diplomatic corps, a line of clients in which she seems to have specialised. The *Revels* comments: 'Tis true her bulk is rather a hindrance to her agility which may in some measure excuse her not being able to get off the ground . . . she still continues to tipple to excess.'

Dubery had to recruit heavily, as did the other King's Place abbesses, in 1792 when a Turkish envoy of prodigious potency and 'insatiable' lust came to London. Yussuf Adji Effendi was said to have 'a Pintle so huge and powerful that it was past all Understanding'. The abbesses were reported to be 'stretched to their utmost limits for the Great Plenipotentiary'. The double entendre was no doubt intentional and Gillray's engraving of the reception of the envoy by George III and his court is an amusing comment on the occasion. Mrs Dubery retired in 1814, 'after a reign of thirty-six years' successful trading'. The *Town and Country Magazine* had once referred to her as 'The Skilful Matron of the Temple of Venus'.

A King's Place bawd, remarkable both for her high connections and her durability was Catherine Windsor, who moved into No. 4 in 1775 and retired in 1821. She was one of the panders regularly employed by Old Q, the Duke of Queensberry, even when he was so elderly that passion had diminished to a faint glow. The patronage of the Prince of Wales and his brother, William, Duke of Clarence, brought her even greater celebrity. The Prince was an enthusiastic lecher but a bad payer and there is a caricature of him being dunned by Mrs Windsor and other brothel-keepers who are presenting him with their bills. One demands £1,000 for 'first slice of a young tit only 12 years' and £1,000 for 'uncommon diversions'. A coloured whore named Black Moll is holding out a bill itemising the delights the Prince has sampled, including 'Tipping the Velvet' for £100. A young girl holds a paper asking for payment for her lost maidenhead. It is most unlikely that she and the other powerless girls who succumbed to the royal satyr were ever paid. The more worldly-wise bawds probably didn't expect payment – royal patronage was worth its weight in gold. A customer who probably did pay when he had the money was the Prince's close friend, Charles James Fox. There is a contemporary caricature, King's Place, or a View of Mr Fox's Best Friends (1784) which shows Perdita Robinson and Elizabeth Armistead talking to the Prince of Wales. Katie Hickman speculates that it was at Mrs Windsor's rather than at Goadby's that Fox first met Armistead. In the cartoon Mrs Windsor is saying: 'He introduced his R—— H—— to my house.'

During Mrs Windsor's long reign many of the best-known members of the Cyprian Corps used her house either for assignations or as a means of supporting their almost impossibly expensive lifestyles. (The term Cyprian derived from the orgiastic worship of Aphrodite on Cyprus in classical times. Other terms for high-class harlots in the eighteenth century included Toasts of the Town and Great Impures.) It was at Mrs Windsor's that the Duke of Clarence met and fell for the actress Dorothea Jordan, according to Burford. She already had four children by Sir Richard Ford, then had another ten by the Duke. He allowed her £840 a year, a figure his father King George III thought much too high. When she was not having babies she appeared on stage at Drury Lane. She seems to have been an excellent actress, and was enthusiastically praised by Hazlitt, Lamb and Byron. She was described as 'beautiful and warm-hearted, but indolent, capricious, imprudent and refractory'.

Perhaps more typical of the beauties at Mrs Windsor's was Miss Meredith, a Welsh girl who, besides the eccentric rake Lord Barrymore, captivated London's small coterie of Welsh noblemen. One reason, apparently, was an anatomical oddity: 'those females being modelled differently from English ladies . . . the Seat of Bliss is placed somewhat higher'. The Nocturnal Revels says of Windsor's protégée Mary Newsham that she would accept any customer 'whether it be a Soubise or little Isaac from St Mary Axe – the Spankers [gold coins] will prevail, for she cannot discover any more sin in yielding to a Blackamoor or a Jew than a Christian – even a Methodist'. The actress Perdita Robinson, who had come down in the world after the Prince of Wales cast her off, was another courtesan forced to seek sanctuary and profit at Mrs Windsor's (Burford).

The Rambler had much fun at Mrs Windsor's expense as she took her girls to Bath, Tunbridge Wells and Brighton in pursuit of the holidaying ton, or promenaded them in St James's Park to catch the attention of the officers of the Guards. The royal connections meant that she was seldom out of the papers, and while good copy for journalists her house also provided caricaturists such as Gillray and Rowlandson with an inexhaustible source of fun. Mammy Windsor, as she was sometimes known, retired in 1821. She was remembered as 'the perfect mistress of the art of conversation'.

Perhaps the most unusual brothels, apart from those which catered for perversions, were the three 'temples of love' opened by Elizabeth Keep in the 1760s in St James's Street. Because she had been the mistress of a member of the aristocratic Falkland family, she adopted the name Fawkland, and the three adjoining houses were known as the Fawkland Temples of Love.

They were patronised by among others Lords Cornwallis, Buckingham, Loudoun, Falkland, Bolingbroke and Hamilton. The first house was the Temple of Aurora. It specialised in girls aged between twelve and sixteen (at the time the age of consent was twelve). Here elderly customers were allowed to fondle the girls but not to have sex with them, at least in theory. These little virgins were said to be 'handpicked from those brought to the establishment by their parents'. Every day they were taken walking in St James's Park, as usual to advertise their charms. From Aurora the girls could graduate to the next-door Temple of Flora, run as a luxury brothel, when they reached the age of sixteen. Finally, there was the Temple of Mysteries, which catered for those interested in flagellation and other sado-masochistic practices. Only those girls who had shown special talents made this final move. Presumably those who did not make the grade were turned out on to the streets when they were considered too old. Only a select few very rich roués could afford the subscriptions to this institution. One of them was Henry Carey, Viscount Falkland, the son of Miss Fawkland's lover. As the age of consent was so low she does not seem to have been prosecuted.

Bawds seldom wrote memoirs – discretion was, after all, their stock in trade. Courtesans were more likely to kiss and tell, and when it became known that a celebrated Cyprian was writing the story of her life and amours a collective shudder went through the Quality. Wives might have good reason to suspect their husbands, but no proof. So when in 1794 it became known that the queen of Dublin's bawds, Margaret Leeson, was writing her life story there was consternation throughout the kingdom in those upper-class circles that most needed and valued discretion. Mrs Leeson had long reigned over the city's vice industry, and she knew all its sexual secrets.

Margaret Leeson (1727–97) was beautiful, vivacious, outspoken, fiery, sexually supercharged and audacious. She was painted as the huntress Diana by no less an artist than Pompeo Batoni. Her prey had included the highest in the land, and her memoirs blew the lid right off the Dublin demi-monde: they are quite as much fun as those of the Regency courtesan Harriette Wilson. On a visit to London she managed to insult the Prince of Wales twice. She died after being gang-raped; at the time it was supposed that she died of syphilis, although this seems unlikely. Her memoirs give a detailed picture of high and low life in a city not unlike London, and so her story is included here.

Peg Leeson, as she was called, followed the conventional path to whoredom: 'ruin' by a lover, pregnancy, rejection, a gradual descent into loose living. She packed a great many lovers and babies into her early years. Her high spirits meant that a lover could not take his eyes off her but she would be in someone else's bed. When the hard times came she told her story with unequalled frankness and great vivacity and style.

She ran several brothels before settling in Pitt Street, where she held court as the city's most important, if also its most eccentric, madam. Here she recounts how she rebuffed the Earl of Westmoreland, Lord Lieutenant of Ireland, when he visited her looking for a good time. She objected to his treatment of his late wife. She follows the convention of thinly disguising personages by using dashes:

> I had the honour of a visit from the Earl of W——, the Lord L——t of I——, whose amiable Countess, as I said before, died of a broken heart in consequence of his connection with that celebrated demy rep the honourable (heaven how that word is prostituted!) Mrs ——. On his Excellency's entrance I arose and received him with much respect, blended with *hauteur and contempt*, but on his attempting to be *too familiar*, I told him he must positively excuse me. . . .

Mrs Leeson then picked a quarrel with the Earl, the pretence being some matter of his domestic arrangements impossible now to understand. All too clear, however, was the result:

> He and [a companion] much chagrined, made a precipitate retreat, forgetting even to pay for the flask of Champaigne the noble Vice-Roy had ordered upon his arrival. Pitiful! despicable! mean wretch! (Leeson, 1995)

Here is her description of her encounters with the Prince of Wales in London:

> One morning walking down the Strand, I saw a fine dashing person, attended by another, go into a shop near Temple Bar. My curiosity to know who it was

led me to follow him in; where I soon found it was the Prince of Wales, and fixed my eyes full upon him until he had finished giving his orders, which were for some stripes for waistcoats. I then addressed the shopkeeper, and desired he would cut off enough to make two waistcoats of the same stripe, and pack it up very well, as I wanted to send it as a present to my shoe-maker in Dublin. The Prince turned, and looked steadfastly at me, and then walked out of the shop.

Quite why she insulted the Prince in this way is not clear. Probably just mischievousness. She got another chance a few days later:

Some days later I was riding to dine at Richmond, in company with one lady and three English gentlemen. I heard a great noise of clear the way, clear the way: I looked behind and saw the Prince come, driving furiously in a very high phaeton, with the same gentleman with him, and a train of servants. The gentlemen who were with me said, Ride on one side, and make room for his Royal Highness. Not I indeed, answered I. There is room sufficient, there is one-half the road for him; and I have as much right to the other half as he or anyone else; ye are three cowards, and I shall laugh at you for as long as I live for mean servility. By this time the Prince had come abreast of us, and as he passed he stared at me, and looked as sour as if he would have bitten my nose off. But that did not intimidate me, I galloped off and kept up with him until he came to a gate, which opened to that part of the park wherein he lived; into which he turned after he had given me half a dozen as crabbed looks, as ever I saw on any gentleman's countenance.

The same combination of high spirits and pugnacity led to a contretemps with the famously elegant English actress-courtesan Ann Cateley when the latter was in Dublin for an engagement at the theatre. Cateley was a leader of fashion 'so fêted ... that the term "Cateley-fied" was coined by the ladies who copied her elegant hairstyles and dress' (K. Hickman, 2003).

Whilst I was in my highest prosperity, I was told the celebrated Miss Cateley had spoken very scurrilously of me at the house of a gentleman where I visited; I therefore resolved to affront her openly the first time I could meet her. Some days elapsed without an opportunity, my passion had not cooled but was rather

irritated by the delay . . . About two days after, as I was driving down Fownes's
Street, I saw her come out of the stage-door. I bid the postillion stop, and I
called to her. She came to the carriage door, when I asked her how she could
presume to revile me, and speak of me in so scandalous a manner as she had
done. She denied that she had ever said any thing about me; adding, that whoever told me was an infamous liar, and if I believed them nobody would believe
me. So saying she turned away; when, not thinking her reply in any way satis-
factory, I filled with spite called her a little street-walking London ballad-singer,
and told her I would have her hissed every time she came upon the stage. About
an hour after, I saw her coming down Dame Street, and wanted to have another
wrangle with her, as my spleen was far from being exhausted by the few words
I had said, bitter as they were. I accordingly stopped at a mercer's shop . . . that
I might speak to her as she passed; and again repeated my former words; she
immediately caught up one of her sons who was with her, went into the shop
and fainted, or pretended to do so.

This led to a lawsuit, Cateley claiming Leeson had ordered her postillion
to drive over her and what Leeson called 'her bastards'. The lawsuit was
thrown out by a grand jury, on the basis, Leeson claimed, that she was
known as a generous supporter of the trades of the city while Cateley was
known for meanness, who 'never laid out a farthing in Dublin that she
could avoid'. These excerpts show what a combative and perhaps difficult
woman Leeson was. But what about business? The following account of a
riotous night in her brothel describes a scene not unlike the game Richard
Head played at Mother Cunny's brothel in the seventeenth century. Leeson
was playing whist with three of her girls when four customers arrived.

We were interrupted by four inebriated bloods, who swore we must leave off
playing and retire with them to another game: They were very young handsome fellows, and so urgent, that we complied on certain conditions, that they
should deposit with us ten guineas each, and we agreed on our part that for
every perfect enjoyment, one should be returned; our sparks closed the agreement with a   burning smack [kiss] each, and thus coupled we retired to our
respective apartments, under promise of a disclosure of particulars the next
morning at breakfast; when lo! my gallant was the only person who was able to

draw a single guinea; the other girls retained ten guineas each [more than £700 today] and I nine, and that, I must confess, was owing to my own wonderful exertions, as I wished to lose a guinea or two if possible; as our beaux were so deadly drunk, that they as soon as they got into bed, dropped instantly into the arms of *Morpheus*. This whimsical affair caused great laughter ...

Leeson does not tell us what proportion of her girls' earnings she took for herself. She had to pay rent, hire servants, provide food and drink and repair the house after the numerous riots that took place there. Dublin bucks seem to have been considerably more volatile than their London counterparts, likely to smash the place up when drunk or cross. And occasionally there was much more serious trouble.

In London in the first decades of the eighteenth century there was a series of outrages perpetrated by upper-class thugs, some of whom were known as Mohocks, who murdered and maimed for amusement. In March 1712 five 'peers and persons of quality' were involved in a scuffle in a tavern in the Strand during which the landlady was killed. 'The gentlemen laughed and ordered that she should be added to their bill.' Queen Anne ordered an inquiry and the High Constable who had released the five from custody was sacked. At a subsequent trial their rank ensured that they were all acquitted. Other Mohocks attacked innocent men and women in the streets at night, raping, slitting noses, cutting off ears and rolling people downhill in barrels. The author L.O. Pike described 'roisterers who made night hideous in the eighteenth century. The "Mohocks", the "Nickers", the "Tumblers", the "Dancing Masters" and the various bully-captains .. . If they met an unprotected woman, they showed they had no sense of decency; if they met a man who was unarmed or weaker than themselves they assaulted and, perhaps, killed him.' The Sweaters would surround a victim and prick his buttocks with swords as he tried to flee. The Bold Bucks specialised in rape. If they could not find victims in the streets they would enter houses and drag out screaming women. They would first drink so much 'they were quite beyond the possibility of attending to any notions of reason or humanity' (Hibbert, 1963).

Dublin's equivalent of these thugs were the Pinking-dindies, mainly students from Trinity College, led by Richard Crosbie. Mrs Leeson says they 'ran drunk through the streets, knocking down whomever they met; attacked, beat and cut the Watch; and with great valour, broke open the habitations of unfortunate girls, demolished the furniture of their rooms, and treated the unhappy sufferers with a barbarity and savageness at which a gang of drunken coal-porters would have blushed'. Crosbie led his gang on a raid on one of Mrs Leeson's brothels, in Drogheda Street. When she refused to let them in they smashed all the windows, battered down the front door, wrecked all the furniture and with swords drawn searched the house for Leeson's lover, a Mr Lawless, 'though he had not given offence to either [any] of the party'.

> Luckily he was absent. This shock, with the ill-treatment I received from these self-called gentlemen, at a time of my being so very big with child, would have moved compassion in the hearts of wild Indians, threw me into a fit. I lay as dead, when some of my neighbours took me out lifeless, and carried me in that state to one of their houses. Still these ruffians continued their outrage, until the Watch came. They then turned and gave battle, and many cuts and hurts were received on both sides. At length, the riot continuing, to the terror of the whole street, the . . . Sheriffs . . . arrived with a party of the military, at whose approach the rioters dispersed.

Mrs Leeson had been roughed up by the students, and gave birth to a still-born baby that had a broken leg. She sued Crosbie for the damage to her brothel, and he was jailed and fined. Later she forgave him and even shook his hand, but 'taught by this affair, I never after would have any acquaintance with Collegians, nor ever entertained one of them'.

One evening – it's not clear when, as Mrs Leeson is not good with dates – two politicians of whom Leeson disapproved came to her Pitt Street brothel. Having heard how they had bilked a poor publisher who had printed their election addresses, Leeson, in her own words, sent them away with a flea in their ear. In the course of her rant she reflected on her own career, winding herself up to such a pitch that she fell to her knees and begged God's forgiveness. She decided on the spot to retire, which she did. She had little savings, but had amassed a vast collection of IOUs from her customers. Once she retired, however, these proved worthless, as she no longer had any bargaining power. (Mrs Haddock was also owed a vast sum when she died.) Hard pressed for cash, she had to let the house in Pitt Street go, attempted suicide and ended up in a debtors' prison. Like many another sinner she decided to publish her memoirs, to raise cash and also, quite candidly, to embarrass former lovers and customers who refused to redeem their IOUs. The first two volumes sold well, repairing much of the damage to her finances; the third was published after her death. She had completed it, and was optimistic about its reception and her future, when she went for a walk one evening with her servant Peggy Collins:

> On our return in the dusk of the evening, we were attacked by five ruffians, who dragged us into an adjoining field, and after stripping us to our shifts, and robbing us of what cash we had about us, actually compelled us by force to comply with their infamous desires and otherwise used us most cruelly, as we made as much resistance as was in our power; particularly poor Mrs Collins, who in her rage thrust her scissors into one of the villains' bellies, at the very moment he was enjoying her, after they severally satiated their brutal appetites, they left us ... stripped to our shifts ...

The two women soon found they had been infected with syphilis. Mrs Leeson was treated with mercury, but died some months later. Even given the supposed great potency of syphilis in the eighteenth century, this seems a remarkably swift demise. She had a decent funeral, attended by 'many respectable citizens'.

Leeson was probably not straightforwardly greedy enough to be a successful bawd – the mountain of IOUs is telling in that respect. She was a kind of good-time girl who couldn't always keep her mind on her trade. Unlike the more businesslike bawds of the Hayes and Needham stamp, she treated her girls well and some of them became close friends. She recognised her faults, and her memoirs are refreshingly free of guilty hand-wringing about her chosen profession.

Brothels dedicated solely to the gratification of women were rare. Mary Wilson, an interesting woman who both translated and published foreign erotic novels and already had brothels in Old Bond Street, St Pancras and Hall Place, St John's Wood, set up what she called 'an Eleusinian Institution'. In 1824 she described it in her book *The Voluptarian Cabinet*. The 'Institution' was divided into two sections, one for married women and their lovers, the other for women seeking sex.

> I have purchased very extensive premises, which are situated between two great thoroughfares and are entered from each by means of shops, devoted entirely to such trades as are exclusively resorted to by ladies. In the area between the two rows of houses, I have erected a most elegant temple, in the centre of which are large saloons, entirely surrounded by boudoirs most elegantly and commodiously fitted up. In these saloons, according to their classes, are to be seen the finest men of their species I can procure, occupied in whatever amusements are adapted to their taste, and all kept in a high state of excitement by good living and idleness ...

The women customers first viewed these studs through a window and when they saw one they fancied they would ring for a chambermaid and point him out. Mary Wilson wrote that the woman client could 'enjoy him in the dark, or have a light, and keep on her mask. She can stay an hour or a night, and have one or two dozen men as she pleases, without being known to any of them. . . .' Two dozen men would have been extravagant in every sense. As in the case of Charlotte Hayes's brothel, where Lady Loveit had to pay a premium, women's pleasure was much more expensive than men's. The subscription alone was 100 guineas, and the fine food and wine also had to be paid for separately, as in a restaurant. The fittings were sumptuous, and the walls were decorated with pornographic paintings after the manner of the Renaissance artist Giulio Romano (Henriques, 1962–8). However, all high-class brothels, whose whores had their own coaches and servants in livery, were prohibitively expensive. Von Archenholz, writing about King's Place, says:

> The admission into these temples is so exorbitant, that the mob are entirely excluded: there are, indeed, only a few rich people who can aspire to the favours of such venal divinities. . . . The houses were magnificent and the furniture worthy of a prince's palace. . . . The celebrated Fox [politician Charles James Fox

(1749–1806), leader of the Whigs] used to frequent these places often before he became a minister; and even afterwards, drunk, as it were, with the pleasures he had enjoyed, he went from thence to move, astonish, and direct the House of Commons, by means of his manly and moving eloquence.

The Covent Garden area fairly seethed with brothels. Mother Burgess specialised in flagellation, a fact which got her a handsome mention in the *Paphian Grove* (1738):

Burgess now does bemoan her absent fair
And wishes their quick return:
But let my Muse advise, to ease your pain
Back to your flogging shop return again.
With breeches down, there let some lusty Lad
(To desp'rate sickness desp'rate cures are had!)
With honest birch excoriate your hide
And flog the Cupid from your scourged backside!

Mother Burgess came from a family of bawds: Thomas had five houses in Drury Lane from 1711, James owned one in James's Street, William operated in Hart Street for more than thirty years, and despite the presence of the police office there John had a brothel in Bow Street from 1727 to 1733 (Burford and Wotton, 1995).

Mother Cane had a brothel in Bedfordbury. The number of her aliases – Row, Dixon, Shute, Monk – however, suggests she was often in trouble with the law. In December 1730 she was fined two marks and imprisoned for six months for keeping a disorderly house. Seven years later she was in trouble again, and sent to the Bridewell at Tothill Fields for three months. This time she was fined only a shilling 'on account of her extreme poverty'. A crony of Moll King, she perhaps had a greater claim to fame: she may have been related to Elizabeth Cane, who as Mrs Armistead married the Whig leader Charles James Fox.

The Coles were another family of Covent Garden bawds. Best known was Mother Cole, 'a sanctimonious Bawd, an infamous Governante' and originally a fruit-seller in the gallery at the Playhouse, a direct conduit to prostitution. Later she ran a milliner's shop in Russell Street where 'three lovely young Harlots served the gentlemen in a spacious Drawing-room at the back in which a select Band of young Fops were wont to gather'. Other shops in the area offered the same service, and in Victorian times exclusive West End shops, were known to have rooms where men and women could retire. Sometimes the pretty shop girls themselves were available.

A special place in this world of fashionable vice around Covent Garden was held by the bath-houses, or bagnios, in a sense a revival of the medieval stews. They were very expensive but popular, and those who went there, both men and women, had other things on their mind than bathing or washing. As we have seen, the Haddocks made a fortune from their bagnios in the Covent Garden area. Men could send out for the prostitute of their choice, or relax after the rigours of an encounter. Casanova, who visited one in the 1760s, wrote: 'I also visited the bagnios, where a rich man can sup, bathe and sleep with a fashionable courtesan, of which species there are many in London. It makes a magnificent debauch, and only costs six guineas.' (Casanova was flush with cash at the time, and could regard 6 guineas as a trifle, but it amounts to about £500 today.) Von Archenholz, a knowledgeable observer of London's low life, describes the bagnios in detail:

> In London there is a certain kind of house, called bagnios, which are supposed to be baths; their real purpose, however, is to provide persons of both sexes with pleasure. These houses are well, and often richly furnished, and every device for exciting the senses is either at hand or can be provided. Girls do not live here, but they are fetched in [sedan] chairs when required. None but those who are specially attractive in all ways are so honoured, and for this reason they often send their address to a hundred of these bagnios in order to make themselves known. A girl who is sent for and does not please receives no gratuity, the chair alone being paid for. The English retain their solemnity even as regards their pleasures, and consequently the business of such a house is conducted with a seriousness and propriety which is hard to credit. All noise and uproar is banned here; no loud footsteps are heard, every corner is carpeted and the numerous attendants speak quietly among themselves. Old

people and degenerates can here receive flagellation, for which all establishments are prepared. In every bagnio there is found a formula regarding baths,
but they are seldom needed. . . . More money is exhausted in one night in
these Bagnios . . . than would maintain all the Seven United Provinces for six
months. Most of them are quite close to the theatres, and many taverns are in
the same neighbourhood.

The Georgian luxury brothel was part club, part salon, a place where
a gentleman could go for pleasant company or for a debauch, or both.
The atmosphere implied that everyone involved knew how to enjoy
themselves, and that the customers had the time and money to do so. For
a brief moment a few square miles of central London existed in a moral
vacuum, devoted to a spirit of *carpe diem*.

FIVE

BUCKS, BLOODS, DEMI-REPS AND CHOICE SPIRITS

Around Covent Garden there were establishments – not quite broth-els but certainly not respectable – where the louche elements of London society could meet. Foremost among them from the 1720s to the 1740s was Moll King's coffee house in front of the church of St Paul's. Here the worlds of fashion, harlotry high and low, crime and bohemian intellectualism mingled and played. It was the haunt of 'Bucks, Bloods, Demi-reps and Choice Spirits of all London . . . the *All-Night Lads*, oth-erwise the *Peep-o-Day Boys*'. Men went there to pick up tarts, the great bawds to find new talent, penniless and supperless girls in the hope of meeting a man who would buy them a drink and a lamb chop and take them to a room for the night. For the price of a cup of coffee they could sit in a corner or sleep off a skinful on a bench.

Moll was born nearby in the venerable slum of St Giles-in-the-Fields in 1696. As a teenager she had a barrow in the Garden, selling nuts. She was loved for her peculiar sweetness of temper and good looks, both eventually lost, as the anonymous *Life and Character of Moll King* of 1747 makes clear. Among her friends were celebrated whores and courtesans, including Sally Salisbury, like Moll a working-class girl, and most of the bawds with establishments around the Garden. In 1717 Moll married Tom King, an Eton and Cambridge scholar who left the university under a cloud and became a Covent Garden waiter. Although he was regarded as a handsome charmer she complained that he beat her, and she left him and briefly became mistress of William Murray, later a corrupt Lord Chief Justice and the first Earl of Mansfield. Through Murray she made contacts with the world of gallantry and fashion, connections which

were useful when she later ran her coffee shop. The Kings were reconciled – Moll claimed she had always loved her husband, and left him only
because he was having an affair with a vicious prostitute who attacked
her. The couple then went into business in a small way selling coffee at
a penny a dish in Covent Garden from 'a little hovel'. Evidently popular,
their shop soon expanded into a row of shacks, becoming a magnet for
'young rakes and their pritty misses . . . Every swain, even from the Star
and Garter to the coffee house boy, might be sure of finding a nymph
in waiting at Moll's Fair Reception House, as she was pleased to term it,
and the most squeamish beau, surely, could not refuse such dainties and
the very sweetest too that ever Covent Garden afforded.' The place was
also a magnet for police spies, and many of the criminals and their molls
who met there talked flash, the underworld dialect, because informers
were ever ready to 'peach' for money. We can eavesdrop, as it were, on
a flash conversation at Moll's. A contemporary pamphlet entitled *The
Humours of the Flashy Boys at Moll King's* gives this exchange between
Moll and a customer named Harry Moythen, who was later murdered:

Harry: To pay, Moll, for I must hike.

Moll: Let me see! There's a Grunter's Gig, is a Si-Buxom; Five Cats' Heads, a
Whyn; a double Gage of Rum Slobber, is Thrums; and a quartern of
Max is three Megs. That makes a Traveller, all but a Meg.

Harry: Here, take your Traveller, and tip the Meg to the Kinchin . . . But Moll,
don't Puff, you must tip me your Clout before I Derrick, for my Bloss has
Milled me of mine. But I shall catch her at Maddox's gin-ken, Sluicing her
Gob by the Tinney. And if she has Morric'd it, Knocks and Socks, Thumps
and Plumps shall attend the Froe-File-Buttocking bitch . . .

To Hike meant to go home, a Grunter's Gig was a hog's cheek, Si-Buxom
was sixpence, a Cat's Head a ha'penny roll, a Whyn a penny, a Gage of
Rum-Slobber a pot of porter, Thrums was threepence, Max was gin,
Kinchin a little child; to Puff, to impeach; Clout, a handkerchief; Derrick,
to go away; Froe-file-buttock, a woman pickpocket-prostitute, and so on.

By all accounts, Moll was a forceful businesswoman, fully the equal of the great bawds of her time. It is interesting that it was her biography that was written, and not Tom's. Although during his lifetime the coffee shop was known as Tom King's – the sign over the door in Hogarth's engraving *Morning* from *The Four Times of the Day* describes it so – Moll was universally acknowledged to be the boss. She lent money to the poor market traders at 2s or half a crown in £1 interest (about 12 per cent). 'Town Misses', as whores were sometimes known, had to pay more. However, she 'made a great distinction between industry and vice'. Courtesans who squandered their huge incomes on drink had to pay the highest interest; poor drabs of streetwalkers got better rates and more time to pay. Moll remembered from her own time in the demi-monde that the lives and finances of the marginal were perilous. 'Notwithstanding her temper, we do not find that she ever put anyone in prison [for debt] unless they used her very ill', records *The Life*. The reference to her temper suggests a change in character. As she grew older she put on weight, lost her looks and became a toper and a bully. She had been known for her sweet temperament and for remaining sober while all about her, including her husband Tom, got completely drunk.

Her coffee house became the most talked-about resort of whores and their customers. The Toasts of the Town, including Betsy Careless and the newly arrived Fanny Murray, used it like a club, and the great bawds, among them Mothers Needham, Burgess and Griffiths, met there to exchange intelligence about their customers. Mother Hayward was a particular favourite. Moll presided over this chaos of disorder and vice with aplomb.

Predictably, the owners of some nearby brothels were dismayed to find their girls taking time off to have a drink at Moll's, or worse, meeting men there and taking them somewhere else to seal their bargains. The *Paphian Grove* (1738) has this to say:

Each vacant bagnio is desert seen
From Haddock's, Hayward's – down to Mother Green.
Refrain from tears, ye Haggs of Hell, refrain
Each girl will soon return and bring a swain

Loaded with gold – who at vast expence
For to support your cursed extravagance!

After midnight things became riotous. Drunken whores fought over customers, swords would be drawn and cudgels swung, desperate fights would spill out into the Piazza where gallants made a game of roughing up the men of the Watch. Moll's evident success and sharp tongue riled the owners of some nearby brothels, and they stirred up more trouble by informing against her. Her coffee house was often raided by that scourge of early eighteenth-century whores, the magistrate Sir John Gonson, but because Moll always insisted that there should be no beds in her shacks he could not accuse her of running a brothel. Her customers could pick up girls at her coffee house but had to take them elsewhere for consummation. Nevertheless, she was sometimes in trouble with the law. In May 1736 four men 'heated with liquor' caused a riot at the chapel of the Sardinian ambassador in Lincoln's Inn Fields, 'abusing and striking several persons'. They had been to Moll's, and she and her nephew were censured. In November of the following year after three men were assaulted at the coffee shacks she and a servant were accused of keeping a disorderly house 'at which sexual offences were committed'. The two women and two doormen were fined.

The artist William Hogarth found abundant material for his moralising series of engravings at establishments like Moll's. In *Morning* he shows a riot at the coffee house, and the woman in the doorway trying to break it up is probably Moll herself. The link boy seen with the pious woman on her way to church is the troublemaker Little Cazey, who invariably accompanied the Toast of the Town Betsy Careless. Is this emaciated woman supposed to be the lovely Careless? Perhaps Hogarth is implying that with time, this is what she will become. In fact Betsy didn't have much time: she was too careless of her money and her health and died young and broke in 1739, three years after Hogarth painted the scenes on which the engravings are based.

The sleepy-eyed rakes fondling their girls outside Moll's have evidently been in the coffee house much of the night. In her *Hogarth, A Life and a World* (1997), Jenny Uglow states that Moll opened her doors after the taverns closed and did not shut up shop until dawn:'. . . the beaux went there straight from Court, in full dress with their swords, mingling in their rich brocaded coats with porters and soldiers and sweeps'.They would also find there the players from the nearby theatres, the Toasts of the Town 'all dressed up fine and pretty and elegantly as if going to a box at the opera'. By two in the morning a hot time was being had by all. George Alexander Stevens (1788) described the shack known as The Long Room:'you might see grave-looking Men, half mizzy-eyed, looking askance at a poor supper-less Strumpet asleep on a Bench, her ragged Handkerchief fallen exposing her bare Bosom on which these old Lechers were doating' (Stevens, 1788). Nearby were 'half-a-dozen Ladies of the Town fighting and scratching one another for the possession of a man about whose person they cared as much as a Sexton cares for a Corpse'. In the smaller shack, where much drinking went on, 'Jolly Claret drinkers' of both sexes 'were making a Jollity, joking and horsing around until the scene turned to shrieking, rioting, the break-ing of bowls and even murder'. Among the court figures who came to gawp at all this was the King himself, George II, who turned up one night with his equerry, Viscount Gage. When the King began to ogle a woman at a nearby table her escort became abusive and drew his sword. Gage drew his too but was restrained by the King, who is said to have murmured 'The gentleman perhaps does not know me', and left (Burford, 1986).

Eventually it would be time for even the most determined reveller to go home or to find a night's lodging, or for the penniless a chilly night could be spent on one of Moll's benches. The *Nocturnal Revels* reports:

> From this gambling set many a broken gamester has repaired to Moll King's to snore out the remainder of the night, for want of a shilling to obtain a lodg-ing. If he should chance to have a watch or a pair of silver buckles remaining, while he was paying his devotion to Morpheus the nimble-handed gentry of either sex were labouring in their vocation, and the unhappy victim of fortune became the still more unhappy victim to Mercury and his votaries. From this receptacle the son of Bacchus reeled home at day-break, the Buck took his doxy to a bagnio, and the Blood carried off his moll in triumph in a chair, himself at the top of it with a broken sword and a tattered shirt, escorted by link-boys, watchmen and pick-pockets.

There is a contemporary engraving, called *The Covent Garden Morning Frolic*, which illustrates just such a scene. It shows Betsy Careless being carried home dead drunk in her sedan chair with her protector Captain 'Mad Jack' Montague, later the notorious Earl of Sandwich, on the roof with a broken sword. Her link-boy Laurence Casey, known as Little Cazey, leads the procession. The playwright, novelist and reforming magistrate Henry Fielding observed: 'I consider Captain Laroun and his friend Captain Montague and their constant companion Little Cazey the link boy as the three most troublesome and difficult to manage of all my Bow Street visitors.' There were troublemakers too among the revellers who after midnight would pour out of the Field of Blood brothel in nearby Charles Court and pile into Moll's.

The Kings became wealthy, and Tom bought an estate at Haverstock Hill on the way to Hampstead and built 'a very genteel country house'. In fact it was a row of houses, which still exists. There is a story that Moll was looking out from a window there one day when a party of gentlemen came by and one remarked: 'Look, there's Moll King's folly.' Moll called back: 'No, ye bantling, it's your folly and some more Jack-an-Apes as silly as yourself, for you know fools' pence flew fast enough about, and they helped to build it.' Tom drank himself into a decline and died in his country house in 1739.

Moll had become addicted to the rough and tumble of her London life and refused to retire. Perhaps she just didn't fancy the country life. 'I love to be in town because I shall see what my pretty Birds are doing.' She was also by now addicted to drink and had become quarrelsome, having long been renowned for sobriety. She became a bloated termagant, her house even more disorderly, 'the haunt of every kind of Intemperance, Idleness and the Eccentric and Notorious in every Walk of Life'. Moll, a '*Fat Priestess* of portly Mien and Voice sonorous ... inviting all to join the Bacchanalian rites', would sit toping with her crony Mother Hayward and occasionally, doubtless to add to their amusement, the pair would 'play a finesse' – a confidence trick – on a drunken customer. A waiter would approach the befuddled gallant with a tray of broken crockery kept specially for the purpose and present him with a bill for up to £20 'for the damage done ... and extra for the broken china'.

After a riot at the coffee house in June 1739 Moll was accused of assaulting a young gentleman whom she had thrashed in a drunken rage. Usually Moll escaped prison by bribing the witnesses against her not to appear, but this time she was fined the enormous sum of £200 (more than £22,000 today) and sent to the King's Bench prison until she paid up. She refused to pay, saying the fine was excessive, and was sent to Newgate to cool off. For three months she negotiated with the High Bailiff, and eventually got the fine reduced to £50. Life in prison was irksome but comfortable for someone as rich as Moll, and when she was released she found her nephew William, whom she had left in charge, had run the business competently. She married a man named Hoff, who was after her money, but she had already willed it to her son Tom, who had been educated at Westminster School. Moll, prematurely worn out by her own nocturnal revels, finally overcame her earlier reluctance and 'retired to live upon a very easy fortune' (*Nocturnal Revels*). She lived at Haverstock Hill, and when she died in 1747, 'one of her favourite customers' wrote an elegy from which these lines are taken:

Here lies my love, who often drove
Wheelbarrows in the street;
From which low state, to Billingsgate,
With wickedness replete
She sold a dish of stinking fish
With oaths and imprecations;
And swore her ware were better far
Than any in the nation.
From thence she came to be in fame
Among the rogues and whores
But now she's gone to her long home
To settle all her scores.

Moll's coffee house was taken over by George Carpenter, a one-time Covent Garden porter who had made a fortune in property, and it was named after him. William Hickey wrote of the unappetising beverage sold there: 'they still continued to dole out a Spartan mixture, difficult to ascertain the ingredients of, but which was served as coffee'. Under the circumstances it was probably fortunate that most of the customers were more interested in the doxies who continued to use the shacks for pick-ups. William Hickey described it as 'the last of those nocturnal Resorts for which Covent Garden was famous ... it bore the same horrid repu-tation as the Soup Shop ale house in nearby Brydges Street'. Carpenter's was also known as The Finish. (Interestingly, in Victorian times certain late-night boozing dens were also known as 'finishes'.)

After Carpenter died in about 1785 the lease passed through vari-ous hands but the premises acquired no more respectability. Nor did its reputation appear to change much – in 1825 the lease was owned by one Jack Rowbottom, and Pierce Egan, the Regency sporting author, wrote of it in his famous satire *Tom and Jerry*: '. . . a notorious Night-House [to which] Swells, bundled out of Offley's in Henrietta Street at four in the morning would bundle-in at Jack's till nine and ten a.m.' The coffee house was demolished in 1866.

Another Covent Garden attraction was a toned-down version of the 'chuck' game made famous by the seventeenth-century bawd Priss Fotheringham. In the following century it was played in the Rose Tavern near Drury Lane Theatre in Russell Street. It involved one of the women, known as 'posture molls', performing a kind of warm-up act for the whores and their customers who congregated there, by strip-ping naked and dancing on an enormous pewter plate, then lying on her back, drawing her knees up under her chin and clasping her hands under her thighs. Drunken customers would crowd round as the posture moll went into her routine, which was of an explicitness seldom if ever seen in public in London since the seventeenth century. At some point she would dance and snuff out a lighted candle in an obscene mock-ery of sex. Plate 3 of Hogarth's *The Rake's Progress* depicts the room at the tavern as the act is about to begin. In the foreground the posture woman strips off and in the background a porter known as Leathercoat or Lethercote brings in the platter and the candle. (Leathercoat, a man of prodigious strength, would for the price of a drink lie down in the street and allow a carriage to pass over his chest.) The satirical writer

Thomas Browne in his *Midnight Spy* (1701) told of 'girls who stripped naked and mounted upon the middle of the table to show their beauties'. He observed one who offered 'just those parts of her body that, were she not without shame, she would most zealously seek to hide', saying of her that she 'usually arrives half-drunk and after a few glasses of Madeira exposes herself in this unseemly manner. Look, she is on all fours like an animal ... men gloat over such prostitution of incomparable beauty!' Brown said it was a place where men 'who by proficiency in the Science of Debauchery [are] called *Flogging Cullies* ... pay an excellent Price for being scourged on their posteriors by *Posture Molls*'.

A witness described how when 'Miss M the famous Posture Girl had stripped and climbed on to the table each Gentleman filled a Glass of Wine and placed their Glasses on her Mound of Venus ... (what time all of them were drinking their Bumpers)'. Burford claims that the best-known of these striptease artists was a girl called Amy Lyon, who later went by the name of Emma Hart and later still was Nelson's mistress Lady Hamilton, but this seems unlikely.

The molls were not prostitutes, and resented being asked for sex. 'They had a great aversion to whoring ... their function was to flagellate or be flagellated to arouse sexual desire in the gentlemen.' Once when some customers, inflamed by the performance, suggested a mass orgy, the posture molls attacked them, starting a riot.

The Rose, although not a brothel, was another 'very sink of iniquity' where 'the real Rake gambles fucks drinks and turns night into day'. Hogarth's marvellous eponymous print shows drunken whores robbing their customers, becoming quarrelsome and getting ready for a night of riot. The whore spitting gin in the face of her rival, so wonderfully observed, is surely based on something Hogarth witnessed. The Rose had a reputation for good food and Pepys ate there with one of his lovers, Doll Lane. Through its rooms over the generations passed the great Toasts of the Town, Sally Salisbury, Betsy Careless, Lucy Cooper, Elizabeth Thomas and Fanny Murray, as well as princes and paupers, poets and playwrights, merchants and broken servants, conmen, mountebanks, rakes, lawyers and distinguished foreigners. Orange Moll, who had the monopoly to sell oranges, lemons and 'other sweetmeats' at Drury Lane Theatre, was often to be seen at the Rose. She also sold her orange girls to wealthy playgo-ers. In 1700 Sir Andrew Slanning, who enjoyed an immense income of £20,000 a year, picked up an orange girl in the theatre pit. When the play ended he left with her and was followed by a gentleman named John Cowland and some of his friends. Cowland put his arm around the orange girl's neck and Slanning objected, saying the girl was his wife. Knowing him to be married to 'a woman of honour', Cowland accused him of lying. The insult called for swords to be drawn but the men were parted, and all agreed to go to the nearby Rose to make it up over a glass of wine. As they were going up the stairs Cowland drew his sword and stabbed Sir Andrew fatally in the stomach. Cowland tried to escape by jumping down the stairs, but was caught. The *Newgate Calendar* reports: 'Mr Cowland being found guilty on the clearest evidence received sentence of death, and, though great efforts were made to obtain a pardon for him, he was executed at Tyburn, on the 20th of December, 1700.'

While the Rose was a popular haunt of actors and managers from the nearby theatre, including David Garrick, Richard Brinsley Sheridan, Jack Kemble, Sarah Siddons, Peg Woffington, George Ann Bellamy and Sophia Baddeley, it was also 'the Resort of the worst Characters in Town, male and female, who make it the Headquarters of Midnight Orgies and Drunken Broils where Murders and Assaults frequently occur'. It was a dangerous place for respectable gentlemen to go, and they went armed. The 'Covent Garden Eclogue', published in 1735, catches something of the atmosphere:

> The Watch had cried 'Past One' with hollow strain
> And to their stands returned to sleep again.
> Grave Cits and bullies, rakes and squeamish Beaux
> Came reeling with their doxies from the Rose ...

After Moll King's death in 1747 Elizabeth Weatherby's Ben Jonson's Head tavern in Russell Street, famous simply as Weatherby's, attracted many of her low-life clients. Some famous harlots began their careers there, including Lucy Cooper and Betsy Weems, or Wemyss. William Hickey describes in his memoirs a visit to Weatherby's, 'an absolute hell upon earth', with some friends equally 'brimfull of wine'.

Upon ringing at a door, strongly secured with knobs of iron, a cut-throat looking rascal opened a small wicket, which was also secured with narrow iron
bars, who in a hoarse and ferocious voice asked: 'Who's there?' Being answered
'Friends' we were cautiously admitted one at a time, and when the last had
entered, the door was instantly closed and secured, not only by an immense
lock and key, but a massy iron bolt and chain. I had then never been within the
walls of a prison, yet this struck me like entering one of the most horrible kind.
My companions conducted me into a room where such a scene was exhibit-
ing that I involuntarily shrunk back with disgust and dismay, and would have
retreated from the apartment, but that I found that my surprize and alarm were
so visible in my countenance as to have attracted the attention of several people
who came up, and good naturedly enough encouraged me, observing that I was
a young hand but should soon be familiarised and enjoy the fun.

At this time the whole room was in an uproar, men and women promiscuously mounted upon chairs, tables and benches, in order to see a sort of
general conflict carried on upon the floor. Two she devils, for they scarce had
a human appearance, were engaged in a scratching and boxing match, their
faces entirely covered with blood, bosoms bare, and clothes nearly torn from
their bodies. For several minutes not a creature interfered between them, or
seemed to care a straw what mischief they might do each other, and the con-
test went on with unabated fury.

In another corner of the same room, an uncommonly athletic young man
of about twenty-five seemed to be the object of universal attack. No less than
three Amazonian tigresses were pummelling him with all their might, and it
appeared to me that some of the males at times dealt him blows with their sticks.
He however made a capital defence, not sparing the women a bit more than the
men, but knocking each down as opportunity occurred. As fresh hands continued pouring in upon him, he must at last have been miserably beaten, had not
two of the gentlemen who went with me (both very stout fellows), offended at
the shameful odds used against a single person, interfered, and after a few knock
me down arguments succeeded in putting an end to the unequal conflict.

The *Nocturnal Revels* of 1779 says Weatherby's was a 'receptacle' for rakes,
highwaymen, pickpockets, swindlers and prostitutes, 'from the charioted
kept mistress down to the twopenny bunter [prostitute] who plies under

the Piazza . . .' which makes it sound a worthy successor to Moll King's. The *Nocturnal Revels* paints a wretched picture of such a poor harlot: 'the unfortunate strumpet who had been starving in a garret all day long while washing her only and last shift, upon making her appearance here, might probably meet with a greenhorn apprentice boy who could treat her with a mutton chop and a pot of porter . . .'. With luck he might also be persuaded to take her to a low lodging house for the night, one more night rescued from oblivion.

A highly fashionable pleasure resort in the 1760s was Carlisle House in Soho Square, run by Madame Theresa Cornelys. Born in Venice, she had once been the mistress of Casanova, by whom she had a daughter. Interestingly, her father had been the lover of Casanova's mother. She married a dancer, then for a time was the mistress of the Margrave of Bayreuth and afterwards Prince Charles de Lorraine; later she became director of theatres at Brussels, but had to flee because of debts. Arriving in London in 1763, after a failed career as a singer she went into business, for which she showed great flair, with a wealthy English parson, John Fermor, who bankrolled the acquisition of Carlisle House where she held recitals, balls and masquerades. It was a kind of nightclub, renowned for the opulent extravagance of its decor. One year the theme was rural, involving real pine trees and fountains, 'an elegant erection of Gothick arches' and 'a moving spiral pillar of lights'. In his memoirs William Hickey describes a visit to her 'truly magnificent suite of apartments . . . So much did it take that the first people of the kingdom attended it, as did also the whole beauty of the metropolis, from the Duchess of Devonshire down to the little milliner's apprentice from Cranbourn Alley.' Another contemporary described her house as 'by far the most magnificent place of public entertainment in Europe'. It was patronised by a fast set of society beauties led by the scandalous Lady Elizabeth Chudleigh, Duchess of Kingston, who formed an improbable attachment to the low-born Cornelys, a relationship most beneficial to the latter since it helped attract high society and, on occasions, royalty to this fashionably decadent nightspot. When in January 1764 the Duke of Brunswick was married to Princess Augusta, sister of George III, a subscription ball to celebrate the occasion was held at Carlisle House.

The Duchess of Kingston herself would have been quite a draw: she was famous for several reasons, none of them respectable. She had appeared almost naked at Ranelagh Gardens in June 1749, and thereafter equally disrobed at other gatherings. As Elizabeth Chudleigh she had been a Maid of Honour to the Princess of Wales and was courted by the Duke of Hamilton who promised to marry her when he returned from the Grand Tour. However, while he was away she met and married the noted philanderer Lieutenant Augustus Hervey RN in 1774. They kept the marriage secret, otherwise Elizabeth would have lost her position in the royal household and her £400-a-year salary. After the ceremony Hervey sailed away to a life of further sexual adventures. Elizabeth seems to have had a good time too. After she appeared at the Venetian ambassador's ball at Somerset House in a costume which revealed all, Mrs Elizabeth Montague, founder of the Blue Stocking Society, wrote: 'Miss Chudleigh's undress was remarkable . . . The Maids of Honour were so offended they were lost for words.'

She became the mistress of the wealthy and elderly Duke of Kingston, and in March 1769 they married, Elizabeth having conveniently convinced herself that the marriage ceremony she and Hervey had gone through was 'such a scrambling shabby business and so much incomplete' that it had not really amounted to a wedding. However, she was so tense that when the marriage ceremony was over she fainted. Hervey threatened to tell all, but in the end remained silent. His marriage to Chudleigh was an open secret, anyway, the subject of much society gossip, and when the Duke of Kingston died in 1763 the eldest of his heirs, who had been disinherited, challenged the will. Chudleigh was tried for bigamy in the Great Hall of Westminster. Hervey had recently succeeded to the title of Earl of Bristol, so if Chudleigh lost she was still Countess of Bristol. She was found guilty, and the Attorney General tried to have her burned in the hand, a common punishment for minor crimes. However, strings were pulled and even this punishment was waived. The judges ordered her not to leave the kingdom, but she went to France and eventually Russia, where she became a friend of Catherine the Great. She died in Paris in 1788. Horace Walpole commented wryly: 'So all this combination of knavery receives no punishment but the loss of the duchy.' Chudleigh had become Countess of Bristol in 1777.

With the Chudleigh connection and her considerable flair for show-manship, Mrs Cornelys made a great deal of money – tickets to her glamorous balls were exorbitantly expensive. But she spent it even faster, and it became impossible to keep the Toasts of the Town out of her masked balls, which became fronts for pick-ups. 'The whole Design of the libidinous Assembly seems to terminate in Assignations and Intrigues', said a contemporary. Burford says that another of the Chudleigh clique, the debauched Countess of Harrington, who sold the tickets for Mrs Cornelys's balls, acted as 'unpaid procuress'. To quote Horace Walpole again, Carlisle House attracted 'both righteous and ungodly'.

Gradually Carlisle House fell out of fashion, not least because of com-petition from the newly opened Pantheon. The Quality began to stay away and the guests became more disreputable. Neighbours complained about the noise, and there were suggestions that the house had become a brothel. But it was her debts that finally overwhelmed Cornelys. She quarrelled with Fermor and other creditors, and had spells in debtors' prisons, a not-uncommon experience in the eighteenth century. She was finally committed to the King's Bench prison in November 1779 by a group of creditors who included Thomas Chippendale, the great cabinet maker. She was freed by the mob who burned London's prisons during the Gordon Riots in June 1780, only to be recaptured a few weeks later. She was discharged the following February. Although she was sixty-nine she tried several times to make a comeback, though not at Carlisle House, which had now passed out of her hands. She was arrested again for debt, and held in Newgate. An old friend persuaded the authorities to move her to the slightly less noisome Fleet Prison, where she died in August 1797, after a painful struggle with cancer. The following death notice appeared in the *Gentlemen's Magazine*: 'In the Fleet prison, at a very advanced age, Mrs Cornelly, a distinguished priestess of fashion, who once made much noise in the world of gaiety.' Thus passed away one of that group of dauntless pioneering women who did so much to make London nights memorable in the eighteenth century.

SIX

JACK HARRIS

PIMPMASTER GENERAL

With so much to offer, Covent Garden needed a publicity agent, and in about 1740 it got one far ahead of his time in the art. Jack Harris was at least for a while head waiter at the Shakespeare's Head Tavern under the Piazza, where the marvellous cook John Twigg presided over a kitchen renowned for many years for its excellence. Twigg's turtle soup had such a following that the proprietor bought fifty turtles at a time, so great was the demand from out-of-town customers. Harris, popularly known as the Pimpmaster General because of the Whores' Club he ran there on Sunday evenings in a private room, was also the author of *The List of Covent Garden Ladies*, a guide to local harlots, their charms, specialities and prices. His publishing venture had begun in a modest way with his circulating hand-written lists of whores in the 1740s, but soon he was selling 8,000 printed copies of each edition and for almost twenty years this *vade mecum* was a necessity for every serious man about town. Not all the descriptions are flattering, but the list launched many young women into fame and fortune, including the most celebrated of her time, Fanny Murray. Harris was accused of being a pimp, a charge he was proud to admit. 'The whole amount of the Charge against me is that I am a Pimp . . . I grant it. I need not be ashamed of the Profession from its Antiquity. Nay!'

Describing himself as 'insinuating, dissembling, flattering, cringing, fawning, conniving, with philosophy enough to bear a kicking and a face as great a (seeming) barrier to incontinence as eunuchism', Harris claimed he was well born, and had been educated at Westminster School. He maintained a kind of control over the sex industry in the Covent Garden area, at that time the epicentre of vice. The earliest account of his rackets is in Fanny Murray's *Memoirs*. He charged the whores a fifth of their income for the advertisements, making them sign a legal contract, and set up a form of whores' trade union, with one of its main functions being the collection of his fees. Harris had agents all over London seeking out new faces for his *List*. Every stagecoach and wagon would be met, and once a year he went to Ireland, where he said the girls were among his most beautiful recruits. He was proud he was responsible for seeing that London was so well stocked with fine whores, whom he had taught himself to become 'perfect adepts'. Although he is disparaging of his looks he must have been a very experienced and successful seducer. Fanny's *Memoir* indicates to what an art Harris had raised his pimping operation: 'Mr Harris, the celebrated negotiator in women, applied to get her enrolled upon his parchment list. . . . The ceremony was performed with all the *punctilios* attending that great institution.' Fanny was examined by a surgeon to prove she was free of venereal disease, and a lawyer was on hand as she signed the solemn agreement to pay Harris a fifth of her earnings, and also to hand over £20 if she lied about the state of her health.

Harris's book bears the title *Harris's List of Covent-Garden Ladies Or New Atlantis*, and the subtitle *Containing an exact description of the Persons, Tempers and Accomplishments of the several Ladies of Pleasure who frequent COVENT-GARDEN and other Parts of the Metropolis*. In the introduction, presumably written by Harris himself, he says that 'were there no common women, young fellows would be more earnest and assiduous in their attacks on the virtuous'. This theme, that the world is full of vice and that virtuous women would be ravished or seduced but for the safety valve of the whore, is repeated:

> It cannot be denied by anyone, that is not utterly unacquainted with the world, that public stews are an absolute necessity for the preservation of chastity and virtue; and it must be acknowledged that there was never a greater occasion for such licence than at present, in order to oppose the prevailing schemes of gallantry, the intent of which seems to be to corrupt all without distinction, and to make a grand seraglio of the whole nation. May then both Laws and Magistrates be kind to those public-spirited Nymphs, who contribute to stem the torrent of corruption. . . .

He then has some tongue-in-cheek advice for the whores themselves.

> Attach yourselves with constancy to your keepers, soothe their amorous
> flames, preserve their ardour unabated. With every artifice rouse ancient desire,
> and make them young once more. Reflect, that if you neglect your keeper,
> your lusty gallant must lack his necessary supply. Keepers are the sinews of
> your trade; may they multiply instead of decreasing; may they always be ready
> and willing to keep up the call as honest Nature bids; so shall the public good
> be invigorated, the cause of virtue promoted, and the most abominable of all
> vices entirely rooted out.

The style of *The List of Covent Garden Ladies* is facetious. Harris's weakness
for double entendres is evident in his puff for a Miss Devonshire of Queen
Anne Street: 'Many a man of war has been her willing prisoner, and paid a
proper ransom; her port is said to be well-guarded by a light brown *chev-
aux-de-frieze* . . . the entry is rather straight; but when once in there is very
good riding . . . she is ever ready for an engagement, cares not how soon
she comes to close quarters, and loves to fight yard arm and yard arm, and
be briskly boarded.' Sometimes the pornography is more frankly hardcore.
This is Miss Wilkinson of 10 Bull and Mouth Street:

> . . . a pair of sweet lips that demand the burning kiss and never receive it with-
> out paying interest. . . . Descend a little lower and behold the semi snowballs .
> . . that want not the support of stays; whose truly elastic state never suffers the
> pressure, however severe, to remain but boldly recovers its tempting smooth-
> ness. Next take a view of nature *centrally*; no *folding lapel*; no *gaping orifice*; no
> *horrid gulph* is here, but the *loving lips* tenderly kiss each other, and shelter from
> the cold a small but easily stretched passage, whose *depth* none but the *blind
> boy* has liberty to fathom. . . .

Miss South, who lived in Thatched House Court, St James's, is 'Young,
genteelly educated, a fine Woman full of Fashion and as sound as a
Roach, with black piercing Eyes, much Tenderness in Looks, dark Hair
and delicate Features, snowy Bosom and elegant Shoulders and Sprightly
Behaviour – but she will have her Price.' Her price started at 5 guineas.

His description in the 1764 edition of Lucy Seales of York Buildings, Duke Street, is less enthusiastic: '... very genteel and well-made Lass, with black eyes and light brown hair ... she has not seen much service yet ... she shows little passion in her amours'.

Many of the entries are ambiguous, obviously, to suggest that Harris is an impartial judge. 'Mrs Paterson *alias* Jackson. Haymarket. This piece of affectation is the daughter of a strolling player and was for some time an actress ... returning to England was taken into keeping by a Jew whom she soon left ... because the Israelite, who was not one of the richest, paid her but poorly.' Polly Gold of Spring Gardens gets a better press: 'Short pretty and very agreeable as to her Person and sings a good song. Has been on the Town about ten years ... she is like a *Kite*, sometimes high and sometimes low.'

Poll Talbot of Bow Street is a bawd and a veteran of the sex industry. 'A fair comely Dame who by long intercourse ... has learnt that the profession of a Purveyor is more profitable than that of a Private Trader, and for that reason has opened a House for the amusement of genteel Company where Gentlemen and Ladies will meet with a Civic Reception. She loves the smack of the Whip sometimes. ...' Poll Davis of Manchester Square charges not less than 10 guineas, and a half a crown for her servant. This puts her fairly high up in the scale of charges, and indeed Harris calls her 'a delicate genteel Lady of the First Fashion and Price ... seldom to be seen in the street unless in a Sedan-chair ... her connections are mostly with Gentlemen of Rank and Fortune'. Working out of Russell Street, Covent Garden, Poll Johnson obviously had to take what she could get: 'Prices from ten shillings to Five Guineas, according to the pocket of the *Cull*. Her principal Trade is with Petty Officers, some of whom have paid handsomely for their frolics.' Miss Bird of Brydges Street, Covent Garden is 'a tall thin genteel girl agreeable in her manners ... seen every night in the *Ben Jonsons Head*. She has a northern brogue and is too often in a state of intoxication.'

Some of the little tales are poignant, telling of lives wrecked by abandonment and deceit. Miss M—nt—n, a twenty-year-old of 55 Berwick Street, was the victim of a young aristocrat. 'A young baronet in this lady's spring of life, unrobed her of her virgin suit. Almost as soon as possession was granted indifference took place, and desire entirely vanished, and he left his much-dejected fair one to seek support in the wide field of fortune.' While she had a good complexion and 'a lively sparkling dark eye' poor Miss M——nt——n was disfigured by smallpox and suffered from low spirits, 'which in general require three or four cheerful glasses to dissipate'. Miss W——ll——m of 17 Goodge Street had been abandoned by a naval officer, leaving her 'prey to the precarious buffetings of fortune, who soon after threw her in the common road, and gave her up as public property'. But she had a better chance than poor Miss M——nt——n, having 'a most elegant figure, a beautiful face, and has a skin so fair, that were it possible to paint its equal, would require the utmost sketch of the most fertile fancy'. Harris also informs us that Lord Chesterfield, urbane writer of the famous *Letters*, liked to have his eyelids 'licked by two naked whores'.

Harris died in 1765, probably wealthy, as he had many irons in the fire. One night he had heard Fanny Murray arguing with a client who couldn't afford her price of 2 guineas, as he had only 5s 6d. Obligingly, Harris lent him the remainder on the security of his sword and peruke. No doubt he made a profit on this transaction. Incidentally, Fanny was soon charging a lot more than 2 guineas. It was a lucky man who got her for so little before her stock rose, just as the apprentices who paid the teenage Sally Salisbury a few pennies could hardly imagine the real value of what they bought so cheaply. After Harris died hack writers were employed to keep the *List* going and some of the later entries are more like hatchet jobs than advertisements. Harris's own *Lists* had contained the occasional acerbic aside, but the *Lists* compiled after his death go much further. For example, it is difficult to believe that Miss Grafton of Bow Street paid for this entry:

> . . . that bubble vanity has so elated her that *self* alone engrosses all her thoughts, and *little I*, the heroine of all her thoughts, is sure eternally to be her table talk . . . a woman of her cast is hardly worth notice unless for mere amusement; no intimate acquaintance or connection should be made with her, as she is well known to have as tender a regard for the male part of the sex as a wolf for a lamb . . . a poor ignorant Irishman piping hot arrived, fell into her clutches and she fleeced the poor devil so much that she scarce left him with a coat to his back, and insolently laughed at him in prison where he was confined for debts

contracted for her use; she may be found at the Cat in the Strand almost every evening, and sometimes at the Blakeney's Head in Bow Street, though this house is not calculated for this lady, as they preserve decency and good order.

The later editions make it clear that the Covent Garden area was no longer the main focus of high-class harlotry, as many of the women have addresses elsewhere. This is Mrs Griffin with an address near Union Stairs in Wapping, a long way to the east. The entry makes it clear that she is a sailor's woman, and her price, 5s, gives the game away.

This is a comely woman, about forty, and boasts she can give more pleasure than a dozen raw girls. Indeed she has acquired great experience in the course of twenty years of study.... She is perfect mistress of her actions, and can proceed regularly from the dart of her tongue, the soft tickle of her hand, to the ecstatic squeeze of her thighs; the enchanting twine of her legs; the elaborate suction of her lower lips, and the melting flood of delights with which she constantly bedews the mossy root of the tree of life ... 'tho past her meridian, she is still agreeable, her eyes are black as well as her hair.... Five shillings is her price, and she earns it with great industry....

The *List* for 1788 advertises the services of a Miss Johnson of Goodge Street:

The raven-coloured tresses of Miss Johnson are pleasing, and one characteristic of strength and ability in the wars of Venus. Indeed this fair one is not afraid of work, but will undergo a great deal of labour in the action; she sings, dances, will drink a cheerful glass and is a good companion. She has such a noble elasticity in her loins that she can cast her lover to a pleasing height and receive him again with the utmost dexterity. Her price is one pound one and for her person and amorous qualifications she is well worth the money.

Some of the later entries, however, lack Jack Harris's playfulness, suggesting that a change had come over the business of selling sex. The official attitude also seems to have changed. In 1795 two booksellers were jailed for publishing versions of the *List*.

Through his little book and his widespread contacts Harris exercised a degree of control over the sex industry. His Whores' Club, which met each every Sunday night at the Shakespeare's Head Tavern, was another sign of his hegemony. There were about one hundred members of this mutual-aid organisation, of which he was the main benefactor.

Harris's Club was not a new idea. The brothel-keeper Mother Wisebourne had established a 'society' or committee of whores in the eighteenth century, apparently with the intention of establishing some kind of code for the industry. Anodyne Tanner, author of *The Life of the Late Celebrated Mrs Elizabeth Wisebourn, Vulgarly Called Mother Wybourn* ... (1721), suggests that the society carried on successfully after her death in 1720 and gives an instance of how it worked. A courtesan caught her lover in bed with another member of the society at Mrs Wisebourne's. When she complained Wisebourne suggested that the matter be put to the full committee for a ruling. They decided that no woman could claim a monopoly of a man, whatever their relationship. The good mother also proposed setting up an insurance scheme for men who caught VD from prostitutes, but the proposal was not taken up.

The aim of Harris's Shakespeare's Head club was to help whores who were down on their luck or in prison. The rules indicate what a gulf has opened up in manners between the twenty-first century and the eighteenth.

1. Every girl must have been 'debauched' before she was fifteen.
2. All members must be on Harris's *List*.
3. No *modest* woman to be admitted.
4. Members must not have been in Bridewell more than once.
5. Any girl tried at the Old Bailey for any crime except picking pockets to remain a member as long as she had not pleaded her belly [told the court she was pregnant].
6. Any member who becomes pregnant to be struck off.
7. Each member to contribute half a crown, one shilling of which to go to support members who cannot earn a living because they are being treated for venereal disease, or who cannot get into the Lock Hospital. Another sixpence to go to Harris for 'his great care and assiduity in the proper con-ducting of this worthy society'. The remaining shilling to be spent on drink, 'gin not excluded'.

8. Any member who finds a wealthy protector to make a suit-able donation to the club before quitting.

9. No men to be allowed in except Harris, who can choose any girl he fancies for his bedfellow that night.

10. No religion or politics to be discussed.

11. Any member who gets too drunk to walk to be sent home in a coach or sedan chair at the expense of the society, the fare to be paid back at the next meeting.

12. Any member who breaks glasses, bottles etc. or behaves in a 'riotous manner' to be expelled until she pays for the damage.

13. Any member 'overcharged' with liquor who in 'clearing her stomach' soils another's clothes must replace them.

This final rule conjures up Hogarthian images of excess on Sunday nights at the Shakespeare's Head as these spirited young women, many of them still in their teens, let their hair down. However, the regulations also convey a note of desperation, an awareness that though their nights may be merry their days will be sad or wretched. Too many of these girls shared the fate of Sally Salisbury and Betsy Careless – dead too young of drink and disease.

SEVEN

ALMIGHTY CURTEZAN

If the bawd was the impresario of the sex industry, the Toast was the star, what the playwright Aphra Behn had called the 'Almighty Curtezan, that glorious insolent thing'. Free-spending aristocrats, magnates and businessmen would be drawn to a brothel by the quality of its girls, and the bawds competed for the best. Easy money meant many of these women could live gaudy lives of great extravagance, suddenly rich and as suddenly bankrupt and flung into the debtors' prison. They were young women of great sexual allure and, if contemporary accounts and memoirs are to be relied on, with a powerful sex drive. Most were only adequately intelligent, but they had star quality. Aristocrats, beginning themselves to live in a fantasy world increasingly financed by the exploitation of the labouring poor and Britain's rich natural resources, were happy to indulge them.

One of the hottest properties, in every sense, was Sally Salisbury, the first working-class Toast of the Town. Before Sally courtesans of the first rank were usually well born or acquired in youth those aspects of courtly education and polish that men liked – elegance, good manners, a measure of culture and some knowledge of current affairs. Into this muted world of music and fairly genteel conversation Sally burst like a grenade, a tempestuous, witty, dan-gerous, foul-mouthed and irresistible beauty.

Born Sarah Pridden in 1692, the daughter of a bricklayer, she grew up wretchedly poor in the slums of St Giles, north of Covent Garden. One of her biographers wrote: 'At different seasons of the year she shelled beans and peas, cried nose-gays and newspapers, peeled walnuts, made matches, turned bunter &c., well knowing that a wagging hand always gets a penny' (Walker, 1723). Her first lover was the notorious rake Colonel Charteris, who seduced her when she was barely into her teens.

Perhaps her hair-trigger temper was too hot even for him to handle, and he abandoned her at Bath, whence she returned to London, where her disapproving mother stripped her of her fine clothes and sent her out to work. She began selling newspapers and then herself at the corner of Pope's Head Alley in Cornhill. Her clients were apprentices, several of whom were lucky enough to have her for a few pennies before word spread of this fresh young beauty selling her charms on the streets of the City. Soon she would sell herself for considerably more. According to the anonymous *The Genuine History of Mrs Sarah Pridden, usually called Sally Salisbury*, she was taken up by 'a wealthy Dutchman', who determined to marry her, kitting her out in finery and lavishing money and affection on her. In return she stole more than £20 in gold from him and treated him with contempt, soon tiring of this 'ancient kisser' and his maudlin lovemaking. 'One day, as he kissed her unseasonably, and asked her a hundred times if she could love him, and him alone, she unluckily cried, "D—— you and your broken tongue, can I love rotten teeth and stinking fifty?" And so flew off his knee.'

Not for the last time Sally had burned her boats. She seems to have gone back to Charteris, and her drunken madcap behaviour got him involved in a duel, in which he crippled a man. Although he owned to having 'very frequent satisfaction of Sally, in a house of pleasure, for the damage sustained', Charteris was a coward and felt that this pleasure was too dearly bought: he kicked Sally out for the last time. She became the star of Mother Wisebourne's estab-lishment, the bawd having earlier in her career cured her of the pox and re-virginised her. At the age of about seventeen Sally was an almost priceless asset, unabashed in high society and drawing a stream of aristocratic lovers to Mother Wisebourne's. They included Viscount Bolingbroke, Secretary of State, who paid 'the highest price for the greatest pleasure'. Particularly smitten were the Duke of Richmond, the Duke of St Albans, who was Nell Gwyn's son, the poet Matthew Prior and the Prince of Wales, later to become King George II. For a while Sally was part of the Duke of Buckingham's 'harem', and a ballad says she played the 'chuck game' (see page 19). Her madcap escapades were famous. She and another girl went to Newmarket races with George Brudenall, Earl of Cardigan, got him blind drunk, bundled him into bed and made off with all his clothes and jewels. Reunited with him in London the girls returned the clothes and the Earl treated the whole affair as a huge joke – fortunately for them. He could have had them hanged.

Sally was dangerous company. An early friend, the great actress Elizabeth Barry, dropped her because of her rough manners and unpredictable temper. She used Mother Wisebourne's establishment to entertain her rich and riotous friends and after a drunken spree there in 1713 Sally was sent to Newgate. She was released on the order of Judge Blagney, who had fallen for her. Blagney wrote to the jailer asking him not to punish Sally as he had something else in mind for her – what he seems to have had in mind was becoming her sex slave. He was later reprimanded for corruption. With Sally were arrested several noblemen, including the Earls of Scarborough and Ossory and Robert Henley, later Lord Northington and Lord Chancellor. Also arrested was Sally's friend Mrs Elizabeth Marsham, later Lady Marsham.

The death of Mother Wisebourne in 1719 was a blow to Sally, who lost not only a congenial base for her professional activities but a friend who accepted her with all her faults. Sally next became allied with the vicious Mother Needham, whose brothel was in Park Place, St James's, the centre of high-class bawdry, patronised by courtiers. The great courtesans often found semi-permanent keepers at brothels. If the bawd had groomed and promoted the girl, losing her in this way would be a considerable financial blow, so the lover would be expected to reach a suitable settlement with the bawd before taking the girl away. After leaving she would often continue to make guest appearances, bringing her fine friends and spending money.

Like other working-class courtesans Sally picked up a veneer of sophistication from her aristocratic clients. She was notoriously waspish, particularly if she suspected she was being patronised. At a grand society ball the hostess, outshone by Sally, had the temerity to comment on the splendour of the whore's jewels.

'They had need be finer than yours, my Lady,' said Sally. 'You have but one Lord to keep you, and to buy you jewels, but I have at least half a score, of which number, Madam, your Ladyship's husband is not the most inconsiderable.'

'Nay, my Lady' cried another guest. 'You had better let Mrs Salisbury alone, for she'll lay claim to all our husbands else, by and by.'

'Not much to yours, indeed, Madam,' replied Sally tartly. 'I tried him once and am resolved I'll never try him again; for I was forced to kick him out of bed, because his —— is good for nothing at all.' (Walker, 1723)

It was her ferocious temper that proved her undoing. In December 1722 Lady Mary Wortley Montague described in a letter the incident that led to her death: 'The freshest news in Town is the fatal accident happened three Nights ago to a very pritty young Fellow, brother to Lord Finch, who was drinking with a dearly beloved *Drab* whom you may have heard of by the name of Sally Salisbury. In a jealous *Pique* she stabbed him to the Heart with a Knife. He fell down dead immediately but a surgeon being called and the Knife being drawn out of his Body, he opened his Eyes and his first Words were to ask her to be Friends with him, and he kissed her.'

The cause of the quarrel emerged later. Sally's lover Jack Finch had turned up drunk at the Three Tuns Tavern in Chandos Street around midnight on 22 December. Sally arrived with her sister Jenny about four o'clock in the morning. She too was drunk and angry because Finch had given Jenny some opera tickets, which she took to mean that he favoured Jenny, as the *Newgate Calendar* says, 'with a view to ingratiate her affections, and debauch her'. After she stabbed Finch she became distraught, and cried out, 'Jacky! You are not so bad as you imagine.' She called for a surgeon and as he staunched the blood she cried out again to Finch, 'Jacky! Forgive me.' Finch is said to have replied: 'I die at pleasure from your hand.' When he appeared to recover she said she wanted to go home with him so she could care for him, but when he demurred she went home alone, where she was arrested and charged with attempted murder.

Finch lived, but Sally was sentenced to a year in Newgate and fined £100 – about £11,000 today. In spite of Finch's pleas she remained in Newgate, where she caught jail fever and wasted away. Here is how a Swiss visitor and commentator, César de Saussure, described her death:

You will suppose her lovers abandoned her in her distress. They did no such thing, but crowded into the prison, presenting her with every comfort and luxury possible. As soon as the wounded man – who, by the way, belongs to one of the best-known English families – was sufficiently recovered, he asked for her discharge, but Sally Salisbury died of brain fever, brought on by debauch, before she was able to leave the prison (Saussure, 1902).

Sally was buried at St Andrew's Holborn in February 1724. Her coffin was followed by four coaches, and six gentlemen bore it to the church. She was about thirty-two. Hogarth's print series *A Harlot's Progress* and John Cleland's *Fanny Hill* owe much to her life and legend. In February 1735 the *Weekly Oracle* published an amusing memorial which catches something of Sally's breakneck progress:

> Here flat on her Back, but unactive at last
> Poor Sally lies under grim Death;
> Through the course of her Vices she galloped so fast
> No wonder she's now out of Breath.
> The Goal of her Pleasures she drove very hard
> But was tripped up e'er half way she ran;
> And though everyone fancied her Life was a Yard
> Yet it proved to be less than a Span.

(The effectiveness of the pun on Yard and Span depended on knowing that a Yard also signified an erect penis.) Walker's *Authentick Memoirs* is less kind. He claims Sally once had an abortion, 'but was so affectionate she always preserved the embryo in spirits'.

Sally Salisbury's place as Premier Toast was filled for a time by Betsy Carless, known as Careless, but she was aptly careless and died young and broke in 1739. 'The gayest and wittiest of all the courtesans around Covent Garden', her brief career followed the shallow arc of so many working-class whores: poverty, beauty, celebrity, dissipation, prison, illness, death. Her passing caused a pang to the playwright and magistrate Henry Fielding, who remembered seeing her in his youth on the balcony at the Playhouse, and recalled her 'modest and innocent appearance, and a pity she was on the way to ruin in such company'. Then he recalled that a few days earlier he had seen her in bed at a bagnio, 'smoking tobacco, drinking punch, talking and swearing obscenely and cursing with all the impudence and impiety of the lowest most abandoned trull of a soldier'. In the Bedlam scene of his series *The Rake's Progress* Hogarth depicted among the other madmen William Ellis, who was unhinged by his infatuation for the sweet-looking young harlot. On the stair rails he has written, 'Charming Betty Careless'.

Betsy's first protector had been the dissolute young barrister Robert Henley, once Sally Salisbury's friend. She was too wild even for him, and after he gave her the brush-off she was taken up by the sponger Sir Charles Wyndham, 'an unexampled instance of debauchery'. Betsy was working from a house in the Piazza in Covent Garden, and it was an elegant address for Wyndham, later Earl of Egremont, to idle away his days. Betsy's drinking and profligacy meant her tenure there was short. In 1735 she advertised in the *London Journal*:

> Mrs Betsy Careless from the Piazza in Covent Garden not being able to make an end of her affairs as soon as expected intends on Monday next to open a coffee house in Prujeans Court in the Old Bailey, where she hopes all her friends will favour her with their company notwithstanding the ill-situation and remoteness of the place since her misfortunes oblige her to stay there.

Within four years she was dead. The *Gentlemen's Magazine* reported in October 1739: 'Was buried from the Poor-house of St Paul's, Covent Garden the famed Betty Careless, who helped the gay gentlemen of this country to squander £50,000.' She had been 'a peerless beauty'.

The next great Toast, Lucy Cooper, rose higher and fell faster than most, propelled by appetites for drink, sex and mischief rare even then. Lucy was born in one of the alleys around Covent Garden to poor parents in about 1733. She became a fruit-seller in Covent Garden market, and when she was fourteen was befriended by the tavern-keeper Elizabeth Weatherby, who was struck by the girl's beauty and wit. It may have been at Weatherby's that Lucy met the ancient and wealthy debauchee Sir Orlando Bridgeman, who became infatuated in equal measure with her burgeoning beauty as with her repartee. Indeed, the *Nocturnal Revels* valued her quick tongue even higher than her looks, saying it 'was the greatest attraction she possessed'. Thompson's *Meretriciad* says that Lucy was 'exalted from a basket to a coach' by Bridgeman, who proved his love by giving her a free hand with his purse. The feeling was not mutual, but she allowed him to set her up in a 'voluptuous manner' in an elegant house in Parliament Street with her own 'chariot'. Sir Orlando wanted to marry her, says the *Nocturnal Revels*, but she was 'so generous as to refuse his hand that she might not bring a scandal upon his family'. Lucy did not want his company, either, and spent many drunken nights at Weatherby's: her carriage was known to have been seen standing outside for forty-eight hours at a time. 'Dissipation was her motto.' She was generous to a fault with Bridgeman's money, entertaining lavishly friends and lovers who included the actor John Palmer, the poet Charles Churchill, the rival one-eyed Toast Bet Wemyss, the penniless hack Sam Derrick and 'some more choice geniuses . . . wit, frolic and fun circulated at her expence'. Sometimes the frolics became so lively Wemyss lost her glass eye, and there would be a scramble on the floor to find it. Lucy's appetite for drink and sex earned this breathless tribute from the *Meretriciad* of 1765:

> Lewder than all the whores in Charles's reign . . .
> At famed Bob Derry's where the harlots throng
> My muse has listened to thy luscious song
> And heard thee swear like worser Drury's Punk,
> The man should have thee, who could make thee drunk,
> Cit, soldier, sailor or some bearded Jew
> In triumph, reeling, bore thee to some stew.

Bridgeman died in 1764, and Mrs Weatherby the following year. Apparently Bridgeman left Lucy a generous annuity on condition she mended her ways. She couldn't. The *Meretriciad* reinforces the point:

> When Bridgeman made his last dear will and groan,
> A good annuity was then thy own
> With this proviso – that you'd rake no more

> Nor play the vagrant mercenary whore.
> Alas! Thy many actions since have shown
> Thou could'st not quit the bottle and the town;
> Oft has the Muse beheld thy tottering feet,
> And prayed that instant for the widest street.

Without her friends and protectors Lucy grew wilder and more drunken. She began frequenting that last resort of low whores, Bob Derry's Cider Cellar in Maiden Lane, of which a contemporary visitor recorded that he found there 'a scene of confusion, drunk-enness and stupidity . . . the many prostitutes . . . were like so many dressed-up carcasses in the shambles, drinking away to keep up their spirits'.

It was a dangerous place. One evening two Jews were murdered there, and the *Meretriciad* describes the fracas in heroic terms – 'A greater ruin Derry's never saw'. Lucy was involved in some way, and the poem suggests what a troublemaker she could be:

> At other times more riotous than lewd,
> Then nought but swords, blood, tears and oaths ensued,
> So dire a conflict surely ne'er was known,
> A worse sedition *Helen* could not sown.

Lucy was arrested and held overnight in the Bridewell. 'She in her arms embraced a drunken Beau/And with him snored upon a truss of straw.' The poem seems to suggest that she was not jailed, and she was soon back in business.

> Debates being done, with Bewley she returned
> And with dear Usher for fresh riots burned;
> The Shakespeare's Head, the Rose and Bedford Arms
> Each alike profit from my Cooper's charms.
> But oh! Alas! how fully can we weep,
> Fat Weatherby sunk in eternal sleep;
> She rests, large Queen, from her kitchen's greezy storms
> And's wheeled in solemn dirge for hungry worms.

Weep, weep my Lucy, Weatherby's no more,
A loss like this, you never knew before;
Usher, Orlando, Weatherby are gone
In dismal sackcloth the dear worthies moan.

Soon Lucy was in prison again, this time for debt. William Hickey and
some friends had a whip-round for her in 1766. 'Tomkyns [a tavern-
keeper] . . . had that very day received a letter from Lucy Cooper, who
had long been a prisoner for debt in the King's Bench [prison], stating
that she was almost naked and starving, without a penny in her pocket to
purchase food, raiment or coal to warm herself.' Hickey and his friends
sent her £50: '. . . this seasonable aid had probably saved the life of a
deserving woman who, in her prosperity, had done a thousand generous actions'. After her release she opened a bagnio in Bond Street but
it failed and she was again arrested for debt. The 1770 edition of the
Meretriciad records the acceleration of her downfall:

But Oh! my luscious dissipated wench
How come ye lately to the close King's Bench? . . .
Thou art the tennis ball of Drury Lane,
For ev'ry stroke you get, you rise again
Yet don't rebound so very strong, to rise
Next to that parlour nearest to the skies . . .

She was released in 1769, 'after a long confinement being left without
friends or money and now destitute of beauty and past the time when
youth supplied the place of charm'. She died in poverty in 1772. Shortly
afterwards Weatherby's closed. The new owner was refused a licence
because of nightly affrays and riots, and when he was indicted for causing a nuisance he was pilloried and jailed.

Lucy's friend Sam Derrick is an interesting example of the period's
numerous penurious hacks. He was probably the author of the *Memoirs
of the Bedford Coffee-house*, published anonymously as by 'a Genius'. He
coached the actress-whore Jane Lessingham for her first appearance at
Covent Garden, which was a triumph, and she repaid him by leaving

him for the theatre's proprietor Thomas Harris. She became a success-
ful comedy actress but refused to help Derrick. After Jack Harris's death,
Derrick was employed by the publisher H. Ranger to edit the *List of
Covent Garden Ladies* and was then surprisingly appointed to succeed Beau
Nash as Master of Ceremonies at Bath. After this sudden rise in status he
called on Jane, but her servant said she 'knew no one of that name'. When
Derrick forced his way in she threatened to call out the Watch. Faithless
Jane took up with Henry Addington, later Lord Chief Justice and Earl of
Sidmouth. In 1777 she was described spitefully as 'a pompous celebrated
actress and a plump lascivious harlot'. She died in 1801.

There is an endearing story about Derrick's stoical humour: one night,
penniless as ever, he was sleeping on a stall outside a shop. A young actor
named Floyd, also homeless, happened upon him, and Derrick said: 'My
dear Floyd, I'm sorry to see you in this destitute state. Will you go home
with me to my lodgings?' When he died he left a will thanking the many
profligate women who had helped him when 'he had not shoes for his
feet', among them his friend, one Charlotte Hayes.

Long before Lucy Cooper died she had been supplanted by Frances Murray,
who attracted superlatives such as 'incomparable'. There are portraits of her
in the British Museum which, although not great works of art, suggest her
allure: one shows her dressed for a mas-querade, and she is undoubtedly a
beauty. She became, by force of circumstance rather than sheer inclination,
the greatest Toast of the second half of the eighteenth century.

Frances, known as Fanny, had been whoring for four years without
much success when Jack Harris included her in his *List*. She became
an overnight success. Her story, told in the anonymous *Memoirs of the
Celebrated Miss Fanny Murray* in 1759, suggests that Fanny was not enough
of a businesswoman to begin with to make the most of her charms. Like
Sally Salisbury she took a while to make her mark, and then for some
reason became irresistible. It is a measure of the fickleness of men that
what one day is an unconsidered trifle is a treasure the next.

Fanny was born in Bath in 1729, where her father was a musician
named Rudman. She was orphaned at the age of twelve, and became
a flower-seller in the Rooms. Unfortunately for her, when she was still

only twelve the incipient beauty attracted the attention of the 'proverbial rake' the Honourable Jack Spencer 'of libertine memory', grandson of Sarah, Duchess of Marlborough. Horace Bleackley comments in *Ladies Fair and Frail* (1909) that Spencer had inherited some of the virtues and all of the vices of his Churchill ancestors. After 'a few tawdry gifts, some earnest promises' Fanny succumbed, but her immature charms did not long detain the practised seducer, and he left her after a few weeks. She had several affairs, including one with Beau Nash, Bath's arbiter of taste, who was then in his middle sixties. When he was criticised for sexually exploiting the child and called a whoremonger, Nash wittily replied that since one didn't call a man who kept a cheese in his house a cheese-monger, so there was no reason to describe a man who kept a whore in his house as a whoremonger. Under his instruction the uneducated child, generally agreed as not including high intelligence among her gifts, learned how to behave in society. At the age of fourteen she was described thus: 'Fanny's person, which already began to testify marks of womanhood, was extremely beautiful; her face a perfect oval with eyes that conversed love, and every other feature in agreeable symmetry. . . .' She was also unfailingly cheerful and sweet-tempered.

Given the great difference in age, this too was a doomed relation-ship: they quarrelled and Fanny left for London. She lodged with a Mrs Softing, who introduced her to randy old men. One of them must have been considerably entranced for he gave her a snuffbox with £40 in it, about £4,700 today. Clearly there was good money to be made out of such undemanding lovers, but the flighty young girl quarrelled with Mrs Softing who threw her out, and she became a common prostitute. 'What must be the ultimate end of such variegated concupiscence? Infection.' Fanny caught her first dose of the pox, and she had no money for treat-ment. She had to pawn her clothes, the doctor's last fee being produced by her last gown. At this low ebb in her career her new landlady told her that a procuress in Old Bailey was looking for 'any clean fresh country goods' to replace girls who had been imprisoned. Fanny was reluctant to allow herself to sink into this form of slavery, but really she had left her-self no choice. The results of her first week's efforts were earnings of £5 10s 6d, and outgoings of £5 10s. Fanny's problem, like that of many other whores, was that she had to hire her clothes at exorbitant rates from her bawd. Here is how she – or rather the anonymous author of the *Memoir*, for it seems unlikely to have been Fanny – detailed her expenditure:

Board and lodging (in a garret, on small beer and sprats)	£1 15s
Washing (two smocks, 2 handkerchiefs, two pairs stockings)	7s
Use of brocade gown (worth a crown [5s])	8s
Use of pair of stays (not worth a shilling)	3s
Use of pair silk shoes (not worth a shilling)	2s 6d
Use of smocks (old, coarse and patched)	7s
Use of ruffles (darned; worth only 2s 6d when new)	2s
Use of petticoats (all of the lowest rank)	4s
Seeing constables to prevent going to Bridewell (Peace officers' fees – in buckram)	10s 6d
Use of a hat (worthless)	2s
Use of ribands (unusable)	3s 6d
A few pins	6d
Use of a Capuchin cloak	8s
Use of gauze aprons (rag-fair quality)	5s
Use of gauze handkerchiefs (the same)	2s 6d
Use of silk stockings (yellow and pierced)	2s 6d
Use of stone buckles (most of stones out)	4s 6d
Carmine and tooth powder and brushes (brick-dust for the first two: brushes unseen)	3s

(The author does not seem to have bothered to add up this sum.) Not only was Fanny being fleeced by her bawd, but she was engaged in a particularly low form of prostitution.

The money thus supplied was mostly gained by apprentice boys who were seduced by the house to spend double the sum they gave to their doxy in bad punch, and worse negus. Perhaps their masters' tills were the only treasure for such debauchery, but good Mrs—— the landlady never troubled herself with such reflections. If Tyburn carried off one set of her customers, which it frequently did, growing vice and the depravity of the times furnished her with another.

The Morning Teſt; or Fanny M—'s Maid, Waſhing her Toes.

The courtesan Fanny Murray at her toilette. This is a merciless caricature. Instead of a polite conversation piece with admirers sipping tea or coffee from elegant china we have a seedy young gent eating oysters – plebeian fare – a lawyer presenting a settlement from a lover, a chamber pot and a painting of copulating dogs. (© *The British Museum*)

Sally Salisbury stabbing her lover. She died in prison, making her story the ideal morality tale, beauty spoiled by vice but redeemed by suffering and death. *(Author's Collection)*

Madam Creſwell
Une Maquerelle
Vecchia ruffiana

R. Gawood ſelat.   P. Tempeſt excu:
                                    cum privilegio

Mother Cresswell, who 'rode admiral' over all the other bawds in Restoration London. She ran an impressive vice empire and warned, 'No money, no cunny'. *(Author's Collection)*

The Cov: Garden: Morning Frolick:

Invented & Engraved by L.P. Boitard. Published According to Act of Parliament, Feb. 5, 1747. Price one Shilling.

Betsy Careless is carried home insensible after a night out in Covent Garden. She climbed higher and fell faster than almost any other Toast. The dwarf is the troublemaker Little Cazey. *(Guildhall Library, Corporation of London)*

Mother Douglas's famous brothel in a detail from William Hogarth's engraving *The March to Finchley*. She is the pious fat woman praying in the window lower right. The cats on the roof indicate a cattery, or brothel. *(Author's Collection)*

Kitty Fisher, as seen by Joshua Reynolds. She snubbed the Duke of York by eating his fee and spurned Giacomo Casanova's offer as wholly inadequate. She was admired for her wit, and was celebrated for 'the elegance with which she sacrificed to Venus'.
(Private Collection)

Moll King, dispenser of coffee and hard words in Covent Garden. Her shop attracted the elites of the social, bohemian and artistic worlds.
(Author's Collection)

Janie Jones (left) and a friend make an impression at a London film premiere. Janie, essentially a
harmless fun-lover, was given a sentence of seven years for controlling prostitutes. (*Mirrorpix*)

The fabulously wealthy lecher the Duke of Queensberry with two whores and the formidable old bawd Mother Windsor. She had a long reign and was remembered as 'the perfect mistress of the art of conversation'. *(Guildhall Library, Corporation of London)*

The vicious bawd Mother Needham sizes up a young girl fresh from the country in a plate from William Hogarth's *The Harlot's Progress*. The man watching from a doorway on the right is the notorious rake Colonel Francis Charteris, known as the Rape-Master of Great Britain. *(Author's Collection)*

Cynthia Payne, the bawd dubbed Madam Sin, leaving prison. She saw herself as providing a public service and wanted to make sex fun. *(Getty Images)*

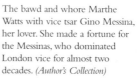

The bawd and whore Marthe Watts with vice tsar Gino Messina, her lover. She made a fortune for the Messinas, who dominated London vice for almost two decades. *(Author's Collection)*

Above left: The kiss-and-tell courtesan Harriette Wilson. When times were hard she wrote her memoirs and invited her lovers to send her £200 'to be left out'. *(Author's Collection)*

Above right: Sophia Baddeley, by Robert Laurie after Johan Zoffany, who squandered a fortune but refused to tie her lovers to a formal financial contract. She died in poverty, a drug addict. *(© The British Museum)*

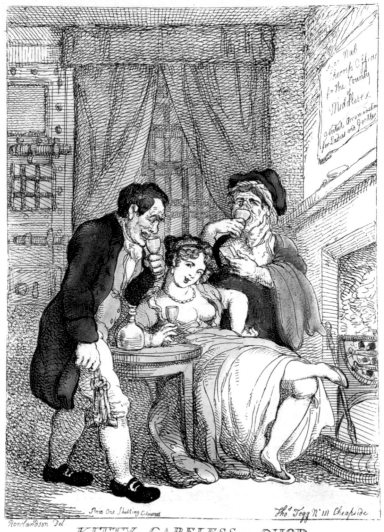

KITTY CARELESS IN QUOD,
OR WAITING FOR JEW BAIL.

A young whore named Kitty Careless making the best of things as she waits to be bailed. She is clearly following the same path as her namesake, Betsy Careless. *(Guildhall Library, Corporation of London)*

SALLY SALISBURY.
Ætat. 32.

AUTHENTICK
MEMOIRS
OF THE
LIFE
INTRIGUES *and* ADVENTURES
Of the CELEBRATED
SALLY SALISBURY.
WITH

True CHARACTERS of her moſt
Conſiderable GALLANTS.

By Capt. CHARLES WALKER.

Don't wonder Others are not with Her ſhown,
She, who no Equal has, muſt be alone.
Ld. ROCHESTER.

LONDON:
Printed in the Year M.DCC.xx.III.
(Price 2ſ. 6d.)

Sally Salisbury, wildest of all the Toasts, and an early biography. She had many aristocratic lovers. (© *The British Library*)

Mrs Armistead, the courtesan who married the Whig leader Charles James Fox, in a painting by Sir Joshua Reynolds. She had specialised in the higher aristocracy, including the Prince of Wales. *(Christie's Images, London/Bridgeman Art Library)*

Giacomo Casanova, legendary lover spurned by Kitty Fisher, by Anton Raphael Mengs. His time in London was spent in a whirl of sexual escapades. *(Private Collection/ Bridgeman Art Library)*

LADY FASHION's SECRETARY's OFFICE, or PETTICOAT RECOMMENDATION the BEST

The only known portrait of

Mrs Cornelys

Theresa Cornelys, proprietor of London's liveliest nightspot in the eighteenth century. It was patronised by a fast set of society ladies, as well as celebrity whores. *(Mary Evans Picture Library)*

Young whores warm up for a night of bad behaviour at the Rose Tavern, near Drury Lane Theatre, in an engraving from William Hogarth's *A Rake's Progress*. The woman undressing on the right is a posture moll, or stripper. *(Author's Collection)*

The interior of Elizabeth Haddock's Turk's Head bagnio at Charing Cross, showing the death of the Earl, provides a rare view of the interior of an eighteenth-century brothel. This engraving is taken from William Hogarth's *Marriage a la Mode. (Author's Collection)*

Fanny was in the trap that faced all powerless whores who had not yet established a reputation and a following. The landlady took all her money and was constantly threatening to have her imprisoned for debt if she didn't earn more. Somehow she managed to save and conceal 7 guineas from her earnings, and with this she fled the brothel and took up with some of her upper-class former lovers. Her luck had changed, and soon 'she had so much business, all in the private lodging, ready-money way, that she could not possibly drive so great a business entirely on her own bottom . . .'. Fanny took an apprentice, and her business was so flourishing that it soon attracted the attention of Jack Harris, publisher of the *List of Covent Garden Ladies*. 'Mr Harris, the celebrated negotiator in women, applied to get her enrolled upon his parchment list.' The *Memoir* shows to what an art Harris had raised his racket; clothing it in semi-legal mumbo-jumbo which would impress and frighten illiterate young girls. A lawyer was on hand as she signed the solemn agreement to pay Harris a fifth of her earnings, and also to hand over £20 if she lied about the state of her health. This is how Harris described her, as though she was a cow at a county show:

> Perfectly sound in Wind and Limb: a fine Brown Girl rising nineteen years next Season. A good Side-box Piece – will show well in the Flesh Market – wear well – may be put off for a virgin any time these twelve months – never common this side Temple Bar, but for six months. Fit for High Keeping with a Jew Merchant – NB a good premium from ditto – then the run of the house. And if she keeps out of the Lock [the VD hospital] may make her Fortune and ruin half the Men in town.

This unflattering advertisement worked, and Fanny became the acknowl-edged Top Toast with the fashionable cachet that went with it, at first charging a minimum of 2 guineas, which seems very low. Another whore on Harris's *List*, Poll Davis of Manchester Square, was said to charge a minimum of 10 guineas and half a crown for her servant. Slightly later in the century the Honourable Charlotte Spencer was charging a minimum of £50 per night. No doubt Fanny soon raised her prices. She was among the more classy whores who became sought-after models for some of the leading painters. The rake Richard Rigby said of her that she was now 'followed by crowds of gallants . . . it would be a crime not to toast her at every meal'. There is a story that one of her temporary lovers, having one evening drunk champagne from her slipper at the Castle tavern in Henrietta Street, asked the chef to cook and serve it. The chef minced the slipper, cooked it in butter and served it garnished with its wooden heels thinly sliced. By now 'the unchallenged Toast of all London', Fanny had several aristocrats paying for her favours and lived in 'an elegant lodging' at 22 St James's Place. There is an anonymous print in the British Museum of Fanny at her morning levée which may show that very address. It is indeed an elegant room, but some of the details are sordid. The seedy young rake who ogles Fanny's leg as her maid washes her foot is eating oysters, cheap food sold by street-criers, as Sheila O'Connell points out in *London 1753*. And the picture on the wall of copulating dogs would not have hung in a respectable home. The lawyer carries a Deed of Settlement from a lover, the ultimate desideratum of the courtesan. However, Fanny lived on the brink of financial disaster, as did most courtesans. From time to time she had to resort to one-night stands, even if she had granted someone a temporary monopoly over her charms. One of her keepers was the Earl of Sandwich, a noted lecher. She was his mistress when Wilkes dedicated the printed version of the obscene *Essay on Women* to her. In November 1763 the House of Commons witnessed a memorable act of hypocrisy and treachery when Sandwich turned on Wilkes and accused him of publishing pornography. He quoted from the *Essay*, and famously shouted: 'Sir, you will either die on the gallows or of the pox.' Wilkes coolly replied, 'That, my Lord, depends on whether I embrace your principles or your mistress.' By then Fanny had moved on.

Fanny became the mistress of the wealthy Sir Richard Atkins, who set her up in a house at Clapham. When he died Fanny, who was only twenty-seven, was arrested for debt. John Spencer, the son of her first seducer, came to her rescue, paid her debts and gave her an annual allowance of £200. (There was a suggestion that he was responding to her threat to publish her memoirs.) She married the actor David Ross and became a respectable housewife, dying, much loved by her many noble friends, in 1778. After her marriage she was untouched by the 'breath of scandal'. One gets the feeling that she had always longed for respectability.

Nancy Parsons had one of the strangest and most eventful careers in pursuit of noble lovers, which continued even when she was on the brink of old age. Gainsborough made her the subject of one of his dazzling portraits and she was clearly a beauty, of a refined and almost aristocratic sort. This coupled with her intelligence, modesty and good taste endeared her to many a lordling.

Parsons was born in London in about 1734, the daughter of a prosperous Bond Street tailor, who was said to have paid for a good education for her at Paris and elsewhere. She went to Jamaica with a Captain Horton, and when he mistreated her she returned penniless to London. She made the best of her good looks and was soon a harlot, much in demand among young aristocrats.

On the evening of 17 April 1768 she was involved in a scandal which if anything increased her attraction. She was observed by the audience sitting in a box at the King's Theatre in the Haymarket with the Prime Minister, the Duke of Grafton. Their affair was common knowledge, but it was unheard of for a great public figure to flaunt his mistress in this way in public. Among those who looked askance was the Duke's estranged wife, seated a few yards away. Many other noble ladies, who had the luck to be married to the men who accompanied them, stared from their boxes. They stared again when the couple descended the broad staircase leading to the main entrance and the Duke called for his mistress's carriage. In the small and tightly knit world of the aristocracy the shock was great.

In the four years they had been lovers, she had become all but a wife to the Duke. At his town houses in Bond Street and Grosvenor Square she 'presided at the head of his table, acting the part of hostess with perfect assurance'. If the Duke, a sportsman at home in the company of grooms and men of the turf, used a coarse expression 'which was not an uncommon incident, she never failed to reprove him with a mild word or a gentle look of reproach' (Bleackley, 1909). This makes her sound rather tiresome, which could be a reason that the acid-penned political commentator known as Junius used her to get at Grafton: 'The Prime Minister of Great Britain, in a rural retirement and in the arms of faded beauty, has lost all memory of his sovereign, his country and himself.' Junius was not to know that the woman whom he suggested was past her prime would continue to dazzle members of the aristocracy for years to come. He continued the attack:

> Did not the Duke of Grafton frequently lead his mistress into public and even place her at the head of his table, as if he had pulled down an ancient temple of Venus, and could bury all decency and shame under its ruins?
>
> It is not that he kept a mistress at home, but that he constantly attended her abroad. It is not the private indulgence, but the public insult of which I complain. The name of Miss Parsons would hardly have been known if the First Lord of the Treasury had not led her in triumph through the Opera House, even in the presence of the Queen. When we see a man in this manner we may admit the shameless depravity of his heart, but what are we to think of his understanding?

In March 1769 the press announced, to general astonishment, that the affair was at an end. It had been widely believed that Grafton would marry his harlot – instead, he gave her a generous annuity, although estimates varied at between £300 and £800. A month later Grafton married Elizabeth Wrottesley, daughter of the Dean of Worcester.

For a while Nancy ricocheted around the available aristos, rumour associating her name with Lord March, later Duke of Queensberry, and Sir George Savile before she settled briefly for Thomas Panton, brother of the Duchess of Ancaster and a former lover of Sophia Baddeley. But the jovial sportsman was no intellectual match for Parsons, and they parted. Then in February 1770 the press announced that her new love was the 25-year-old Duke of Dorset. 'No allowance was made for Nancy, who incurred the hatred of every matron who had a marriageable daughter' (Bleackley, 1909). Much was made of the disparity in their ages – Nancy was about thirty-six – and when they set out on a continental tour it was maliciously suggested that Nancy would need the help of crutches before she returned. Observers feared once again that Parsons was about to break into the aristocracy through marriage to Dorset, but in June 1773 the society busybody Lady Mary Coke, foremost among those who feared this intrusion, was able to record, 'the Duke of Dorset has certainly parted with his mistress'. The Duke had fallen for the ample charms of Elizabeth Armistead. And then Parsons finally pulled it off.

In June 1776 the *Morning Post* announced: 'It is said Lord Viscount M——d was married on Monday last to Mrs H——n, the late very celebrated Nancy Pars——s.' Maynard was twenty-five and believed to be slightly simple. He once remarked of the House of Commons, 'Is that going on still?' Because he had spent most of his fortune on women the pair were obliged to live much of the time abroad, usually in Naples. Early in 1784 it was rumoured that Parsons had added another duke to her collection, this time the improbably youthful and fabulously rich Francis, Duke of Bedford. He was eighteen, she almost fifty. Parsons explained to friends that she was merely saving the boy from worse company. When the inevitable split came Parsons retired to France, where she died aged about eighty in 1814. For some time she had been noted for her charitable giving, and an Englishwoman living in France at the time stated: 'She was an English lady of some renown in the middle of the last century. Her misfortunes and her errors (for which the tears that were shed by the poor over her grave are proof that she had atoned) have been recorded by the celebrated Junius under the name of Miss Anne or Nancy Parsons.' It is not recorded that any of the wealthy young men to whom she had taught the arts of love was present.

One day in March 1759 Kitty Fisher was riding in St James's Park. An expert horsewoman and former pupil of Dick Berenger, author of that equestrian bible *A New System of Horsemanship* and later Gentleman of Horse to George III, Kitty was one of the sights of London as she galloped along the Mall or by the Serpentine. This day, however, her horse was startled by a troop of soldiers and threw her. Kitty was unhurt by the fall, but very bruised by the publicity. The *Universal Magazine* celebrated the event in verse:

> Dear Kitty, had thy only fall
> Been that thou met'st with in the Mall,
> Thou had'st deserved our pity;
> But long before that luckless day,
> With equal justice might we say,
> Alas! poor fallen Kitty!

The whilst you may, dear girl, be wise,
And though time now in pleasure flies
Consider of hereafter;
For know, the wretch that courts thee now
When age has furrowed o'er thy brow,
Will change his sighs to laughter.

Reform thy manners, change thy ways:
For Virtue's sake, to merit praise
Be all thy honest strife:
So shall the world with pleasure say,
'She tasted folly for a day,
And then grew wise for life.'

Fisher was one of that small elite of Toasts of the Town whose doings were news. When she published a riposte two days later in the advertisement columns of the *Public Advertiser* – 'Miss Fisher is forced to sue to that Jurisdiction to protect her from the Baseness of little Scribblers' – the papers mocked her. A ribald mock biography of her, *The Juvenile Adventures of Miss Kitty F——r* had recently been published, and when a second volume appeared it included a parody of Fisher's ill-advised advertisement.

Although much was written about her, it was mostly unreliable. She was probably born in Soho in about 1738, the daughter of a German silver-chaser and her somewhat unfortunate advertisement, if indeed she wrote it herself, shows her to have been educated. She went to work in a milliner's, was picked up and seduced by a handsome young ensign named Martin who was known, we are assured, as 'the military Cupid'. When he was posted abroad she took up with a wealthy landowner named Medlycott who had previously pursued Maria Gunning, who rejected him and became the Countess of Coventry, and the actress Peg Woffington. Medlycott introduced Fisher to the pleasures of society – masquerades at the Opera House, concerts in the Rotunda at Ranelagh where she took supper in one of the boxes in the vast hall, tea at Marlebone Gardens, promenading at Islington Spa. Medlycott could afford to dress her in the latest fashions

and inevitably she caught the eye of wealthier and socially more important men. Her next lover was Captain Augustus Keppel of the House
of Albemarle, and soon 'it was whispered that Admiral Lord Anson had
been captivated by her charms, that General Ligonier was one of her
warmest admirers. Thus she was reputed to enjoy the patronage of the
foremost sailor and the most popular soldier in Great Britain. Her name
grew familiar to the beaux of clubland, and curiosity was piqued when it
was known that she was an exclusive young lady who would accept no
present and grant no interview without a formal introduction' (Bleackley,
1909). She was admired as much for her wit as her beauty, and it was said
that her *bons mots* 'were quoted in the club rooms as frequently as the sal-
lies of [Sam] Foote the player'. A commentator avowed that she was 'the
essence of small talk and the magazine of contemporary anecdote . . . it
was impossible to be dull in her company'. Her drolleries are forgotten,
and she is best remembered today by the series of paintings Reynolds
did of her, although he was by no means the only artist commissioned
to portray her. Casanova's anecdote of meeting her at the brothel of a
bawd named Walsh (or Wells) as she waited for a duke could lead one to
think she was a greedy little mercenary, but who can blame her for knowing her price? She would have been only too aware of the fate of her
near-contemporaries Betsy Careless and Lucy Cooper, and that fortune
would smile on her only so long as her face and her figure lasted. She was
better known for showing her contempt for the Duke of York by eating
the 'present' he left after a night in her bed. Von Archenholz, who wrote
that Kitty was 'indebted to nature for an uncommon portion of beauty,
judgement, and wit, joined in a most agreeable and captivating vivacity'
and for 'the elegance with which she sacrificed to Venus' tells the story in
A Picture of England (1789):

> The union of so many perfections procured the esteem, and fascinated the
> desires of those who prefer Cyprian delights to all the other pleasures of life.
> This lady knew her own merit; she demanded a hundred guineas a night for
> the use of her charms, and she was never without votaries, to whom the offer-
> ing did not seem too exorbitant. Among these was the Duke of York, brother
> to the King; who one morning left fifty pounds on her toilet [dressing table].

This present so offended Miss Fisher that she declared that her doors should ever be shut against him in future; and to show by this most convincing proof how much she despised his present, she clapt the banknote between two slices of bread and butter, and ate it for breakfast.

It should be said that a similar anecdote was told of other courtesans, including Fanny Murray. Casanova, who seems to have had no sense of humour, remarked that the only gainer was the banker who had issued the note. There are many other tales of Fisher's extravagance, some doubtless embellished by jealous gentlewomen who resented Fisher's hold on their husbands. They also told stories meant to ridicule her. One was about Lord Mountford, a diminutive peer who called at her house in New Norfolk Street one evening and found Kitty dressed, patched and powdered ready for an evening at the opera. As he was a good customer she let him in, although she was waiting for her escort, Lord Sandwich, to arrive. As Mountford was about to leave Sandwich's steps were heard on the stairs. The girl raised a corner of her huge hoop petticoat and told the tiny Mountfort to slip inside. She chatted with Sandwich until it was time to leave. She then went into an adjoining room, released Mountfort and went on to the opera.

Another anecdote, with Pitt the Elder as its hero, is probably more reliable, as there were witnesses. Kitty was at a review in Hyde Park attended by the King, George II. Some courtiers suggested mischievously to the King that it would be fun to introduce her to Mr Pitt. The King agreed, and looking towards the young beauty, asked her name. 'It is the Duchess of N——, a foreign lady, whom the Secretary [Pitt] should know,' replied Lord Ligonier. The King said that they should be introduced and Pitt was led by Ligonier towards Kitty. 'This is Mr Secretary Pitt – Miss Kitty Fisher.' Pitt removed his hat, bowed and told the astonished Fisher he regretted not having the honour of knowing her when he was younger. 'For then, Madam, I should have the hope of succeeding in your affections, but old and infirm as you now see me I have no other way of avoiding the force of such beauty but by flying from it.' He hobbled away, and Fisher claimed that even the youngest of the gallants around her had never paid her such a compliment.

Fisher had one of the shortest of all reigns at the top of her profession, roughly from 1758 to 1763. Edward Thompson, the 'Cyprian bard' and author of the *Meretriciad*, advised her:

Kitty, repent, a settlement procure,
Retire and keep the bailiffs from the door.
Put up with wrinkles, and pray paint no more.

She dropped out of the Cyprian scene, and in 1766 married her current lover, John Norris, son of a Kent landowner. He was MP for Rye and governor of Deal Castle, a heavy gambler and deep in debt. Under Fisher's influence he mended his ways, and his father invited them to live with him at Hemsted Park, near Benenden. There Fisher indulged her love of horse-riding and took to the rural life with aplomb. Almost exactly a year later she was dying. There were rumours that, like Lady Coventry, she had been poisoned by lead in her make-up. Bleackley, with sickening sanctimony, reports: 'The disease had another cause. It was the pace that kills, and Kitty Fisher was paying the penalty of the evil-liver.' She died on 23 March 1767, and after she had lain in state, 'dressed as for a ball' in her finest clothes and jewels, she was buried in the family vault in Benenden church.

Of the actress-courtesan Sophia Baddeley it was written that her 'gaudy and fitful career reads like a troubled dream'. By all accounts another great beauty, she was the equal of Kitty Fisher, Fanny Murray or Betsy Careless. The Duke of Ancaster lauded her as 'absolutely one of the wonders of the age . . . no man can gaze on you unwounded. You are in this respect like the Basilisk, whose eyes kill those they fix on.' Another aristocratic admirer, Lord Falmouth, told her: 'Half the world is in love with you.' Wealthy men plied her with gifts and large offers for exclusive access to her favours. Noblewomen, who would normally not countenance actresses, let alone courtesans, particularly if they were of that class themselves, were said to speak of her with rapture. One night in June 1771 as she watched a play from a box in the Little Theatre in the Haymarket the audience rose in tribute to her beauty and applauded her for fifteen minutes.

Yet fifteen years later she was dead, a pauper head-over-heels in debt and a drug addict, the great wealth and the jewels frittered away. If she had more beauty than most she had less sense. As Katie Hickman says in *Courtesans* (2003), 'She was vain, spoilt, impetuous, lazy, spendthrift, only moderately intelligent, and possessed of a great deal of sexual energy.' When her companion Eliza Steele suggested she could economise by cutting back her spending on clothes to £100 a year she replied: 'Christ, that is not enough for millinery! . . . one may as well be dead as not in the fashion.' She was also, says Hickman, 'warm-hearted, affectionate, funny, mercurial, and generous to a fault', another Lucy Cooper, in fact. This was the woman for whom a posse of aristocrats drew their swords to get her admitted to the Pantheon in Oxford Street, and for whom Lord Melbourne would leave vast bundles of banknotes after a night of pleasure. Someone called Fitzgerald wrote: 'No stranger picture of life can be conceived than her singular story; her short and showy course, across which flit royal dukes, infatuated lords, rough and rude colonels, and the gradual fall and degradation, when a footman winds up the procession. . . .'

Born in Westminster in 1745, Sophia was the daughter of a theatre musician who was at one time Sergeant-Trumpeter to George II and so she was from a more respectable background than many of her kind. She had a musical education but found the lessons tedious, and when she was eighteen eloped with an actor named Robert Baddeley, who was twice her age. They married and parted shortly afterwards. They never divorced, probably because of the expense – at the time, it would have required an Act of Parliament. Before they parted company, however, Robert got her a part in a play at Drury Lane. She never liked acting, and she wasn't much good at it, but in the bad times that were to come it brought her a good living, or what would have been a good living for someone less extravagant. As Hickman says, 'she nevertheless became one of the most famous players of her day, achieving the kind of overwhelming celebrity which is rare even in our own celebrity-obsessed age'. If Sophia was an indifferent actress she was a fine singer, and appeared regularly in that role at the pleasure gardens of Ranelagh and Vauxhall. Her fee for these singing engagements alone was £12 a week – equal to the salaries of the best-paid actresses.

Both she and her husband had varied and frenetic sex lives, the *Town and Country Magazine* suggesting that Robert Baddeley acted as her pimp. When a rich Jew named Mendez made a pass at her, Robert remarked that 'so valuable a friend was not to be slighted' and advised her to treat the Jew with 'the greatest civility'. This liaison triggered a series of affairs, including one with the Duke of York. Subsequently she fell for John Hanger, son of the impoverished Irish peer Lord Coleraine, and they set up home in some style in Dean Street. They soon ran through his money and then hers, ending up heavily in debt, despite her high income. Hanger, whom she called Gaby, finally left her. Distraught, she took an overdose of laudanum, the drug to which she became addicted and which would eventually prove her undoing. So severe were its effects that six weeks later she could still barely walk.

When she recovered, serious offers of 'keeping' began to come in from men with old money. 'Keeping' was a very desirable status, high above prostitution, and a woman who managed 'high keeping' with a substantial gentleman almost – but not quite – avoided the stigma of immorality. But she had to be careful how she behaved. In Harris's *List of Covent Garden Ladies* there is a Mrs Cl—pp—o, of Gerrard Street, Soho, who is in keeping.

> This lady bears a strong resemblance to the most celebrated beauty of the town, as such it were almost superfluous to say that her person is elegant, her features regular, her eyes captivating, her teeth charming, and that her coral lips solicit a thousand kisses. She is said to be in keeping by a gentleman, whose name she is known by, and who keeps the house she lives in on purpose for her, she is therefore obliged to keep pretty constantly at home, whilst he is in town, and she never receives any messages or mandates from Bagnios. In those intervals, when her friend is at his villa some distance from the capital, she shines with great splendour at all public places. Her conversation is lively and entertaining, which added to her present situation and corporeal attractions she thinks entitles her to at least a bank note.

She was playing with fire. If her lover discovered her treachery he would almost certainly throw her into the street.

Baddeley's first offer was from Lord Molyneux, who suggested £1,000 to settle her debts and £400 a year – about £30,000 today. Because he was married she refused. For the moment she could afford to – her companion Mrs Steele wrote that her salary at the theatre had been increased from £8 to £14 a week which, according to Hickman, was probably more than any of her fellow actresses earned. George III ordered a portrait of her by Zoffany, and when the theatre impresario David Garrick gave her a benefit, aristocrats took all the boxes, at prices up to £100. Men of distinction, if not their wives – although Sophia would make some inroads into that forbidden territory, too – invited her to dine or attempted to make her aquaintance socially; inevitably, some had intentions that were more than social. Sophie's éclat made her a target for wealthy predators. Lord Melbourne was wealthier than most and at twenty-one, recently married to the beautiful and brilliant but complacent Elizabeth Milbanke, he was eager for new adventures. He sent Sophia a gift of £300 through a friend, and an offer to share his fortune. When Sophia refused he gave her more money. After the total reached the equivalent of about £50,000 in today's terms Sophia gave in.

With Melbourne bankrolling her she went on a spree. Her friend and biographer Mrs Steele, who liked lists, noted her expenditure. There were ten diamond pins at £20 each, nine rings costing £920, a diamond necklace for £450, which was bought by Melbourne himself, silks costing £120, plus 'ribbands, gauses etc' for £70. Cloth for a new coach lining cost £200, a pair of diamond earrings £300. Sophia would set out on these shopping trips in her carriage, making the rounds of the fashionable shops. She must have been a very welcome sight to the likes of Mr Price, the haberdasher in Tavistock Street. Her extravagance was boundless. However expensive a dress, she would wear it only three or four times before giving it to her maidservant. If friends admired her costly trinkets she pressed them to accept these gewgaws as gifts, on one occasion generously bestowing upon a Miss Radley all the jewels she was wearing, worth about £100 (say, £7,000).

When she grew bored with the theatre, Melbourne offered to pay her more than three times her salary. But she was soon bored with Melbourne, too. Mrs Steele said he was 'not the brightest man of the age', and Sophia would sometimes find she had a headache when Melbourne called. What she really loved was extravagance. Her house in Grafton Street just north of Berkeley Square was sumptuously furnished, she had nine servants and she also rented a house at Brighton, with more servants. Then there was another rented house in Hammersmith. And she possessed that emblem of all successful courtesans, a carriage and four, but also drove a phaeton, a light two-seater. She had a fabulously expensive private box at the opera, and she made the full round of masquerades, theatres and pleasure gardens. We have already seen how an armed guard of young aristocrats forced a way for her into the Pantheon, when she had been barred by name. Another actress-courtesan, the Prince of Wales's lover Perdita Robinson, told in her *Memoirs* of seeing Sophia there, and of the effect her beauty had: 'The countenance which most pleased me was that of the late Mrs Baddeley'.

Was Sophia just a greedy trollop, essentially heartless and cold, or simply a thoughtless pleasure seeker like Lucy Cooper or Betsy Careless? It is interesting that women liked her, and she had a gift for friendship. Noblewomen were reported as saying: 'There is that divine face! That beautiful creature!' Others would cry out: 'Here's Mrs Baddeley – what a sweet woman.' (Hickman, 2003). And it should be said in her defence, and in that of other courtesans, that their periods of prosperity might be brief, as the men who besieged them would usually drop them when ardour cooled if something better, in the sense of more fashionable, turned up. A writer in the *Covent Garden Magazine* pointed out: 'I have known several gentlemen turn off a first mistress merely because she was not sufficiently well known, for the sake of a celebrated woman of the town, a dancer or an actress.' To her credit, Sophia was unfailingly kind to servants.

Some of the great rakes of the day paid court including the Duke of Ancaster, Lord Harrington and perhaps the most illustrious of them all, the Duke of Queensberry. Their pursuit was shameless. The Duke of Ancaster sent his servant with £200 to Mrs Steele to procure an introduction – Mrs Steele sent him away with a robust rejection of this 'dishonourable' proposal. Mr Damer offered Sophia £400 a year if he could replace Melbourne in her affections. There were other offers, but the Duke of Northumberland topped them all: £1,000 guineas up front and £500 a year. Sophia said she would be faithful to Melbourne.

At the time it was customary for an experienced courtesan to reach a legally binding financial settlement, called an annuity, with her lover. For some reason, perhaps because she feared losing her freedom of action, Sophia never put her relationship with Melbourne on this footing; it was a decision that would come to haunt her. The wise courtesan knew that looks fade and ardour cools, but a legally binding settlement goes on and on. Perhaps also because of Melbourne's impulsive generosity, despite the advice of her friends, Sophia never made him put pen to parchment. And he was marvellously generous. Sometimes he would leave a pile of bank-notes, amounting to £500 at a time, on the table at the end of a visit.

Northumberland came back with another offer. He would allow her £1,500 a year (£110,000) and pay off all her debts. If she remained faithful – and that meant not seeing another visitor – he would consider making a settlement. When Sophia hesitated Mrs Steele said the enormous allowance the Duke was proposing would hardly last her three months. The Duke made another offer: he would call on her twice a week, when Melbourne was not there, and 'that on his first visit to tea, he would give her £500'. His Grace also said that if she agreed he would 'be her friend for life'. The prissy Mrs Steele records her conversation with Sophia after this encounter:

In short, she told me she gave the gentleman this answer; that she would consider his proposals, and give him her determination the next day. 'And why,' says I, 'did you not give him a positive denial then?' 'Because', returned she, 'I wished to consult you first.' I told her, she knew my sentiments on the subject, and she might assure herself, they would not alter if the Duke had offered her his whole fortune. 'Well', says she, 'suppose we admit him to drink tea?' 'That would only lead to further evils,' replied I, 'and I am determined he shall not come' – 'Good God', says she, 'I can have five hundred pounds for nothing.' 'Certainly,' replied I, laughing at her, 'for nothing. Mankind are too fond of their money to bestow it, but in return for favours received.' 'Surely, my dear Steele,' says she, 'you are not serious; I have partly promised to receive him at tea tomorrow.' At this I lost my temper, and said, you may act as you please, but you must invite him to some other house; for he certainly shall not come here: if he does, as soon as he enters the house I will affront him, and I would do the same if he was the King of England.

The relationship between Sophia and Mrs Steele is difficult to read. Mrs Steele liked to dress as a man at masquerades, and declared her undying love for Sophia. Whether there was more than an element of sex in it is, however, hard to judge.

Sophia did meet Northumberland again, but without Steele. At her house in Hammersmith she succumbed after the Duke gave her £500, and she regretted it. 'Much against my will, he led me to my chamber, I found my resolution give way, and I did what I now repent of.'

Sophia's extravagance grew worse. In spite of Melbourne's generosity her debts mounted until she owed £3,000 – about £180,000. And Melbourne was cooling, perhaps not surprisingly as Sophia was sharing her favours with handsome but penniless young lovers. He became less responsive to her demands, and began to avoid her. When, unwisely as it turned out, Sophia sought him out at a masquerade at Mrs Cornelys's Carlisle House, he was with another lovely courtesan, Harriet Powell, with whom he had lived before his marriage. Melbourne broke with Sophia on the spot, leaving her in serious financial difficulties. She had to pawn her best jewels, which had cost the equivalent of about £100,000, for less than a third of that sum. Her debts had by now more than doubled, to £7,000, and she was forced to give up the elegant house in Grafton Street and move to the one in Hammersmith. She went back on the stage, perhaps in March 1774, but her salary was now £7 a week, and her earning power was declining elsewhere. There were still offers, but they were more likely to come from merchants than wealthy aristocrats. One day there was a peremptory summons from the Duke of Cumberland, a dissolute uncle of the Prince of Wales, to a Covent Garden brothel. Sophia indignantly refused, retorting: 'Go and tell the Duke to send for Lady Grosvenor.' This was the Lady Henrietta Grosvenor who attended Mrs Prendergast's infamous *Bal d'Amour*: she was better known for a delicious society scandal featuring the Duke who had been sued by Lord Grosvenor over his affair with Henrietta. Cumberland's puerile love-letters were a feature of the case. Grosvenor was awarded a colossal £10,000, paid of course ultimately by the state, another reason for radicals to detest the House of Hanover.

Despite her stinging rebuke of the royal lecher, Sophia had to accept her decline in status. Such were her straitened circumstances that she even considered an offer from a Mr Petrie of £100 a year. A contract was drawn up, but Sophia drew back, saying it would be inconvenient to receive visits from a man she disliked. She fell for a politician named Stephen Sayer, a republican, quite unacceptable to her former aristocratic lovers. He sponged off her, to Mrs Steele's despair, and when Sayer moved in the almost ever-loyal Mrs Steele moved out. Sophia became pregnant; Sayer married a wealthy woman; Sophia had children, became ill, and went back to the stage again, where she was a success. She took up with an actor called Webster, with whom she had two more children. When he died she became the mistress of his servant. Mrs Steele, who still saw her from time to time, lamented: 'To think that she should thus far fall....'

Sophia's health began to fail, and her last appearance at Drury Lane was in December 1780. She began to play provincial theatres, in Dublin, Edinburgh and York. Debts, laudanum and ill health were bringing her career to an end. Tate Wilkinson, actor-manager at York, recorded of her last appearance there: 'She was very lame, and to make matters worse, was so stupidly intoxicated with laudanum that it was with great difficulty that she could finish her performance.' She went back to Scotland and continued acting until 1785, dying the following year, aged forty-one.

One of Charlotte Hayes's girls was Emily Warren. Although she was not among the foremost Toasts, we know a good deal about her because she became the mistress of William Hickey's friend Bob Pott. When Pott had to return to India he placed her in Hickey's care and as soon as Pott departed Emily sent for him. Hickey had first seen her at Hayes's in 1776 when the bawd was teaching the young girl deportment and manners. At the time she was 'an unripe and awkward girl, but with features of exquisite beauty'. Hayes managed to impart a veneer of sophistication, but didn't succeed in turning the child into another Harriet Powell. And Emily never learned to read or write. William Hickey finally guessed the truth after noticing that she left the room whenever a letter was delivered to her.

Hayes had spotted Emily, then not quite twelve, as she led her blind father through the streets, begging. Immediately struck by her potential, Hayes enticed the child away, no doubt paying her father off. Hickey said the transformation was total. He wrote of seeing her waiting for him in her splendid coach, their first encounter after Pott's departure: 'But what was all this outside show compared to the lovely creature within, looking more than mortal. Never did I behold so perfect a beauty.' Sir Joshua Reynolds painted Emily several times, and is said to have declared that he never saw 'so faultless and finely formed a human figure'.

Hickey spent much time with Emily over the next few months, and we get a sense of the state of heightened excitement she induced wherever she went. She suffered from a feverish impetuosity, always rushing about, wanting to be seen, to be adored, in a narcissistic whirl of pointless activity. 'Stepping into the carriage, she almost devoured me with kisses, laughed, cried, and was nearly in hysterics, to the surprise and entertainment of several persons who were passing at the time.' At the theatre: 'Her manner towards me drew the attention of the whole house upon us, which made me entreat her to be less ardent. At my gravity she laughed heartily, adding that she was too happy to be considerate and could not help betraying her regard for *her bashful swain!*' Inevitably, all this led fairly soon to a night in her bed. 'I passed a night that many would have given thousands to do.' But Hickey realised that at heart she was empty. 'Although to look upon Emily was to look upon perfection as far as figure and features went, yet my continued intimate acquaintance with her convinced me that she was totally void of feeling, and was indeed as cold as ice.'

Coldness and self-centredness are qualities attributed to many of the great courtesans, but never to Elizabeth Armistead. Hers has often been told as a great love story, of the girl who emerged from a brothel (probably Mrs Goadby's) to rise vertiginously through a string of affairs with aristocrats to become the beloved wife of the greatest orator of the age, Charles James Fox. During that ascent her status gradually changed, and marriage to Fox conferred a degree of respectability equal to that attained by Elizabeth Farren, who married the Earl of Derby, and Harriet Powell, who married the Earl of Seaforth. They married when Fox was thirty-four and she thirty-three – a mature age for a courtesan, who would be competing with girls in their middle teens. By then Armistead was wealthy, having acquired two substantial annuities or settlements from former lovers, and a great deal more besides. This suggests a degree of calculation, but no more than could be expected of anyone forced to make their way in a hostile world since their teens.

Before she became Fox's mistress Armistead had many lovers, so many that it is perhaps surprising that questions were not raised about her status, whether she was not really a whore rather than a courtesan. Among the first to keep her was the Duke of Ancaster. The *Town and Country Magazine's Tête-a-Tête* feature (see Note on Sources) claimed that while they were linked she had a child by a lieutenant in the army. Her next keeper was the Duke of Dorset, who had just parted company with Nancy Parsons. Nancy had first been kept by a man called Horton, whose name she used, the spiteful Horace Walpole writing of 'The Duke of Grafton's Mrs Horton, the Duke of Dorset's Mrs Horton, everybody's Mrs Horton.'

There was much swapping among aristocrats, too. When the Duke of Dorset took up with the Earl of Derby's Countess, the Earl transferred his affections to the Duke's former mistress Elizabeth Armistead. The *Town and Country Magazine* cooed: 'His lordship immediately took a house for her at Hampstead, allowed her his own equipage, besides two very handsome saddle horses; and as he makes no kind of secret of his amour, under his present cir-cumstances, they may frequently be seen riding ensemble in Hyde Park, upon a fine day, and are often met upon the road to Hampstead. They seem perfectly well pleased with each other, and his lordship has had so complete a surfeit of matrimony that this probably may be a lasting alliance.' Katie Hickman (2003) speculates that the Earl's generosity may have been motivated by a desire for revenge on his wife.

Armistead's next lover was Viscount Bolingbroke, known as 'Bully' and with good reason. Previously married to Lady Diana Spencer, he had beaten and generally mistreated her so she had taken a lover, Topham Beauclerk, whom she married when Bully divorced her. She regretted the new marriage almost as much, but at least had achieved a modicum of celebrity under her new name, as the artist Lady Diana Beauclerk.

Moving on, Armistead was next the lover of the very wealthy nabob General Richard Smith. Inevitably the *Town and Country Magazine*, ever with its ear to the ground, had a comment:

There is a fashion in intrigue, as well as other pursuits, and although it must be acknowledged that Mrs A—st—d is a most elegant and beautiful woman, yet if she had not been so highly rated for her charms among the Macaronis of this period, she might probably have escaped unnoticed by Sir Matthew. But as a man of taste, to establish his reputation, must have a mistress as well as a man cook, the degree of his gusto is determined by the happiness of his choice. Who then so proper to establish a man's virtu in amours as Mrs A—st—d, who can claim the conquest of two ducal coronets, a marquess, four earls and a viscount?

Whether the General acquired Armistead as a fashion accessory or out of lust, he made her rich. He conferred her second annuity on her, giving her at last a rare degree of autonomy. She bought two houses in fashionable locations, Bond Street and Clarges Street, and took dancing lessons in order to make an elegant entrance into her box at the opera. She acquired the most fashionable of all lovers, the Prince of Wales. This cannot have been a profitable arrangement, as the Prince did not pay for his pleasures if he could help it. But for the moment Armistead could afford to have a fling at her own expense. The Prince had recently split with one of Armistead's main rivals, the courtesan-actress Mary 'Perdita' Robinson, and no doubt there was an element of triumphalism in Armistead's conquest. The liaison led to an absurd incident. Armistead was at the time involved with Lord George Cavendish, a man who could afford and was willing to pay for her favours. One night, more than a little tipsy, he returned to her house. Noticing a light in a room he forced his way in, despite her entreaties from within. Thrusting his candle into the darkened room, he found the Prince of Wales hiding behind the door. Summoning up more grace than the Prince could manage, he laughed, bowed and left.

Armistead was already showing some signs of that amplitude which the Prince found so beguiling – he had a series of crushes on women of generous figure, a taste which grew with his own girth over the years. His secret wife, Maria Fitzherbert, was given to *embonpoint*, as the contemporary term had it. As he grew older his tastes tended to large aristocratic *grandes dames*, older than himself, some of them grandmothers, Lady

Stafford commenting that 'elderly dames' seemed 'to be his taste'. Lady Bessborough, who suddenly found herself the object of his unwelcome passion, told her lover, Lord Granville Leveson Gower: 'Such a scene I never went through . . . [he] threw himself on his knees, and clasping me round, kissed my neck before I was aware of what he was doing. I screamed with vexation and fright; he continued sometimes struggling with me, sometimes sobbing and crying . . . and then that immense, grotesque figure flouncing about half on the couch, half on the ground.'

Perhaps Armistead realised she could not retain the attention of the Prince for long or perhaps she was growing tired of him, for it appears that she introduced her rivals into his circle. The *Town and Country Magazine* reported: 'Mrs Arm—d, finding that her charms were rather too antiquated, and that Florizel [the Prince] languished after youth and variety, was resolved, at least, to a due regard to the main chance; and as she was acquainted with some who might attract the attentions of the hero . . . administered to his appetites.' By no means for the first time, the magazine had got it wrong. As we have seen, George's lusts were strongly aroused by older, more experienced and masterful women. But on Armistead's side the affair had become a burden, with heavy incidental expenses she knew the Prince would never pay. The expense of running her two houses was large, especially when she entertained the Prince and his friends. When Armistead went abroad after the split with the Prince the *Morning Herald* reported that 'the principal cause of her going abroad was that ill-founded patriotism, which led her to sacrifice so much of her time to the heroic members of opposition, without the receipt of a single guinea'. Already her successor was in place. Grace Dalrymple Eliot, the courtesan known as Dally the Tall, had quarrelled with her French lover the duc de Chartres and hurried back to England, having heard that a greater quarry was free. In 1782 she had a daughter by the Prince, a child he refused to acknowledge. The girl later married into the aristocracy.

For more than ten years, Armistead had been the premier Cyprian, an almost unprecedented reign. (I.M. Davis believes that the longevity of her supremacy was matched only by those of Grace Dalrymple Eliot and Perdita Robinson.) After the Prince dropped her she had affairs with, among others, her old lovers Lord George Cavendish and the Earl of

Derby, who would later marry the actress Elizabeth Farren and be lost to the world of gallantry. Armistead, too, was soon to leave the scene. She had known Charles James Fox for some time. When she returned from the continent he wrote to a friend: 'Mrs Armistead arrived yesterday from Paris and seems to be quite well, tho' she certainly looks (one cannot conceal it) a little old.' Elizabeth was nearly thirty-two. The Prince of Wales laid claim to her again, but this time she insisted he paid, and she apparently got her way. The *Morning Herald*, which habitually called her The Armstead, alluded to this in a particularly obscure and convoluted paragraph: 'The *Armstead*, with very subordinate personal attractions, has contrived to out-jockey the whole *stud* of first-rate *impures*, by the superiority of her understanding – for she has not only outstripped them in the *race amorous* for a certain *Royal sweepstakes*, but has contrived to *touch the plate*, which none of the others could do.' The Prince's interest in Grace Dalrymple Eliot was now waning, and his attention was divided between Armistead and some of her Cyprian rivals.

The promiscuity of the upper classes in the late eighteenth century has often been commented on. It is generally thought to have first become *de rigueur* at the Restoration court of Charles II, 'where sexual promiscuity was almost a hallmark of fashion' (Wagner, 1982). In the eighteenth century this tendency was given new impetus by arranged marriages, in which the personal feelings of both parties were ignored. This left husband and wife free to pursue their inclinations once dynastic considerations had been assured in the form of suitable offspring. Further down the social scale people simply aped their betters, thinking it the fashion to be unfaithful and to have mistresses and lovers. Wagner (1982) has this to say:

In the eighteenth century it became a common practice and eventually a status symbol for the London aristocrats to keep one or even several mistresses. This in turn had an impact on social as well as moral values. Given the frequency of extra-marital relations, a word like *adultery* almost lost its former connotation with sin. The new usage of words of love was partly influenced by French romances of seventeenth and early eighteenth-century origin: formerly negative words were upgraded. Thus adultery became *gallantry*, a love affair was an *amour*, and an attempt at seducing someone became an *intrigue*.

The fast set which gathered round the Prince of Wales and Georgiana, Duchess of Devonshire, set new standards in casual promiscuity. The Prince, married secretly to Mrs Fitzherbert, had a very public affair with Lady Jersey, forty-one years old and the mother of nine children, but still beautiful. Georgiana had a child by the future Prime Minister, Charles Grey. Georgiana's sister Harriet, Countess Bessborough, was the lover of the twenty-year-old Lord Granville Leveson Gower. Georgiana's husband kept a former milliner in a cottage. Georgiana and her best friend lived with him in a *marriage-à-trois*. Newspapers hinted at scandalous goings-on at the Prince's parties, 'promiscuous assemblies', 'midnight bowers and miscellaneous companionships'. The poet and essayist Leigh Hunt was jailed with his brother John in 1813 for criminal libel against the Prince, who was then Regent. In their Sunday paper the *Examiner* they had described him thus: 'This Adonis in loveliness is a corpulent man of fifty ... a libertine over head and ears in debt and disgrace, a despiser of domestic ties, the companion of gamblers and demireps, a man who has just closed half a century without one single claim on the gratitude of his country or the respect of authority.'

In the summer of 1782 the vortex of sexual intrigue at the heart of London high society reached a new intensity. In *The Harlot and the Statesman* I.M. Davis writes:

> The comparative decorum of transient but temporarily exclusive pairings appeared a thing of the past ... as the Prince, his lovers and his friends entangled themselves in a network of multiple liaisons. The Grand Chain of the Cytherean dance seemed broken up into an orgy of promiscuous hands-across: the Prince and the Armistead, the Prince and Dally; Dally and [Lord] Cholmondeley, Cholmondeley and the Armistead; Fox ... and Perdita, Perdita and Banastre Tarleton. Amidst this confusion of couplings there unsurprisingly occurred, some time in August or September, the Ex-Secretary [Fox] and Mrs Armistead. Not long afterwards 'The Armstead' gave up the strenuous fight to stay at the top of her profession and became the permanent mistress, and, eventually, the wife of Charles James Fox.

Harriette Wilson was proof that courtesans were by no means always beautiful. The writer Sir Walter Scott, who recalled supping with her and others where the company was 'fairer than honest', described her as 'far from beautiful . . . a smart saucy girl with good eyes and dark hair and the manners of a wild schoolboy'. But she was lively, witty, stylish, sexy, impudent, amoral and available at a price – qualities some men found irresistible. She captivated an astonishing range of Regency aristos and swells, including the Duke of Wellington and other dukes, earls, marquesses and so on down through the ranks of *Burke's Peerage*. When she fell on hard times she wrote scintillating and revealing memoirs and demanded hush-money from her many lovers 'to be left out'.

Born in 1786, Harriette was one of four daughters of a Mayfair shopkeeper, all of whom became whores. One, Sophia, married Lord Berwick, and snubbed the other three. Harriette got her revenge by taking the box directly above Sophia's at the Opera, and spitting down on her head. From then on Harriette and her two remaining whore sisters were known as the Three Graces, although only she became famous.

Harriette hated hypocrisy. 'Now the English Protestant lady's virtue is chastity!' she wrote. 'There are but two classes of women among them. She is a bad woman the moment she has committed fornication; be she generous, charitable, just, clever, domestic, affectionate and ever ready to sacrifice her own good to serve and benefit those she loves, still her rank in society is with the lowest hired prostitute. Each is indiscriminately avoided, and each is denominated the same – bad woman, while all are virtuous who are chaste.'

Her *Memoirs* characteristically launch straight into the beginning of her career, when she claims she became the mistress of an aristocrat at the age of fifteen.

> I shall not say why and how I became . . . the mistress of the Earl of Craven. Whether it was love, or the severity of my father, the depravity of my own heart, or the winning arts of the noble Lord which induced me to leave my paternal roof and place myself under his protection, does not now much signify: or if it does, I am not in the humour to gratify curiosity in this matter.

Life with her older lover, a military man, soon palled. Craven was a bore, something Harriette could not abide.

I resided on the Marine Parade at Brighton; and I remember that Lord
Craven used to draw cocoa trees, and his fellows, as he called them, on the
best vellum paper, for my amusement. Here stood the enemy, he would say;
and here, my love, are my fellows: there the cocoa trees, etc. It was, in fact, a
dead bore. All these cocoa trees and fellows, at eleven o'clock at night, could
have no peculiar interest for a child like myself. . . .

She and Craven soon parted, and lovers clustered round her. Harriette
had a strong sex drive, and when she felt what she called *le besoin d'aimer*
she would go man-hunting. Two men she claimed to have written to
proposing a meeting were Granville Leveson Gower, later Earl Granville,
and the Prince of Wales. Nothing came of these invitations, but a letter
to the handsome Marquess of Lorne, later Duke of Argyll, led to a
deeply satisfying affair, at least physically. Harriette had suggested that if
he would 'walk up to Duke's Row, Somerstown [where she was living]
he would meet a most lovely girl'. Lorne replied: 'If you are but half as
lovely as you think yourself, you must be well worth knowing; but how
is that to be managed? Not in the street! But come to No. 39 Portland
Street, and ask for me.' Harriette replied: 'No! Our meeting must be in
the high road, in order that I may have room to run away, in case I don't
like you.' In fact they liked each other very much. However, Lorne could
not afford to keep her in the style she demanded. She had moved from
Somerstown into the West End, and hired expensive servants. Her clothes
– she was known for the costly simplicity of her dress – and jewels were
expensive. Although Lorne remained her official lover Harriette frankly
sold sex in brothels when she was short of cash.

The contemporary equivalent of the luxury brothel was the introducing house. They were exclusive, lavish, a kind of upper-class secret. Fifty
years later William Acton (1857) described the very similar Victorian
introducing houses as 'the leading centres of the more select circles of
prostitution', and little had changed:

The leading persons in this line of business . . . make known to the clients
their novel and attractive wares, one might almost say, by circular. A finds a
note at his club telling him that a charming arrival, *de la plus grande fraicheur*,

is on view at Madame de L's. If he has no vacancy for a connexion, he may answer that a mutual friend, C, a very proper man, will call on such and such a day in —— Road, or that Madame —— may drive the object round to his rooms at such another time. All parties handle the affair with mock refinement.

Hickman (2003) says that the principal bawd in the introducing-house line was a Mrs Porter (immortalised by T.S. Eliot in the *Waste Land*: 'O the moon shone bright on Mrs. Porter/And on her daughter/They wash their feet in soda water', lines which seem to be a quotation from an old song or ballad). The courtesan Julia Johnstone, a friend and then an enemy of Harriette, describes Porter when she was about fifty in her *Confessions* (1825) as 'of an agreeable temper and conciliating manners; her face bore the remains of beauty, her figure was fine, and she was in every way calculated to wind herself into the secret recesses of the human heart'. It was Mrs Porter who introduced Harriette to the Duke of Wellington, at the latter's request. At first Harriette feigned reluctance: 'Well, thought I with a sigh, I suppose he must come. I do not understand economy, and I am frightened to death at debts. [Lorne] is going to Scotland; and I shall want a steady sort of friend, of some kind, in case a bailiff should get hold of me.'

Her description of their first meeting is a good example of Harriette's lively style. The portrait of Wellington is unflattering, perhaps because he refused to be blackmailed, reportedly writing – although it is now doubted – 'Publish and be damned' on the copy of her *Memoirs* she sent him with a demand for £200:

I was getting into debt, as well as my sister Amy, when it so came to pass, as I have since heard say, that the —— immortal!!! No; that's common; a very outlandish distinction, fitter for a lady in a balloon. The terrific!!! that will do better. I have seen His Grace in his cotton nightcap. Well, then, the terrific Duke of Wellington!! the wonder of the world!!!

. . . at three on the following day, Wellington made his appearance. He bowed first, then said —— 'How do you do?' then thanked me for giving him permission to call on me; and then wanted to take hold of my hand.

'Really,' said I, withdrawing my hand, 'for such a renowned hero you have very little to say for yourself.'

'Beautiful creature!' uttered Wellington, 'Where is Lorne?'

'Good gracious,' said I, out of all patience with his stupidity —— 'what come you here for, Duke?'

'Beautiful eyes, yours!' reiterated Wellington.

'Aye, man! they are greater conquerors than ever Wellington shall be: but, to be serious, I understand you came here to try to make yourself agreeable?'

'What, child! Do you think I have nothing better to do than to make speeches to please ladies?' said Wellington. . . .

Wellington was now my constant visitor – a most un-entertaining one, Heaven knows! and in the evening, when he wore his broad red ribbon, he looked very like a rat-catcher.

Harriette was hopelessly extravagant, and really needed a wealthy lover to provide her with security. But early on she had decided 'to live free as air from any restraint but that of my conscience'. So when the love of her life came along she was unencumbered by any permanent lover. John Ponsonby was considered the handsomest man in England. His father had been a Foxite MP, his wife was the daughter of the Earl of Jersey and he himself later became Baron of Imokilly. He was, says Hickman, 'related, both by blood and politics, to the very cream of the British aristocracy'. Later he became a much-promoted ambassador – allegedly because King George IV envied his looks and wanted him out of the country.

Harriette's account of their first meetings, after months of stalking each other, is both touching and witty. (She really must have been delightful company.) Ponsonby talked and talked, and Harriette tried to kiss him. 'No,' said Ponsonby, shaking his head, 'I have a thousand things to tell you.'

'I cannot listen to one of them,' said I, faintly, and our lips met in one long, long, delicious kiss! So sweet, so ardent! that it seemed to draw the life's warm current from my youthful heart, to reanimate his with all its wildest passion.

And then! Yes, and then, as Sterne says –

And then – and then – and then – and then – and then we parted.

Three years later they parted for ever. Ponsonby's beautiful wife Fanny seems to have found out about the affair. She was deaf as a result of scarlet fever, and Ponsonby may have been suffering from feelings of guilt about betraying her. He agreed to stop seeing Harriette, and told her by letter. When Harriette received it 'a cold dew, as if from a charnel house, overspread [her] whole frame.' For two weeks Harriette was distraught. She lost weight, wrote letters which Ponsonby ignored, imagined that rats and mice were running over her head 'which thus kept me in a frenzy, from the mere working of a disordered brain'. She wrote that 'the very spark of existence was nearly destroyed'.

Soon, however, it was time to get back to work. Harriette had many older aristocratic clients, but she had acquired a liking for adoring young lovers, and another such soon turned up. The Marquess of Worcester had long admired her from afar, and had tried to get the Duke of Leinster to introduce them. One night at the Opera the Duke pointed him out to Harriette. 'There he is! Do you not observe a very tall young fellow, in silk stockings . . . upon my honour, he won't wear trousers or curl his hair, because he hears that you dislike it.'

When eventually they were introduced, Harriette wrote, 'the young Marquess blushed so deeply, and looked so humble, that it was impossible to treat him without civility . . . the Marquess scarcely spoke, but the little he did find courage to utter was certainly said with good taste, and in a gentlemanly manner'. Worcester was hooked, but she was still involved with another young admirer, the Duke of Leinster. He was soon to leave for the war in Spain, and Harriette told Worcester: 'I [cannot] be tender and true to a dozen of you at a time' and persuaded him to wait. After Leinster set sail she spent a restless night alone – 'no woman ever felt *le besoin d'aimer* with greater ardour than I' – and then, although she did not love him, gave herself into the sole keeping of Worcester. His regiment was based near Brighton, and he took a house for her there. She amused herself by reviewing the troops and was particularly taken by the way Sergeant Whitaker gave sword drill.

'Tik nuttiss!! the wurd dror is oney a carshun. At t'word suards, ye drors um hout, takin a farm un positif grip o'th'hilt! sem time throwing th'shith smartly

backords thus! Dror!!' Here the men, forgetful of the caution which had just
been given them, began to draw. 'Steady there!! Never a finger or a high to
move i'th'hed. Dror! suards!!'

Obviously Harriette was having fun, and Worcester was besotted. His
parents, the Duke and Duchess of Beaufort, grew increasingly alarmed
that their son was about to marry a notorious courtesan. While Harriette
always denied that she intended to marry Worcester, his parents bom-
barded him with bitter hectoring letters. Eventually the Duke's lawyer
approached Harriette and said she could name her price if she handed
over all the letters in which Worcester promised to marry her. She
showed the letters to Henry Brougham, the great statesman and lawyer
who would defend Queen Caroline in 1820 when George IV attempted
to divorce her. Brougham told her that in a court of law the letters could
be worth £20,000. But instead of cashing in Harriette sent all the letters to the Duke, saying 'I will not sell the proofs of respect and affection
which had been generously tendered to me.'

The Duke had Worcester posted to Spain and retracted all promises
to pay Harriette an annuity. When against her undertaking Harriette
wrote to Worcester, the Duke demanded back £100, the only money he
had paid her. His lawyer said: 'His Grace, being no longer obliged to do
anything, will never give you £20 as long as he lives.'

After that Harriette drifted. She went to Paris, quarrelled with a
wealthy lover and in 1823 took up with a swindler and phoney 'colonel' named William Henry Rochfort who may have persuaded her
to write her memoirs. Now in her forties and broke, she desperately
needed money. The book came out in parts between January and April
1825, each instalment carrying an advertisement giving the names of
prominent people to be named in the following one. This gave them the
chance to pay hush-money to be left out. Harriette also wrote blackmailing letters, and one victim sent his copy to the newspapers:

> Sir, People are buying themselves so fast out of my book ... that I have no
> time to attend to them should be sorry not to give each a chance, if they
> chuse to be out. Two noble Dukes have lately taken my word, and I have

never named them, I am sure – would say you might trust me never to publish, or cause to be published, aught about you, if you like to forward £200
directly to me, else it will be too late, as the last volume in which you shine,
will be the property of the Edetor, and in his hands . . . I attack no poor men
because they cannot help themselves.

Adieu. Mind I have no time to write again as what with writing books and
then altering them for those who pay out, I am done up – *frappé en mort*.

What do you think of my French?

Yours, Harriette Rochfort, late Wilson.

The *Memoirs* caused a sensation and a scandal. Sir Walter Scott reported
in his *Journal*:

> The gay world has been kept in hot water lately by the impudent publication
> of the celebrated Harriette Wilson. Wilson from earliest possibility I suppose
> lived with half the gay world at hack and manger; and now obliges such as
> will not pay hush-money with a history of whatever she knows or can invent
> about them . . . there is good retailing of conversation in which the style of
> the speakers . . . is exactly imitated, and some things told as said by individuals
> of each other which will sound unpleasantly in each other's ears.

The *Memoirs* were a bestseller. The Cabinet was said to be engrossed in
reading them, jokes were made in Parliament, members of Brooks's held
a meeting to discuss action but decided there was nothing they could do,
and the publisher, Stockdale, had to erect barricades outside his premises
in the Haymarket to hold back mobs of eager buyers. Harriette was said
to have made £10,000 from sales and hush-money, more than enough to
ensure her a comfortable old age. But Rochfort, who left Harriette for
another woman a few years later, probably squandered it all. Harriette
tried writing novels but without the enlivening touch of her own direct
experience they were a failure. Her former lover Brougham made her a
small allowance. She wrote him begging letters from Dieppe, where she
was living. One, dated 30 June 1828, read: 'Do me the charity to send me
the 20£ on the day you receive this or the next day as I am so miserably
distressed, the least delay in my present very un-fortunate circumstances

will be severely felt. . . .' And from Brighton a few years later:'What did
you gain by obliging me to sell my old favourite good piano forte (in
a hurry to avoid a broker taking it for my landlord's rent) for £5 – for
which I could in a little time easily have got 20£ – and then when all
the mischief was done, and my fever increased by the agitation of these
bailiffs in the house etc. you sent me 25£ instead of the ten I required
to make up the debt. I hate all suspense worse than poverty.' In 1830 she
was charged with assaulting her French maid. 'There was a lot of noisy
recriminations and the newspapers made much of Harriette's vanished
looks, the Colonel's doubtful ancestry and their joint inability to raise
bail' (Wilson, 1964).

Harriette probably died in 1845, aged fifty-nine, and little or nothing is known of her last years. There was a story, probably untrue, that
one of her lovers had once tried to lure her away to live in his house in
the country, but Harriette, 'never one for ruralising', turned him down.
Under the terms of his will the richly furnished house has stood shut-
tered and empty ever since.

Although women such as Mrs Armistead-Fox and Sophia Baddeley
achieved a degree of respectability and even social acceptance rare for
a courtesan, the rise of middle-class morality in the earlier part of the
Victorian period gradually made such people unmentionable. This
changed towards the end of the nineteenth century when high-class
prostitutes once again became news, and were seen as fashion trend-set-
ters. The career of Laura Bell spans this period, although her life was so
full of drama that she would always have been news.

Bell was born in County Antrim in 1829. She worked as a shop-girl in
Belfast, and may have been a prostitute there before leaving for London
when she was twenty. Here she worked first at Jay's General Mourning
House in Regent Street, but was soon supplementing her earnings on
the streets. Blonde, pretty and doll-like, she quickly soared to the top of
her profession and drove daily in Hyde Park in her own carriage. Among
her many wealthy conquests was the Nepalese envoy Jung Bahadoor,
who set her up in Wilton Crescent. He spent the fabulous sum of
£250,000 on her. Nevertheless, in 1852 she married Captain August

Frederick Thistlethwayte, a relative of the Earl of Bathurst. Quite why she married him, and whether she immediately changed her ways, is not known, but her husband was forced to disclaim her debts, so clearly she was still spending lavishly. Thistlethwayte came to a mysterious end. In August 1887 he was found shot dead in his bedroom. Most improbably it was supposed that he had had a fit, in the process knocking over a table which just happened to have a revolver on it. According to this theory, the revolver went off, shooting him dead. By then Laura Bell had certainly altered her ways, having become an evangelical preacher. She chose Scotland to launch this unusual change of career, and her past reputation assured her of large audiences. One observer who heard her preach in 1874 remarked: 'She was getting on in years then, and inclining to be obese. . . .' The society hostess Lady St Helier also heard her preach, and wrote in *Memories of Fifty Years*:

> She was a very striking-looking woman, and the large black mantilla which covered her masses of golden hair, the magnificent jewels she wore around her neck, and the flashing rings on her hands with which she gesticulated, added to the soft tones of her very beautiful voice, made a great impression on those who listened to her.

Strenuous good works and preaching made Laura Bell a modern Magdalen, and long before her death in 1894 she had won grudging acceptance.

By the time Catherine Walters, the last of the great Victorian courtesans, was well into her career things had changed greatly. Courtesans became objects of polite gossip, newspaper headlines, public male rapture and female emulation, at least as regards their manners and dress. Michael Harrison says in *Fanfare of Strumpets* (1971) that in about 1860 the Great Impures, having long been unmentionable, 'became the great subjects of conversation . . . the sight-worth-seeing . . .'. After church on Sunday respectable matrons took their daughters to see the trollops flaunting their wealth in Hyde Park. 'And it was not only the young and not-so-young women who copied the harlot's fashion: the chaste little pork-pie hat worn by the royal princesses and every other mid-Victorian middle-class girl was made fashionable by Catherine Walters – Skittles – whose impudent self-assurance knew no equal. . . .'

Walters was born in Liverpool in 1839, the daughter of a sea-captain and his Irish wife. She told one of her lovers, the poet Wilfrid Scawen Blunt, that she ran away from a convent after a fight with the mother superior. She developed a love of horses, and was employed by the owner of a livery stable to show off his animals on the hunting field. When she was sixteen she became the mistress of George, Lord Fitzwilliam, Master of the Fitzwilliam Hounds. A few years later they separated, Walters being paid off with £300 a year and a lump sum of £2,000. Her 'impudent self-assurance' was more than justified by her next triumph – she hooked Spencer Compton Cavendish, Marquess of Hartington, son and heir of the Duke of Devonshire and a major political figure who later led the Liberals and three times refused the premiership. For all his power and prospective wealth 'Harty-Tarty', as he was called, was hardly a dashing lover for the nineteen-year-old girl. Margot Asquith described him as having 'the figure and appearance of an artisan, with the brevity of a peasant, the courtesy of a king and the noisy sense of humour of a Falstaff. He gave a great wheezy guffaw at all the right things, and was possessed of infinite wisdom' (Leslie, 1972). Hickman (2003) describes him as 'a shy and somewhat immature' man – he was twenty-six. Nevertheless their correspondence shows that for four years they were deeply affectionate lovers.

What was the Marquess getting for his money? Catherine's beauty was of a naturally patrician kind, like that of Nancy Parsons. To quote Hickman once more: 'Photographs of her . . . show a young woman of ravishing natural beauty. Her waist is the requisite handspan, her neck long and graceful, her profile pure; she is dressed with a sobriety which borders on the austere.' Her aristocratic air and expert horsemanship were great assets, although in other ways she was very unladylike. Sir Willoughby Maycock recalls in his *Annals of the Billesdon Hunt* how

Suddenly we heard the sound of horses . . . two people passed by . . . one was a man in black; the other a woman . . . [she] wore a habit that fitted like a glove, and a bit of cherry ribbon round her neck. . . . She made a remark to her pilot as she passed which we both heard distinctly . . . it was to the effect that . . .

a certain part of her anatomy would probably be the same hue as the tie she
wore around her neck. (Quoted in Hardman, 1923)

Another reference to her unladylike propensities has her replying in the
same vein to a man who congratulated her on her healthy flush after a hard
day's hunting: 'You should see my arse.' A story which also had several versions tells how the Countess of Stamford, wife of the Master of the Quorn
Hunt, objected to Walters's presence on the hunting field and asked one
of the whips to get rid of her. Lady Stamford was a gamekeeper's daughter, and it was hinted that her career before her marriage had not been
respectable. As she left the field Walters said: 'Why does Lady Stamford
give herself such airs? *She's* not the queen of our profession, I am.'

Hartington, prospective heir to great wealth but for now living on an
allowance, was as generous to her as he could afford to be. He set Walters
up in a house in Park Street, Mayfair, gave her horses, an allowance and
occasional large gifts of cash. Walters believed he intended to marry her,
but this must have been wishful thinking on both their parts – he was
too much a keystone of the Establishment, and she too notorious. She
was one of that group of courtesans, known as the 'pretty horsebreakers',
who rode in Hyde Park, and had a fan club of men and women who
went there to see them – just like Kitty Fisher a century earlier. There
was even a music hall song commenting on the horsewomen:

> The young swells in Rotten Row all cut it mighty fine,
> And quiz the fair sex, you know, and say it is divine,
> The pretty little horsebreakers are breaking hearts like fun,
> For in Rotten Row they all must go the whole hog or none.

Such was her acclaim that in 1861 the future poet laureate, Alfred Austin
himself, referred to her in verse: 'With slackened rein swift Skittles rules
the Row.'

In September 1861 Hartington wrote explaining that he couldn't come
to see her before making a visit to Scotland, adding ominously: 'I have no
good excuse for going up to London now; and I don't want my people
here to know anything about you Skipsy if I can help it. . . . Poor child,

I am no use to you am I?' A year later he tried to end the affair, also by letter. 'My poor little child . . . you will begin to see that it must have been done some day and that putting it off only made it harder to both of us every day.' Walters set out to see him in New York, whence he had written. She was pursued by a lover who had left his wife for her, the lover in turn being pursued by his father-in-law and uncle. Her affair with Hartington seems to have dragged on for another year. After it ended Walters sold her house in Park Lane and moved to Paris. The Devonshires gave her a generous allowance, said to be £500 a year for life.

It was 1863, Walters was twenty-four, independent and com-fortably off, and ready for new adventures. In Bordeaux she met the young poet, diplomat and traveller Wilfred Scawen Blunt, a man of 'extraordinary physical beauty' (Hickman, 2003). They seem to have become lovers almost immediately. At Biarritz the beautiful young couple – he was a year younger than Walters – caught the eye of the Emperor and Empress, and Blunt was invited to the Empress's parties – without Walters, of course. He was besotted but gradually his possessiveness began to pall on Walters. Hickman says her 'impulsive seduction' of Blunt had been entirely for pleasure, but she was a natural courtesan and did not want to belong to any one man. She told Blunt she was going back to Paris, and he should go back to his diplomatic post in Madrid. Blunt wrote years later: 'I should have kissed my goddess's fair hands and gone my way with benedictions on her head and thanks to Heaven for a pleasure harvested.' Instead he clung weeping to her skirts, until she agreed to take him to Paris. It was a terrible mistake. In Paris Walters was surrounded by admirers who laughed at her gauche young lover. He burst into tears again, and she sent him packing. He went on torturing himself over her, finding her with lovers, creating tremendous scenes and being dismissed. After they ceased to be lovers they wrote to each other for almost forty years. Walters returned to London where, Hickman says, the Prince of Wales was almost certainly among her protectors. Shortly before her death she showed Blunt a drawerful of the Prince's letters to her. As the years passed Walters remained a great courtesan but became much else besides. She took an interest in politics, which she discussed with Blunt and some of the great politicians of the day, and became an unlikely society hostess. Hickman writes:

Catherine's Sunday-afternoon tea-parties at her elegant little house in South Street were soon a Mayfair institution. The Prince of Wales was a regular visitor, and so too was her old friend Blunt. Although Catherine's circle consisted mostly of Establishment gentlemen, some women, mostly singers and actresses, or writers such as the popular novelist Marie Corelli, also attended. Like all good hostesses Catherine took particular pride in bringing her friends together.

Among her visitors was the Prime Minister, Gladstone, known to the prostitutes he attempted to reform as 'old glad-eye'. Walters told Blunt how she had 'captivated no less a personage than . . . the Grand Old Man [Gladstone] himself!' According to Blunt, 'nothing improper seems to have happened, except that the old man kissed her hand saying in a rather formal manner "If it is permitted for an old man"'. Walters hectored him about politics, which he accepted with good humour. He sent her gifts, and on a second visit measured her tiny waist with his hands. He invited her to write to him, telling her to mark her letters with a little cross to indicate they were for the eyes of the Prime Minister only. Although the Prince of Wales warned her not to trouble Gladstone with politics she told Blunt 'when he has got into the habit of coming then I mean to let him have it'. Another visitor was Disraeli, whom she found dull, and her old lover Hartington, now a leading Liberal politician, renewed their friendship. Her last lover, or perhaps companion, was Gerald du Saumarez, who was twenty years her junior and whom she had first known when he was an Eton schoolboy of fifteen. Three weeks before she died of a stroke in her house at South Street in August 1920 she had been planning a visit to Blunt with du Saumarez.

Walters began her career only ten years after Harriette Wilson's early death. By the time she died the world of gallantry of which she had been a part for so long was a dim memory. For more than a hundred years London offered unique opportunities for beautiful young women without money and men with both money and time on their hands to meet and mix to their mutual satisfaction. It is time to look at a few of the more notorious of these men.

EIGHT

MEN OF PLEASURE

A great daily cash flow was needed to keep London's sex industry going, including contributions from many of the wealthiest citizens. Casanova is probably the most famous man of pleasure to have used the London brothels around the middle of the eighteenth century. Particularly flush with money at the time, he could contemplate with equanimity spending 10 or 15 guineas for a bout, although that would not have been enough to buy time with one of the great courtesans. Laura Bell was given £250,000 by the Nepalese Prince Jung Bahadoor – about £12 million today, and whether it was for a single night, as is sometimes suggested, or spread over the whole period of their acquaintance is beside the point. The pearls alone of the English *grande horizontale* Cora Pearl, the glory and the scandal of the Paris demi-monde in the middle of the nineteenth century, were said to be worth £40,000. The Duke of Northumberland offered to pay Sophia Baddeley £500 (£30,000) every time she slept with him, while the nonchalant Lord Melbourne paid her similar amounts.

A man with an enormous appetite for sex, on which he managed to spend as little as possible, was the very wealthy scoundrel Colonel Francis Charteris, who died in 1731. Charteris is a kind of eighteenth-century comic-strip character of awfulness – sly, insin-uating, greedy, dishonest, cowardly, cunning and utterly heartless. His sex drive, a kind a satyriasis, seems to have given him little peace. Charteris made a fortune from South Sea stock and from cheating at cards and had great estates in Lancashire and Scotland. Known as the Rape-Master of Great Britain, he boasted of seducing more than a hundred women, although rape would be a more accurate description; the anonymous *Some Authentic Memoirs of the Life of Colonel C——s, Rape Master of Great Britain* (1730) claims he sent out servants to find 'none but such as were strong, lusty and fresh Country Wenches, of the first size, their B—tt—cks as hard as Cheshire Cheeses, that could make a Dint in a Wooden Chair, and work like a parish Engine at a Conflagration'. He turned his house into a brothel, and his escapades made entertaining reading in a flood of pamphlets. Variously accused of rape, using loaded dice, fraud, bearing false witness, denying his bastard children and, not least, of being an associate of the corrupt First Minister Robert Walpole, he even used his army rank, although he had been cashiered for embezzlement. His aristocratic connections got him out of several scrapes, as when he drew his sword on a constable in St James's Park, or when he raped a young virgin in the Scotch Ale-House in Pall Mall, although he was forced to pay maintenance for the bastard child born to the girl. He was tried for rape at least twice, and sentenced to death once. A Scots woman giving evidence against him said: 'This is the huge raw beast that ... got me with Bairn ... I know him by his nastie Legg for he has wrapt it round my Arse mony a guid time!' (Burford, 1988). In keeping with his interests, Charteris owned brothels, financed by cheating at cards, notoriously winning £3,000 from the Duchess of Queensberry by placing her in front of a mirror in which he could see her cards, a trick that got him banned from several clubs and prompted the Duchess's husband to bring in a law to limit stakes at gambling. Finally, he was reputed to have been the first lover of the noted courtesan Sally Salisbury, when she was little more than a child.

Charteris is depicted in Plate 1 of Hogarth's print series *A Harlot's Progress*. A sweet young country girl newly arrived in town is propositioned by a bawd, easily recognised by contemporaries as the notorious Mother Needham. The Colonel lurks in a nearby doorway watching the progress of this negotiation with his cringing servant Jack Gourlay, who acted as one of his panders. Mother Needham supplied Charteris with many a young and inexperienced girl.

Shortly before Hogarth began his series early in 1730 Charteris was tried for the rape of his servant Anne Bond, who seems to have been recommended to him by Mother Needham. The court was told that as soon as she took up her post he offered her money for sex. She refused, but at seven one morning 'the Colonel rang a Bell and bid the

Clerk of the Kitchen call the Lancashire Bitch into the Dining Room'. Charteris locked the door, threw her on to the couch, gagged her with his nightcap and raped her. When she threatened to tell her friends, he horse-whipped her and took away her clothes and money.

Charteris's rich and aristocratic friends and relatives, including two Knights of the Garter, packed into the court to hear him sentenced to death for rape. He was in Newgate less than a month, and received a royal pardon, negotiated by his son-in-law Lord Wemyss, who bribed Lord President Forbes of Culloden. It also helped that Charteris was the cousin of the Duke of Wharton, himself a notorious rake and the friend and pro-tector of some of the great bawds of the age. In return for his pardon Charteris had to settle a large annuity on Anne Bond. She was also alleged to have received £800 in exchange for signing a petition calling for his reprieve. One paper reported that she was planning to get married, and that she and her husband were going to open a tavern called the Colonel Charteris's Head. The reprieve also cost Charteris a large cash payment to his friend Sir Robert Walpole, leader of the government.

There are many stories told against Charteris. One night at an inn a beautiful young servant girl caught his eye. At first she indignantly refused his gold, but was eventually worn down by his experienced per-sistence and left his room a guinea richer. In the morning Charteris told the landlord that he had given the girl a guinea to change into silver for him, and that she had not yet returned. The girl was called, and had to produce the guinea. Charteris pocketed it, then told the land-lord what had really happened. The girl was dismissed. This unsavoury incident occurred at Lancaster, and many people there never forgot it. When, years later, Charteris was a candidate for a parliamentary seat in Lancaster he found it almost impossible to find a room at any inn. He lost the election.

In 1711 Charteris was found guilty of taking bribes from civilians to allow them to join the army temporarily as a way of escaping prosecution for various reasons. He was cashiered, arrested, taken to London and com-mitted to the custody of the Sergeant-at-Arms of the House of Commons. He had to kneel before the Bar of the House to receive a severe reprimand from the Speaker. The case generated a small literature.

Charteris later raped a miller's wife in Scotland at gunpoint, fled south and was found guilty *in absentia*. Some years afterwards, in 1721, finding it inconvenient not to be able to visit his Scottish estates he petitioned King George I for a pardon. It was granted. *Fog's Weekly Journal* reported: 'We hear a certain Scotch Colonel is charged with a Rape, a misfortune he has been very liable to, but for which he has obtained a *Nolle Prosequi*. It is reported now that he brags that he will solicit for a Patent for ravishing whomever he pleases, in order to put a stop to vexatious suits which may interrupt him in his pleasures hereafter.'

After another girl had been rescued from him by her sister, neighbours stormed Charteris's house with 'Stones, Brickbats, and other such vulgar Ammunition'. When he was released from Newgate following the Anne Bond case, he was set upon by a London crowd. He died in 1731, probably from venereal disease, and the mob threw 'dead dogs &c. into the grave' with him. Pope lampooned him in his *Moral Essays*.

An epitaph for this remarkable man appeared in the *Gentlemen's Magazine* for April 1732:

Here continueth to rot
The Body of Francis Chartres,
Who, with an Inflexible Constancy, and
Inimitable Uniformity of Life,
Persisted,
In spite of Age and Infirmities,
In the Practice of every human Vice,
Excepting Prodigality and Hypocrisy:
His Insatiable Avarice exempting him
From the first,
His matchless Impudence from the second.
Nor was he more singular in the undeviating
Pravity of his Manners
Than successful in accumulating Wealth.
For, without Trade or Profession
Without Trust of Public Money,
And without bribe-worthy Service,

He acquired, or more properly created
A Ministerial Estate.
He was the only Person of his Time
Who could cheat without the Mask of Honesty,
Retain his primeval Meanness
When possessed of ten thousand a year.
And, having daily deserved the Gibbet for what
he did,
Was at last condemned to it for what
He could not do.
O indignant Reader!
Think not his Life useless to Mankind!
Providence connived at his execrable Designs
To give to after-Ages
A conspicuous proof and example
Of how small estimation is exorbitant Wealth
In the Sight of God,
By His bestowing it on the most unworthy of all Mortals.

It is interesting to note that this searing condemnation is almost all about money, and scarcely mentions his other sins. E. Beresford Chancellor, in his *The Lives of the Rakes* (1925), says of Charteris that 'nothing quite like him is to be found in history or fiction'.

Another notoriously debauched character, with a sexual appetite to match Charteris's and the money to indulge it was William Douglas, 4th Duke of Queensberry (1724–1810), known variously as 'Lord Piccadilly' or 'Old Q'. For many years, he lavished his great fortune on the bawds, courtesans and harlots of London, desisting only when he was in his eighties. He was less heartless than Charteris, a good and at times even a generous friend. He helped Emma Hamilton when she was ill and down on her luck, having frittered away her inheritances from Nelson and Sir William Hamilton. Like Charteris he had other passions besides sex: he gambled successfully and on a magnificent scale, he was a patron of the arts and the turf and he was pronounced a dandy. Old Q was a customer of many of the more fashionable brothels, including those kept by Mother Windsor and Sarah Dubery. His housekeeper, Maria Brown, also called Moreton, wrote in her *Memoirs* that he 'employed that skilful Procuress Mrs D—— [Dubery] to procure his *Sultanas* . . . candidates were paraded for inspection . . . she seldom served him with a dish that he could not make at least one meal upon. If he approved, he rang a bell and Mrs D . . . had to school the Novitiate in her duties. . . .'

When he was in his forties he began an affair with La Zamparini, a fifteen-year-old dancer at the Opera, and asked his friend George Selwyn to explain to his current mistress, the 'Contessa' della Rena: 'I love her vastly, but I like this little girl.' Another of his mistresses was Kitty Fredericks, 'the very *Thais* of London'. She had originally been one of Charlotte Hayes's girls, and that great bawd had used her noted expertise at grooming to transform her 'from a shaggy tail'd uncomb'd unwash'd filly' into a delightful child, educated and well spoken, with a knowledge of French and skill at dancing. Charlotte had sold her off 'at a good price' to the Earl of Uxbridge. When he died in 1769 Kitty took up with Captain Richard Fitzpatrick, who was unfortunately killed in the American War of Independence. Kitty had to leave her fine house in Pall Mall and return to the brothel, which was now being run by Catherine Matthews, who had taken over the Hayes establishment at No. 5 King's Place. Mrs Matthews became one of several panders employed by Old Q, and he acquired Kitty for £100 a year, 'a genteel house' and a carriage. Kitty became known as 'Duchess of Queensberry elect' and Old Q's friends fully expected he would marry her. However, in 1779, when Old Q was in his middle fifties, they quarrelled and parted. Kitty became one of the best-known and highest-paid courtesans of the epoch, the darling of high society. Old Q never married.

Four years after the quarrel the *Rambler* carried a caricature of the veteran King's Place bawd Mrs Windsor bargaining with Old Q for the services of three young whores – twenty-year-old Lucy, Polly, aged seventeen, and Priscilla, fifteen. They are depicted in Mrs Windsor's brothel, and she says of Polly that only the previous night she had been 'passed for a Vestal to Father Solomons of St Mary Axe'. But because Q was a regular customer he can have her half-price. Windsor wanted £200 for Priscilla, claiming that 'old Mr Solomons' would pay even more. Old

Q replied: 'They are very young. Will you warrant them?' Mrs Windsor replies: 'Warrant, my Lord! I am astonished at you. . . . They are chaste, virtuous girls. . . . One has almost got her maidenhead!' In the end his lordship takes them all as he is going out of town and doesn't want to be without female company. 'Very well! I'll take them all to Bath with me.'

Old Q was rumoured to have re-enacted the Judgement of Paris, with the goddesses being played by prostitutes, and Paris by himself. He also subsidised the Italian Opera in London for many years, and was indefatigable in his amours with singers and dancers. It was said that his sexual prowess increased with his advancing years, and he presided over tremendous orgies at his houses in Richmond and at 138 Piccadilly. However, Maria Brown, who described herself as 'formerly President of His Grace's Harem', tells a little tale which suggests that Old Q could not always rely on his once superabundant sex drive. She quotes a young woman picked up by Mrs Dubery as a likely candidate for His Grace's bed.

> I had been with a lady to buy a few yards of lace at a shop in New Bond Street, when perceiving an elderly and motherly looking woman looking steadfastly at me in the shop . . . we instantly fell into conversation.

The motherly woman was Mrs Dubery, and she persuaded the young woman to abandon her shopping expedition and go with her to Q's Piccadilly mansion. The girl continued:

> From the Sultan's renown at that time in the annals of gallantry I had framed very high notions of his figure and strength; but I was not in the least displeased to find him otherwise, and there was nothing Herculean about him. . . . We supped together, and after this short tete-a-tete retired to the bedroom. . . . Here I should choose to close the scene with the drawing of the curtains; but . . . it may not here be thought too improper to own, that the Piccadilly Sultan left me as good a maid as he found me; after making a violent fit of coughing his apology for a sudden retreat from the field of love.

Now in his eighties, Old Q really was past it. His longtime friend Sir Nathaniel Wraxhall wrote in his *Memoirs*: 'His person had then become a wreck: but not his mind. Seeing with only one eye, hearing very imperfectly with one ear, nearly toothless and labouring under multiple infirmities. . . .' Thackeray wrote of him in old age in *The Four Georges*: 'This wrinkled, paralysed, toothless old Don Juan died the same corrupt, unrepentant fellow he had been in the most fiery days of his youth. In a house in Piccadilly there is a low window where old Queensberry is said to have sat in order to peer at passing women with voluptuous eyes.'

There are many stories about Old Q we don't have to take too seriously. It was said that a groom was permanently stationed at the door of the house. If a passing woman took the old man's fancy the groom was ordered to accost her, and invite her in. The Duke himself would sit on a balcony eyeing the passing beauties. There is no doubt that some women, attracted by his reputation, pro-menaded by the house in hopes of being chosen for closer inspection, if nothing more. Many a young beauty must have felt a delicious tingle at the thought of so much naughtiness within. Perhaps they were disappointed that the old roué's powers had faded. Women were as fascinated by him as he by them.

In his later years it was the task of his doctor, previously physician to Louis XV, to keep him in a fit state to perform sexually. According to the *Gentlemen's Magazine* a chemist, one Fuller, although receiving a legacy in the Duke's will, claimed £10,000 for 9,340 visits made in the last seven years of the old man's life, and for over 1,000 nights in which he sat up with his patient. He was awarded £7,500.

Old Q died at eighty-five years of age, worn out by a very full life. 'The fact is that in December 1810, when at the point of death, his bed was literally covered with at least 70 *billets doux* and letters written by women of the most varied social positions, from duchesses to semi-prostitutes. Being unable to open and read the letters, he ordered them to be left unopened, and they lay there until his death.' After he died they were gathered up and burned (Jesse, 1847). Three years earlier there had been a premature report of his death, and a wag had penned some verses which caused the Duke much merriment:

And now this may be said of Q,
That long he ran all Folly thro',

For ever seeking something new:
He never cared for me, nor you,
But, to engagements strictly true,
At last he gave the Devil his due;
And died a boy – at eighty-two,
Poor Q of Piccadilly.

For more than sixty years Old Q had contributed generously to the upkeep of what Mother Cresswell had called the 'amorous republic'. He had outlasted all his contemporaries of both sexes in vice. Many of the compliant young girls offered up to him by the bawds of the golden era had gone on to independent careers as Toasts, had died and been succeeded by others. Old Q had seemed to go on for ever. But of course the economy of the amorous republic needed more than one Maecenas, however munificent. Some of the best-known men of pleasure, such as the Honourable Jack Spencer, were very uncertain sources of supply. Others, such as Lord Baltimore, a wealthy eccentric with a sex drive to match, were generous patrons.

Frederick, Lord Baltimore travelled in the East in the 1730s, and when he returned to London used his immense fortune to build a fine house and install a harem, on the lines of those he had seen at Constantinople. His seraglio consisted of 'five white and one black woman'. They were not permitted to go out unchaperoned, but otherwise could have anything they wanted. When he tired of them he loaded them with presents, even dowries, and sent them on their way. They were presided over by his wife, Lady Diane Egerton, who 'acted as the Mistress of her husband's harem . . . chaperoning the girls in their outdoor excursions . . .'.

Songs and satires were written about him and if he had contented himself with the inmates of his personal brothel he would have remained a tolerated figure of fun. But in 1764 he was accused of rape by sixteen-year-old Sarah Woodcock, whom he had kidnapped from her father's shop on Tower Hill. She was a strict Dissenter. To help him break down her resistance he enlisted the help of a corrupt German physician, his wife and a bawd. Sarah was taken to Baltimore's house and held captive while her four kidnappers tried to break her will. She was not allowed eat or sleep for three days. On the fourth, when she was too weak to resist, Baltimore raped her twice. Then they induced her to sign a letter saying she had gone to the house of her own free will. It was this letter that formed the basis of Baltimore's successful defence when he was tried for rape. 'A criminal process was instituted in consequence of this accusation; but his lordship vindicated his innocence, and triumphed over the malice of his enemies. This affair, however, made a lively impression on his mind; he dismissed his mistresses, sold his house ... gave away the magnificent furniture, and in a short time left his native country' (Von Archenholz, 1789). Baltimore died shortly afterwards in Naples.

The Regency period was the heyday of the rake, the court of the Regent himself lending a kind of sanction to heartless philandering just as had the Restoration court of Charles II. The last of the Hanoverians, William IV, was a womaniser. When a young man in Hanover he 'pursued his amours with ladies of the town, up against a wall or in the middle of a parade ground ... he lamented for the pretty girls of Westminster who would never clap or pox him'. In 1787 he had the mercury treatment for two bouts of venereal disease. By the time his niece Victoria came to the throne the moral climate had changed, and although the aristocracy fought a long rearguard action the era of their carefree hedonism was over.

NINE

INTO THE ABYSS

A puritan backlash against the profligacy of the Restoration had begun at the end of the seventeenth century with the backing of the royal couple William and Mary. William issued a *Proclamation for Preventing and Punishing Immorality and Profaneness* in 1698, and zealots like the magistrate Sir John Gonson were soon ranging the haunts of pleasure and rounding up and punishing bawds and whores. Strictly speaking prostitution was not a crime, although soliciting was. Keeping a brothel was also legal, as long as it was not 'disorderly', although this might be a matter of opinion. The Watch and the magistrates would, however, often act if there was sufficient public pressure, and being a 'notorious common prostitute' or bawd might be enough to get a woman hauled up before the courts. Some were so poor there was no point in fining them. Sentencing them to the pillory was a risk: there was at least a chance this dangerous secondary punishment would be much more severe than intended – Mother Needham probably died as the result of injuries inflicted by the mob. Ann Morrow, a Covent Garden brothel-keeper, was sentenced by Sir John Fielding to be pilloried in August 1777. She lost the sight of both eyes. Bawds arrested by constables or the zealots of the vigilance societies could sometimes escape the worst punishments by bribery, but occasionally they came up against an honest or puritan officer who insisted on the full rigour of the law. Then the bawd might be carted – paraded through the streets on a cart, pelted with filth by a jeering mob, preceded by musicians or people beating saucepans to drum up a crowd, taken to a city gate and expelled with a warning to stay away. More severe punishments included whipping and having their noses slit. Usually those expelled were soon back in business.

In 1716 Barbara Jarrett, 'bawd of Wapping', was stripped to the waist and whipped the two miles from Old Gravel Lane to Wapping. Her neighbour Margaret Shadrack was tied to the 'cart's arse' and whipped, then sent to Newgate for a month. A pregnant bawd, Phillis Hansford, was whipped from her brothel, the Adam and Eve in Ratcliffe. Part of her sentence was suspended until after the child was born.

Sometimes the law was little better than a charter for sadists. Under a sixteenth-century statute which was not repealed until 1817 a woman could be chastised in this way. It stipulated that she 'should be stripped naked from the middle upward and whipped till the body should be bloody'. In his *London Spy* the author Ned Ward describes such punishments carried out at the Bridewell gaol by the River Fleet behind Bride Lane:

> A grave gentleman whose awful looks bespoke him some honourable citizen, was mounted in the judgement seat, armed with a hammer . . . and a woman under the lash was in the next room, where folding doors were opened so that the whole court might see the punishment inflicted. At last went down the hammer and the scourging ceased. . . . Another accusation being then delivered by a flat-cap [citizen] against a poor wretch, who had no friend to speak on her behalf, proclamation was made, viz.: 'All you who are willing E——th T——ll should have present punishment, pray hold up your hands.'

The audience having voted for instant punishment, the woman was stripped 'as if it were designed rather to feast the eyes of the spectators than to correct vice or correct manners' and lashed.

Even the more exalted bawds were not safe. Mother Elizabeth Hayward, who catered for the Quality at her establishment in Russell Street and was a crony of Moll King, was pilloried in 1721 with a man named Richard Hayward, presumably her husband. They had to pledge good behaviour for seven years, but were soon back in business in nearby Charles Street. Mother Hayward died in 1743, apparently unmolested again by the law.

At first the campaign to clean up London made little headway, its supporters being regarded as interfering busybodies at best, but by the early nineteenth century a change in moral sensibility had taken place, spearheaded by the growing middle class. What would eventually be known as Victorian values were reinforced by newspapers, writers and a host of religious and social reformers.

Estimates of the numbers of prostitutes in the capital ranged as high as 220,000, but J.B. Talbot, secretary of the deeply puritanical London Rescue Society, suggested the more conservative total of 80,000 based on his own observations 'and the evidence of eight different investigators'. This figure came to be widely accepted. Whatever the true total, it was apparent to all that the streets swarmed with whores, some of them very young, pestering men by plucking at their sleeves and making lewd suggestions.

A German traveller wrote: 'Every ten yards one is beset, even by children of twelve years old, who by the manner of their address save one the trouble of asking whether they know what they want. They attach themselves to you like limpets. . . . Often they seize hold of you after a fashion of which I can give you the best notion by the fact that I say nothing about it.'

The Russian author Fyodor Dostoevsky noticed in the Haymarket how 'mothers brought their little daughters to make them ply the same trade'. He left a heart-rending description of one exploited child. The little girl was 'not older than six, all in rags, dirty, bare-foot and hollow cheeked; she had been severely beaten and her body, which showed through the rags, was covered with bruises. . . . Nobody was paying any attention to her . . . the look of such distress, such hopeless despair on her face . . . . She kept on shaking her tousled head as if arguing about something, gesticulated and spread her little hands and then suddenly clasped them together and pressed them to her little bare breast. . . .'

The Haymarket was known as 'Hell Corner'. The French historian Hippolyte Taine recorded a stroll down the Haymarket and the Strand in the 1860s: 'Every hundred steps one jostles twenty harlots; some of them ask for a glass of gin; others say, "Sir, it is to pay my lodging." This is not debauchery which flaunts itself, but destitution — and such destitution! The deplorable procession in the shades of the monumental streets is sickening; it seems to me a march of the dead. That is a plague-spot — the real plague-spot of English society.' As late as 1881 a police witness told a Select Committee of the House of Lords:

The state of affairs which exists in this capital is such that from four o'clock, or one may say from three o'clock in the afternoon, it is impossible for any respectable woman to walk from the top of the Haymarket to Wellington Street, Strand. From three or four o'clock in the afternoon Villiers Street and Charing Cross Station and the Strand are crowded with prostitutes, who are openly soliciting prostitution in broad daylight.

At half-past twelve at night a calculation was made a short time ago that there were 500 prostitutes between Piccadilly Circus and the bottom of Waterloo Place.

In an effort to gauge the extent of the problem investigators penetrated areas of the city unknown to all respectable citizens except the police, coroners' officers and a few intrepid journalists such as Dickens. They entered the rookeries, the 'ancient citadels of vice and crime' which extended in a rough kind of arc west to east through the city. This began in the west with Devil's Acre in the shadows of Westminster Abbey, then ran east to the Covent Garden– Drury Lane area and north to St Giles, known as the Holy Land, because it attracted so many Irish Catholics. It took a diversion south to Alsatia, between Fleet Street and the River Thames, the area which gave its name to all criminal ghettoes, then turned north and east again to Saffron Hill and out into the East End. Beyond the City limits stretched Whitechapel and Shoreditch, *terra incognita*. Places such as Wentworth Street, which in 1836 had six consecutive houses that were all brothels, were just ugly rumours even to the intrepid crusaders of the rescue societies. It wasn't until Jack the Ripper made his unique contribution to social reform in 1888 that the area was, in a sense, opened up, like a dark continent. His killings were all committed within 500 yards of Whitechapel High Street, 'where the wealth of the City met the poverty and mystery of the East End'. South of the river Southwark, that most ancient haunt of vice, although no longer so fashionable, still had many brothels.

In 1817 the London Guardian Society reported to the Parliamentary Committee on the State of the Police the results of its survey of prostitutes. In three parishes – St Botolph without Aldgate, St Leonard's, Shoreditch and St Paul's, Shadwell – there were 360 brothels and 2,000 prostitutes in a population of 59,050. St Paul's, Shadwell alone had 200 brothels and 1,000 prostitutes out of 9,855 inhabitants and 1,082 houses. In other words, nearly a fifth of the houses in the parish functioned as brothels. In Stepney, four streets abutting on the Commercial Road contained 65 brothels and 194 prostitutes. Southwark's parish of St George the Martyr had 370 prostitutes, and Lambeth, which housed many of the women who plied their trade in Vauxhall Gardens, had 1,176 brothels and 2,033 prostitutes. In the City, there were 22 brothels housing 150 prostitutes 'in the vicinity of New Court'. Even at Westminster Abbey the Almonry was a haunt of whores.

The Police Committee heard evidence that among the reasons Southwark still attracted prostitutes were the area's theatres and circus, the three nearby bridges to the City and the fashionable parts of town, and the 'great numbers of small houses lately built in that parish, which are particularly suited for such occupants', which mainly attracted whores who plied their trade in the brothels and accommodation houses of the West End.

In 1840 the French socialist and feminist Flora Tristan published *Promenades dans Londres*, an account of visits to the capital between 1826 and 1839. This is her description of a visit to the western fringe of the Southwark area:

There are so many prostitutes in London that one sees them everywhere at any time of day; all the streets are full of them, but at certain times they flock in from outlying districts in which most of them live, and mingle with the crowds in theatres and public places. It is rare for them to take men home; their landlords would object, and besides their lodgings are unfit. They take their 'captures' to the houses reserved for their trade....

Between seven and eight o'clock one evening, accompanied by two friends armed with canes, I went to take a look at the new suburb which lies on either side of the long broad thoroughfare called Waterloo Road at the end of Waterloo Bridge. This neighbourhood is almost entirely inhabited by prostitutes and people who live off prostitution; it is courting danger to go there alone at night. It was a hot summer evening; in every window and doorway women were laughing and joking with their protectors. Half dressed, some of them *naked to the waist*, they were a revolting sight, and the criminal, cynical expressions of their companions filled me with apprehension. These men are for the most part very good looking – young, vigorous and well made – but their coarse and common air marks them as animals whose sole instinct is to satisfy their appetites. . . .

We went on our way and explored all the streets in the vicinity of Waterloo Road, then we sat upon the bridge to watch the women of the neighbourhood flock past, as they do every night between the hours of eight and nine, on their way to the West End, where they ply their trade all through the night and return home between eight and nine in the morning.

A particularly distressing aspect of vice was juvenile prostitution. The children involved inevitably came from the poorer parts of the city. The crusading newspaper editor W.T. Stead raised the profile of the problem in a series of articles in his *Pall Mall Gazette*. Entitled 'The Maiden Tribute of Modern Babylon' and written in a hard-hitting style, the articles created a sensation.

'Here,' said the keeper of a fashionable villa, where in days bygone a prince of the blood is said to have kept for some months one of his innumerable sultanas, as she showed her visitor over the well-appointed rooms, 'Here is a room where you can be perfectly secure. The walls are thick, there is a double carpet on the floor. The window, which fronts on the back garden, is doubly secured, first with shutters, then with heavy curtains. You lock the door and then you do as you please. The girl may scream blue murder, but not a sound will be heard. The servants will be far away at the other end of the house. I will only be about seeing that all is snug.

Stead asked an experienced police officer if it would be possible to buy a genuine young virgin.

'Certainly' he replied without a moment's hesitation. 'But', I continued, 'are these maids willing or unwilling parties to the transaction – that is, are they really maiden, not merely in being each a *virgo intacta* in the physical sense, but as being chaste girls who are not consenting parties to their seduction?' He looked surprised at my question. . . . 'Of course they are rarely willing, and as a rule they do not know what they are coming for.'

In the issue of 6 July 1885 Stead quoted a former brothel-keeper:

> Did they begin willingly? Some; others had no choice. How had they no choice?
> Because they never knew anything about it till the gentleman was in their bed-
> room, and then it was too late. I or my girls would entice fresh girls in, and
> persuade them to stay out too late till they were locked out, and then a pinch of
> snuff in their beer would keep them snug until the gentleman had his way.

This man admitted picking up a girl of thirteen on the pretext that he
would employ her as a maid, a common ruse of procurers. Instead he
took her to his brothel. 'A gentleman paid me £13 for the first of her,
soon after she came to town. She was asleep when he did it – sound
asleep. To tell the truth, she was drugged. It is often done.'

Stead said unwilling girls would be taken to soundproofed rooms and
raped. Many would scream and fight, so they were held down by the
brothel-keeper or strapped to the bed.

> To oblige a wealthy customer ... an eminently respectable lady undertook that
> whenever the girl was fourteen or fifteen years of age she would be strapped
> down hand and foot to the four posts of the bedstead, so that all resistance
> except that of unavailing screaming would be impossible. ... Strapping down
> for violation used to be a common occurrence in Half Moon Street.

Howard Vincent, director of the Criminal Investigation Department of
the Metropolitan Police, told the 1881 select committee:

> There are houses in London, in many parts of London, where there are people
> who will procure children for the purposes of immorality and prostitution,
> without any difficulty whatsoever above the age of 13, children without
> number at 14, 15 and 16 years of age. Superintendent Dunlap will tell you that
> juvenile prostitution is rampant at this moment, and that in the streets about
> the Haymarket, Waterloo Place and Piccadilly, from nightfall there are chil-
> dren of 14, 15 and 16 years of age, going about openly soliciting prostitution
> ... this prostitution actually takes place with the knowledge and connivance
> of the mother and to the profit of the household. ... These procuresses ...

have an understanding with the mother of the girl that she shall come to that house at a certain hour, and the mother perfectly well knows for what purpose she goes there, and it is with her knowledge and connivance, and with her consent that the girl goes....

One reason for this demand for young girls was a kind of mania for defloration among Victorian debauchees. There was a belief that sex with a virgin could cure venereal disease. Another was men's anxiety about infecting their wives with VD. If they had sex only with virgins that would not happen. The result was an un-precedented demand for girls under the age of consent. Until 1875 it was twelve: from 1876 to 1883 it was thirteen, and thereafter it was raised to the present level of sixteen.

Prices for virgins in a superior London brothel in the 1880s could range from £50 upwards, and Chesney says in *The Victorian Underworld* that on occasions £100 or more would be offered. But demand outstripped supply, and the diarist 'Walter' suggested in *The Secret Life* that this was because most working-class girls lost their virginity to members of their own class by their early teens:

> Few of the tens of thousands of whores in London have given their virginities to gentlemen, or to young men, or to old men, or to men at all: their own low-class lads had them before anyone else ... that is the truth of the matter, though greatly to be regretted, for street boys cannot appreciate the treasure they destroy. A virginity taken by a street boy of sixteen is like a pearl cast before swine.

The evidence of child prostitution in Victorian London was all around. Girls from twelve to fifteen paraded up and down between Piccadilly Circus and Waterloo Place, and there was even a market where children could be bought for any purpose (Henriques, 1962–8, Vol. 3). W.T. Stead revealed a particularly revolting means of supplying the market with virgins. He quotes a brothel-keeper:

> Another very simple mode of supplying maids is by breeding them. Many women who are on the streets have female children. They are worth keeping. When they get to be twelve or thirteen they become merchantable. For a

very likely 'mark' of this kind you may get as much as £20 or £40. I sent my
own daughter on the streets from my own brothel. I know a couple of very
fine little girls who will be sold before very long. They are bred and trained
for the life. They must take the first steps some time, and it is bad business not
to make as much out of that as possible. Drunken parents often sell their children to brothel-keepers. In one street in Dalston you might buy a dozen....

The police were powerless to stop men taking advantage of girls who were
only just over the age of consent, or the girls from prostituting themselves.
The 1881 select committee report already quoted contained this evidence
from a police superintendent about a visit to a house in Windmill Street:

I went in with my chief inspector, and in each of the rooms in that house I
found an elderly gentleman in bed with two of these children. They knew
perfectly well that I could not touch them in the house; and they laughed and
joked me, and I could not get any direct answer whatever. I questioned them,
in the presence of the brothel keeper, as to what they were paid, and so on.
They were to receive six shillings each from the gentleman, two of them; and
the gentlemen had paid six shillings each for the room. It was four shillings if
there was only one girl, but six shillings if there were two girls for the room.

To meet the demand for young virgins procurers placed advertisements
in provincial newspapers offering jobs in domestic service. When the
girls arrived in London they would be taken to a brothel and forced into
prostitution, having been drugged or made drunk first. There was little
the girls could do: the local police would have been bribed and it was
useless appealing to them for help – Stead cited a brothel in the East End
which paid the Metropolitan Police £500 a year for protection.

Procurers for brothels preyed on Irish girls coming to England in search
of work. They would be met on the wharf at Liverpool by a stranger
who offered to take them to a cheap hotel – really a brothel. Those lucky
enough to evade the traps at Liverpool and make it to London were still
in danger. 'A woman dressed as a Sister of Mercy would approach them
saying she had been sent from a convent to meet them, and take care
of them. Introduced to the brothel the system worked as in the other

methods – drink, no money, and the life of luxury awaiting them' (Henriques, 1962–8, Vol. 3). The Society for the Protection of Young Females stated:

> It has been proved that upwards of four hundred individuals procure a living by trepanning [trapping] females from eleven to fifteen years of age, for the purposes of Prostitution ... when an innocent child appears in the streets without a protector, she is insidiously watched by one of these merciless wretches and decoyed, under some plausible pretext, to the abode of infamy and degradation.... She is stripped of the apparel with which parental care, or friendly solicitude has clothed her, and then decked with the gaudy trappings of her shame, she is compelled to walk the streets ... should she attempt to escape from the clutches of her seducers she is threatened with instant punishment, and is often barbarously treated.

There is probably an element of exaggeration here, particularly in the figure of more than four hundred procurers, but nevertheless there was a real problem. Flora Tristan quotes a document produced by the Society for the Prevention of Juvenile Prostitution in 1838. It concerned a brothel specialising in young girls, mostly foreign, which had been prosecuted by the Society. The madam, a Frenchwoman named Marie Aubrey, had fled abroad.

> The house in question was situated in Seymour Place, Bryanston Square. It was an establishment of great notoriety, visited by some of the most distinguished foreigners and others .... The house consisted of twelve or fourteen rooms, besides those appropriated to domestic use, each of which was genteely and fashionably furnished ... a service of solid silver plate was ordinarily in use when visitors required it.... At the time when the prosecution was instituted, there were about twelve or fourteen young females in the house, mostly from France and Italy . .. Marie Aubrey had lived at the house a number of years, and had amassed a fortune.... Upon receiving a fresh importation of females, it was the practice of this woman to send a circular, stating the circumstance, to the parties who were in the habit of visiting the establishment.... There are a number of houses of this description at the West End now under the cognizance of the Society....
>
> Your Committee desire to lay before this meeting the means adopted by the agents of these houses. As soon as they arrive on the Continent they

obtain information respecting those families who have daughters and who are desirous of placing them in respectable situations; they then introduce themselves, and by fair promise induce the parents to allow the stranger to accompany [the girl] to London, with the understanding that they are to be engaged as tambour [embroidery] workers, or in some other genteel occupation. . . . While they remain in the house they were first taken to, the money is duly forwarded, and the parents are thus unconsciously receiving the means of support from the prostitution of their own children; if they remove, letters are sent to the parents to apprize them that their daughters have left the employ of their former mistress, and the money is accordingly stopped.

The 1844 tract *Miseries of Prostitution* quotes a letter from a procurer offering a client a young girl who is 'fresh', that is a virgin.

Sir, When I was at your office, to bring you a letter from Miss Villiers, I promised to let you know when I knew of any lady – *fresh*. I can recommend you a very pretty fair young girl, just come from the country, and I think you will like her much; and if it is convenient to you to meet her tomorrow at — Lichfield Street, at the bottom of St Martin's Lane, at eight o'clock, she shall be there waiting for you. If it is not convenient, will you have the kindness to send me a note by post, and inform me when it will suit your convenience.

Child prostitution was vile, but we should be cautious about unquestioningly accepting the rescue societies' propaganda. They regarded prostitution as a fate worse than death, but for most girls it was infinitely preferable to a life of servitude as a 'domestic' or the sweated labour of millinery. It suited many girls of a restless or independent character. Frederick Merrick, chaplain of Millbank Prison, reported that out of 16,000 prostitutes he interviewed 14,000 were attracted by the promise of 'nothing to do; plenty of money; your own mistress; perfect liberty; being a lady'. The profession offered girls the chance to save enough to start a small business or attract a respectable husband, perhaps a small trader. Most got off the streets or out of the brothels by their middle twenties. In the meanwhile they had experienced a degree of independence rare for women of their time.

TEN

HAUNTS OF PLEASURE

The places where Victorian whores went for pick-ups were many and varied. One told Henry Mayhew's collaborator Bracebridge Hemyng of her daily routine, which except in one important particular resembled that of a woman of leisure. She rose and dined at about four in the afternoon and went on the streets for an hour or two 'if I want money'. Afterwards she would go to the Holborn Casino, 'and if anyone likes me I take him home with me'. If she was unsuccessful she would go to various cafés in the Haymarket, and try her luck there. If she was again unsuccessful she would go to the 'cigar divans', but that was almost the last resort: 'you don't as a rule find any good men at the divans'. These divans were places men went late at night to buy and smoke cigars, drink and pick up whores.

Casinos – large dance halls – were popular places for pick-ups. The Holborn Casino was an enormous dance hall, 'glittering with a myriad prisms', where young middle-class men could pick up working-class whores who 'dressed up flash'. The men were 'medical students, apprentice lawyers, young ships' officers, clerks, well-off tradesmen' (Chesney, 1999). The city's growing wealth meant that there were many more such men about and, con-sequently, more prostitutes.

The most luxurious and fashionable of the dance halls was the Portland Rooms, known as Mott's, where the most expensive courtesans sought customers between midnight and four or five in the morning. A dress code was enforced: gentlemen not wearing dress coats and white waistcoats were refused admission. That lively memoir of the mid-nineteenth-century capital, Shaw's *London in the Sixties*, sets the scene:

> The ladies who frequented Mott's, moreover, were not the tawdry make-believes who haunt the modern 'Palaces' but actresses of note, who if not

Magdalens [prostitutes] sympathised with them; girls of education and refinement who had succumbed to the blandishments of youthful lordlings, fair
women here and there who had not yet developed into peeresses and pro-
genitors of future legislators. Among them were 'Skittles' [Catherine Walters],
celebrated for her ponies, and sweet Nelly Fowler, the undisputed Queen of
beauty in those long-ago days.

In the 1850s and 1860s the most celebrated of the cafés, or night houses,
was the Café Royal in Princess Street, Leicester Square, known after the
woman who ran it as Kate Hamilton's. It was approached down a long
passage and carefully guarded to keep out the lowest and poorest prostitutes. Kate weighed 20 stone 'with a countenance that had weathered
countless convivial nights'. *London in the Sixties* describes her as 'shaking with laughter like a giant blancmange' as she sat all night with her
favourites drinking champagne. There is an engraving of her sitting with
these cronies on a platform above the fray, her powerful voice keeping
order. High-class night houses such as Kate's made their money by selling food and drink at outrageous prices – champagne and Moselle cost
12s a bottle.

Mayhew's *London Labour and the London Poor* says that Kate was so
selective – only men prepared and able to spend £5 or £6, or even more,
were admitted – that 'these supper rooms are frequented by a better set
of men and women than perhaps any other in London'. These were
people who would 'shrink' from appearing in the Haymarket cafés, or
the supper rooms of the surrounding streets, 'nor would they go to any
other casino than Mott's'.

Not even Kate's was immune to raids by the police, although generous bribes probably ensured no harm came of them. *London in the Sixties*
describes what happened when a raiding party was spotted: 'An alarm gave
immediate notice of the approach of the police. Finding oneself within
the "salon" during one of these periodical raids was not without interest.
Carpets were turned up in the twinkling of an eye, boards were raised and
glasses and bottles – empty or full – were thrust promiscuously in; everyone assumed a sweet and virtuous air and talked in subdued tones, whilst
a bevy of police, headed by an inspector, marched solemnly in and having

completed the farce, marched solemnly out. What the subsidy attached to this duty, and when and how paid, it is needless to inquire.'

The lively Argyll Rooms by Windmill Street was one of the most famous of the Haymarket's places of entertainment. It had a dance floor and gallery, and on one occasion Lord Hastings, known as something of a sportsman, emptied a sack of rats among the dancers. This is how D. Shaw in *London in the Sixties* depicts the scene, although he places it at Mott's: 'To describe what followed is impossible. Two hundred men and women and two hundred sewer rats compressed within the compass of forty feet by thirty, and in a darkness as profound as any that was ever experienced in Egypt.' Hastings was a man of legendary generosity: 'Six cases of champagne invariably formed the first order' as he treated all and sundry.

The Argyll was regarded as a pick-up place for prostitutes; the author Dr William Acton said of it: 'The women are of course all prostitutes. They are for the most part pretty, and quietly though expensively dressed, while delicate complexions, unaccompanied by the pallor of ill-health, are neither few nor far between. This appearance is doubtless due in part to the artistic manner of the make-up by powder and cosmetics, on the employment of which extreme care is bestowed.' Although for a long time the authorities tolerated the Argyll because they felt it was better to have its prostitutes in one place rather than dispersed in the streets, it fell victim to the rising tide of Victorian morality and closed in 1878.

D. Shaw writes of the Haymarket he had known in his youth that it 'literally blazed with light' from such temples as the Blue Posts, Barnes's, the Burmese and Barron's Oyster Rooms. 'The decorous Panton Street of today was another very sink of iniquity. Night houses abounded, and Rose Burton's and Jack Percival's were sandwiched between hot baths of questionable respectability and abominations of every kind.' All these places, and many more, had one thing in common: respectable women did not go there. Men could and did eat in supper rooms and drink in night houses without seeking female company, but the fact remained that prostitution kept the houses in business.

Prostitutes who did not work in a brothel needed somewhere to take their clients. The poorest and cheapest would take a man into an alley for

brief sex against a wall – Boswell describes several such encounters – but
girls further up the scale needed a room and a bed. High-class courtesans would have houses of their own, perhaps as far away as Fulham or
St John's Wood. All other prostitutes found their lives and their working practices dominated by this problem. They could take the clients
to lodging houses which were in effect brothels, in that all the rooms
would be rented by prostitutes, or to the more comfortable and convenient accommodation houses, where rooms were let by the night or
even the hour. Lodging-house brothels were found all over London, and
varied enormously in the rents they charged the whores. William Acton
tells how a kind of communal life in the kitchens of these houses had a
corrupting effect on the girls:

> Her company is sought for novelty's sake when she is a newcomer, and her
> absence or reserve is considered insulting when she is fairly settled in; so if she
> had any previous idea of keeping herself to herself, it is very soon dissipated.
> . . . They are usually during the day, unless called upon by their followers, or
> employed in dressing, to be found dishevelled, dirty, slipshod and dressing-
> gowned in this kitchen, where the mistress keeps her table-d'hote. Stupid
> from beer, or fractious from gin, they swear and chatter brainless stuff all day,
> about men and millinery, their own schemes and adventures, and the faults
> of others of the sisterhood. . . . As a heap of rubbish will ferment, so surely
> will a number of unvirtuous women deteriorate, whatever their antecedents
> or good qualities previous to their being herded under the semi-tyranny of a
> lodging-house-keeper of this kind. In such a household, all the projections of
> decency, modesty, propriety and conscience must, to preserve harmony and
> republican equality, be planed down, and the woman hammered out, not by
> the practice of her own profession or the company of men, but by her associ-
> ation with her own sex and class, to the dead level of harlotry. (Acton, 1857)

Another option, and one chosen by many prostitutes, was the accommodation house. These establishments were more like hotels, but they let rooms
by the hour or the night. In the better ones food and drink were available. The anonymity suited many of them. They could keep their working
and home lives separate, vital if they wanted to maintain a façade of

respectability, which a lot of married prostitutes did (there are several stories of apparently respectable women who were secret prostitutes). Although they had to pay for the room it was cheaper than living in a lodging-house brothel. A room in a slum accommodation house might cost 1s, a more discreet and luxurious house in the centre of the city a guinea or two. The average was about 5s. The owner of a successful establishment in the Haymarket retired to a villa in Camberwell and called it Dollar House after all the 'dollars' (slang for 5s) she earned by letting her rooms repeatedly throughout each day. Moreover, prostitutes patrolling their 'beats' would know that they were never far from an accommodation house, for they abounded in many parts of London. The important vice area around the Haymarket and Leicester Square had its share, and there was a string of such premises all the way from Bond Street to beyond Covent Garden. There were large houses in the slums of St Giles and Seven Dials, one of which had thirty-two bedrooms. Soho and the slums north of Leicester Square also offered cheap rooms for assignations.

There was a large house in Bow Street, near the Opera House, and the diarist Walter described how a prostitute called Brighton Bessie took him there. For wealthy Walter the fact that it was dearer than the usual house of its type was less important than the fact that couples were not interrupted by the landlord asking them to hurry up. 'In it there must have been twenty rooms, and there were more sighs of pleasure in that house nightly than in any other house in London, I should think.' In winter there were large fires in the rooms, and wine and liquor 'of fair quality' were available. The beds, 'large enough for three', always had clean linen. 'It was one of the most quiet, comfortable accommodation-shops I ever was in, and with Brighton Bessie I passed there many voluptuous evenings.'

As well as the lodging-house brothels and the accommodation houses, prostitutes could take their customers to a wide variety of places which offered rooms for assignations. Cigar divans, chop houses, coffee rooms and particularly and perhaps, surprisingly, shops. The latter included some exclusive West End establishments, and some of the elegant fronts in the Burlington Arcade were known among the cognoscenti to have rooms where a man and woman, entering the shop separately, might discreetly retire. Sometimes the girls behind the counter were available.

Life as a brothel whore was less challenging than having to advertise one's attractions in person in the streets or in a theatre or tavern. It was also less lucrative, and could amount to little more than slavery. In *London Labour and the London Poor* Henry Mayhew recounts the life of a young prostitute in a brothel off Langham Place. He does not give a date for the interview, but the book was published in 1851, so he is describing conditions in an early Victorian brothel.

The room he was shown into was well if cheaply furnished, having coburg chairs and sofas, handsome green curtains and even chandeliers. He does not describe the girl, whom he guessed was aged about twenty-three, although she said she was twenty – 'but statements of a similar nature, when made by this class, are never to be relied on'. The girl asked for a drink, and Mayhew bought her a bottle of wine.

> What she told us briefly was this. Her life was a life of perfect slavery, she was seldom if ever allowed to go out, and then not without being watched. Why was this? Because she would 'cut it' if she got a chance, they knew that very well, and took very good care that she shouldn't have much opportunity. Their house was rather popular, and they had lots of visitors; she had some particular friends who always came to see her. They paid her well, but she hardly ever got any of the money. Where was the odds, she couldn't go out to spend it? What did she want with money, except now and then for a drain of white satin [gin]. . . .

The girl told Mayhew how she had been 'ticed' (enticed) into prostitution by the mistress of the house, who met her one day in the street. The woman began talking to her in a friendly way about her family, then invited her home for tea. She was then sent to a 'branch establishment' south of the river where she was 'broken in'. They made her drunk and got her to 'sign some papers', which she was told gave them great power over her. They clothed and fed her well, and after about two months of being gradually introduced to the life of a prostitute she was moved to Langham Place. The girl said 'she lived in the present, and never went blubbering about as some did. She tried to be as jolly as she could; where was the fun of being miserable?'

The keepers of brothel-lodging houses were notoriously mean towards their whores, but they had justified fears of the girls 'chousing', or absconding without paying their debts. This was particularly so in the case of 'dress lodgers', girls who were lent 'tawdry ball costumes' to wear as they sought customers in the streets and theatres. Such girls had to take the customers back to their rooms, and pay most of their takings to the brothel owner, which meant they would never save enough to buy their own smart clothes. Dress lodgers were naturally tempted to disappear with the clothes, or to take their customers to another house without their landlady knowing.

Bawds often used a form of blackmail to force girls to work for them. In his *The Seven Curses of London* (1869) the influential journalist and author James Greenwood tells the story of a 'really handsome' girl who was tricked by a woman brothel-keeper into a form of slavery. The girl, obviously an independent prostitute, had taken a room in the brothel, for which she paid the considerable rent of 9s a week, but refused to work for the bawd. One night when she returned she found a 'detective' waiting for her who accused her of stealing a diamond shirt pin from a customer, and claimed he had found it in her room. He said he was arresting her, and the terrified girl pleaded with the bawd to intercede on her behalf. The bawd and the detective went into another room, and the bawd returned to say that he had agreed to accept £10 to cover up the 'crime'. The girl had no money, and the bawd agreed to lend it to her in return for all her clothes and belongings and a signed paper saying the girl still owed £5. Later the girl discovered that the 'detective' was a bully from another brothel.

'That's how I came to be a dress lodger. She didn't wait long before she opened her mind to me. She told me that very night:"You've got a new landlady now, my fine madam", said she;"you've got to work for your living now; to work for *me*, d'ye understand?You can't work – can't earn a penny without you dress spicy, and every rag you've got on is mine; and if you say one wry word I'll have them off and bundle you out." So what could I do or say?' continued the poor wretch, tears streaming down her really handsome face. 'I've been a dress lodger ever since, not being able to get a shilling for myself, for she takes away all I get, and besides is always threatening to strip me and turn me out, and to sue me for the five pounds I owe her.'

When dress lodgers ventured out at night in search of customers they were closely watched by a brothel servant, usually a former prostitute whose looks had faded, to see that they didn't cheat. Mayhew's colleague Hemyng came across a whore named Lizzie in the Strand who was regularly followed by an old woman in a dirty cotton dress. Hemyng plied the old woman with gin and she agreed to tell him her story.

A former prostitute, she was now a servant in a brothel. One of her duties, apart from serving the bawds and their prostitutes, was to watch Lizzie as she walked the streets. Lizzie's dress was too garish for her to attract upper-class customers. Her clients were usually men who worked in shops, commercial travellers and impecunious medical students. Sometimes she picked up a clergyman from nearby Exeter Hall. None of these would have more than a few pounds to spend, and now and then Lizzie and her broken-down old companion tramped the streets in vain, no doubt to the fury of her bawd. . . . Occasionally there were better times, and that particular night, the old woman said, Lizzie had had three clients in as many hours and had earned 45s 'for herself'. At the time, seamstresses might be paid as little as 3s a week.

Mayhew tells us that the old elite brothel area around King's Place was still flourishing, although the splendour of its Georgian heyday had vanished. The area now boasted a mixture of accommodation houses and brothels. 'Men may take their women there, and pay so much for a room and temporary accommodation, or they may be supplied with women who live in the house. The unfortunate creatures who live in these houses are completely in the power of the bawds, who grow fat on their prostitution.' The dress-lodging racket was not new – on 10 May 1786 *The Times* had told of prostitutes 'attended by an old ragged harridan, who supplied them with cloathes for the purpose of enticing passengers'.

Not all bawds were inhuman leeches, however. Mother Willit of Gerard Street had the sense to feed and clothe her girls. 'So help her kidnies, she al'us turned her gals out with a clean arse and good tog [outfit]; and as she turned 'em out, she didn't care who turned 'em up, cause 'em was clean as a smelt and as fresh as a daisy – she vouldn't have a speck'd 'un if she know'd it' (quoted in Pearsall, 1969).

ELEVEN

MARY JEFFRIES

'THE WICKEDEST WOMAN
OF THE CENTURY'

There were chains of Victorian luxury brothels, but we know much less about them than their Georgian equivalents because of the reticence about sexual matters that affected polite discourse from the late eighteenth century on. The long afterglow of Stuart libertinism would not fade, among the upper classes at least, until well into the twentieth century. After the Tory politician Lord Lambton resigned over a minor sexual scandal in the 1970s he appeared to sum up this attitude when he said: 'Surely all men visit whores?' Marthe Watts, madam for the Messina brothers, vicious overlords of vice in London's West End in the 1940s and 1950s, recalled how an aristocrat descending the stairs from her flat met his son coming up. They smiled at each other as they passed. But upper-class nonchalance had lost much of its self-confidence under assault from the rising middle classes, and public attitudes to sexual licence reflected this. The scandal of Mary Jeffries, which involved an Establishment cover-up of sexual high jinks in high places, reflected the clash of these two competing moralities.

Jeffries was the most important brothel-keeper in London in the last quarter of the nineteenth century. Once described with wild journalistic hyperbole as 'the wickedest woman of the century', she started her career as a prostitute at the exclusive establishment of a Madam Berthe in the 1840s. 'Berthe's had been operating since the 1820s under different owners, and had built up an almost exclusively aristocratic clientele. But it had refused to move with the times – it merely provided straightforward commercial sex with no concessions to the growing appetite for "perversion"' (Henriques, 1962–8,Vol. 3). Mrs Jeffries, who wanted to cater for all forms of perversion, saw the possibilities of such a gap in the market and with finance provided by wealthy clients opened an establishment in Church Street, Chelsea, which catered to the latest tastes in sexual matters. She got the formula right and soon she was running four houses in the street – numbers 125, 127, 129 and 155. There was also a brothel which specialised in flagellation in Rose Cottage, Hampstead, among other venues. Mrs Jeffries lived at 125 Church Street with two young ladies who were said to be her 'nieces'. Among her clients, or so she claimed, were the King of the Belgians and what she described as 'patrons of the highest social order'. Her threat to expose these aristocratic patrons was believed to have saved her from prison when she was first prosecuted.

One evening a police inspector named Jeremiah Minahan, who was also something of a moral crusader and had been watching the daily and nightly arrivals of 'toffs' in their carriages at the houses in Church Street, was passing and struck up a conversation with Jeffries over her garden wall. She had seen him keeping watch and had decided to warn him off. At the same time she was remarkably frank about her business. According to Minahan she told him that in addition to the businesses in Church Street she had establishments at 4 Thurloe Place, 29 Fulham Road and 15 Brompton Square. She even named some celebrated ladies of the town who had first been seduced under her auspices by men of distinction, whom she also named. One of the whores she claimed as a protégée was Mabel Gray. However, Mabel's heyday predated even Jeffries's long-established empire. Finally Jeffries told Minahan, or so he claimed, that she sent girls for prostitution to Brussels, Paris and Berlin. Then she tried to bribe him, offering him a sovereign and a half. She made it plain that she was in the habit of bribing policemen on the Church Street beat, and told him that he would be wasting his time if he tried to prosecute her. Her houses were not disorderly – on the contrary, they were 'properly conducted for persons of high position' who would not tolerate interference by the police.

Minahan claimed that when he tried to get his superiors to act he met with a series of rebuffs. First his notes on the case were taken from his desk, and when he told a superior of Jeffries's attempt to bribe him he was told he was a fool to refuse the money. When he submitted a detailed report he was threatened with demotion. The Assistant Commissioner of Police, Colonel Labalmondiere, saw the words 'brothels for the nobility' and said that was a 'highly improper' remark for a police officer to make. As we say today, the fix was in, even if it was just a case of the Establishment instinctively protecting itself.

Doubtless disappointed, even disgusted, Minahan resigned and became a paid investigator for the London Committee for the Exposure and Suppression of the Traffic of English Girls for the Purposes of Continental Prostitution. For some time Benjamin Scott, Chamberlain of the City of London and chairman of the committee, had been trying to nail Jeffries. He was particularly interested in Minahan's allegations that Jeffries sent girls abroad, as there was a story that she had a 'white-slave house' by the river at Kew, and that drugged girls were sent abroad in closed coffins with air-holes in the lids. This was just one of the many exaggerated tales of pure young English girls lured to shady dens and drugged, only to wake terrified in some continental hell-hole. However, presumably the committee could find no real evidence for this, and instead on 16 April 1885 Jeffries was charged with keeping a disorderly house. At the preliminary police court hearing a prostitute testified that she had 'received gentlemen' at one of Mrs Jeffries's Church Street brothels, and for some time afterwards remained on call. Another whore, Kate Kennedy, said that when she was starting out in her profession a 'gentleman' had given her a letter of introduction to Mrs Jeffries. Former servants from the Church Street houses also gave evidence, one telling how ladies and gentlemen would arrive separately and the latter would leave money on the hall table. Usually this would be £5, out of which Mrs Jeffries would sometimes take £2 for herself, and sometimes £3. Jeffries's former coachman told how he delivered her messages to the homes of various women, and to gentlemen at their clubs, including the Army and Navy. Both prosecution and defence counsel were careful that the names of these 'gentlemen' should not be disclosed. On the other hand, they encouraged witnesses to be free with the names of the women, and so the court heard of Miss West of Alfred Street, Miss Stewart of Thurloe Place and Miss Grace Waynan of Marylebone Road.

There was one slip, of the kind that at the time was said by newspapers to have caused 'a sensation in court' (Playfair, 1969). The coachman told how he was driving Jeffries in her carriage in Hyde Park one evening. She was in an unusually talkative mood, and boasted that the King of the Belgians paid her £800 a month to supply him with women. She had lured him away from a rival bawd, Madam James of Lodge Row.

There was clearly evidence that Jeffries was running a brothel, but the Establishment was rattled by the possibility of revelations about upper-class clients. The Home Office paid a barrister to keep a watching brief during the police court hearing. The committee's counsel, a Mr Besley, accused the police of trying to 'screen the woman Jeffries'. Her counsel, Montague Williams, called this 'a scandalous assertion', but the police had refused to be associated with the case, and there was no explanation of what the Home Office barrister was doing there. A police officer called by the prosecution under subpoena claimed that though he had watched Mrs Jeffries's houses he had never seen prostitutes or 'gentlemen' entering or leaving, nor seen any cabs outside. A string of witnesses contradicted him. One, butler to the Revd Alfred Povah, one of Mrs Jeffries's neighbours, watched the comings and goings from a window. Sometimes women would call at his master's house by mistake and ask for Mrs Jeffries. One of them called him 'ducky'. The cook from another neighbour's said early morning callers at the brothels included police officers.

When the full case against her was heard in May 1885 Mrs Jeffries arrived at court in a carriage provided by a member of the House of Lords. Before the trial began counsel for the prosecution and the defence had a private interview with the assistant judge, a Mr Edlin. Questions were later asked in Parliament about this interview, and although Mr Edlin denied through the Home Secretary that he had agreed to a deal which would keep Mrs Jeffries out of prison if she pleaded guilty, 'it is difficult to imagine what else opposing counsel could have wished to discuss with him in private' (Playfair). Mrs Jeffries was fined £200 and ordered to find a surety of £400. A titled Guards officer stood surety for her, and before the day was over she was back in business.

Purity campaigners were outraged. At a public meeting James B. Wookey, secretary of the Gospel Purity Association, named the distinguished men he said were responsible for 'this conspiracy': they included Lords Fyfe, Douglas Gordon, Lennox and Aylesford and the Prince of Wales. Wookey made no mention of Cavendish Bentinck, believed to represent the interests of brothel-keepers, particularly Mrs Jeffries, and who as the Member of Parliament for Whitehaven had fought a rearguard action in the Commons against efforts to raise the age of consent for girls from thirteen to sixteen. *The Sentinel*, one of the purity campaigners' journals, thundered: 'The inferences point to a state of moral corruption, heartless cruelty, and prostitution of authority almost sufficient, even in this country, to goad the industrial classes into revolution.'

Stead, the campaigning journalist and enemy of Mrs Jeffries, used the columns of his *Pall Mall Gazette* to press for greater protection for young girls. After Mrs Jeffries was fined he launched an all-out attack on the forces of reaction. His lurid 'Maiden Tribute' articles about the exploitation of young virgins caused near-riots as readers fought to lay their hands on copies of the paper. Circulation shot up from around thirteen thousand to hundreds of thousands of copies, and newsboys were said to be selling copies for half a crown. Still Parliament refused to raise the age of consent. At this point Stead staged a sensational and silly stunt. He 'bought' a thirteen-year-old girl, Eliza Armstrong, from her parents and after having her medically examined to confirm she was a virgin spirited her away to Paris to show how easily it could be done. Senior officers of the Salvation Army were complicit in this farrago. Stead was arrested and sentenced to three months in prison for indecent assault (the medical examination). But his action had the desired result. Parliament passed legislation to protect young girls. The Prince of Wales cancelled his subscription to the *Pall Mall Gazette*.

When Stead stood trial Mrs Jeffries was seen handing out rotten fruit for crowds outside the courthouse to throw at him. By then she had her own troubles. Many of her clients in the Guards had been sent to Egypt to defend it against invasion by the army of the Mahdi. She was reported as saying: 'Business is very bad. I have been very slack since the Guards went to Egypt.'

The law had not finished with Mrs Jeffries. The Revd Povah complained that the nuisance caused by her brothels in Church Street was 'as bad as ever', and this time the Home Office instructed the police to make enquiries. They reported that nothing untoward was going on in Church Street, but a house in Brompton Square, which was registered to Jeffries, appeared to be disorderly. Eventually she was prosecuted over the Brompton Square address, although it had been occupied by a series of sub-tenants at the time of the offences. It had been run as a brothel, but there was no real evidence against Jeffries. When she appeared before Mr Edlin at Middlesex Sessions in November 1887 there was no plea bargain. She got six months. Stead was shocked. He wrote in the *Pall Mall Gazette*:

> Mrs Jeffries will probably die in gaol. She is 72, suffering from diabetes. . . . We wonder what the kings, princes, peers and officers, who found the old lady so convenient for the gratification of their pleasures, think of her now. Probably, if the truth be told, they never spare a thought for their fallen flesh broker. Yet, if the truth must be told, so far as she deserves to be there, so much more do they to share cells by her side. They supplied the gold with which she tempted others to ruin. She was but their go-between. They were the principals. They go forth scot-free, honoured by men and women, to swagger in the forefront of the state. She, despised, broken and dying, is hurried off to end her days in gaol.

It is not known whether Jeffries died in prison. We hear no more of her.

TWELVE

WAR AND GANGSTERS

The decline of aristocratic spending power at the beginning of the twentieth century seems to have marked a corresponding decline in the prevalence of the luxury brothel. The long fantasy of upper-class moral and economic invulnerability faded before the harsh new realities of taxes, democracy and war. The vice industry gradually regressed to an almost medieval condition of squalor. The ten-minute rule, introduced during the Second World War, was the application of industrial techniques to a business which had once emphasised other kinds of sensual gratification – music, food and drink, pleasant surroundings and behaviour which at least implied mutual respect. There was a time when men sometimes went to brothels just to gossip with a well-informed bawd or harlot. It is inconceivable that anyone went to a brothel run by the Messina brothers, overlords of vice in London in the middle of the twentieth century, for more than momentary gratification.

The golden age of the great courtesans, the Toasts of the Town or *Grandes Horizontales*, was over. Catherine Walters, 'Skittles', lived on until 1920 and seemed like a ghost from another age. Newspapers no longer found ready copy in the doings of the Ten Thousand or even the Manchester House set. The Prince of Wales, later Edward VII, largely escaped censure because of a conspiracy of silence by newspaper editors and proprietors who connived in a culture of deference that lasted until the 1960s and the arrival of *Private Eye*. Of course it applied only to the Establishment; those further down the social ladder were fair game. Many of the victims of this prurience were those who took advantage of the Divorce Reform Act of 1923, which made it possible for women to get a divorce on the grounds of a single act of adultery by their husbands. A witness was needed, and Brighton was often the venue

for these stage-managed one-night stands, sometimes involving compliant out-of-work actresses. The *News of the World* flourished.

The twentieth century got off to a promising start, as far as the popular
newspapers were concerned, with the case of Queenie Gerald. This attractive young woman ran a brothel in the Haymarket, and police raided it in
June 1913. Queenie was in the bathroom with two girls, aged seventeen and
eighteen, who were said to be 'almost nude'. Queenie said to the officer
leading the raid: 'This *is* a surprise.' She claimed she was giving the girls a
bath. That was suggestive enough, but some of the contents of the brothel
hinted at an exciting and exotic world. There were letters from men, a
revolver, a whip, a cane, some photographs and rather a lot of money – in
excess of £200. Poor Queenie was sent to prison for three months for
living off immoral earnings. That should have been the end of it, but there
were rumours that things were not quite right, that virgins were being procured for wealthy men – the old Victorian bugbear of white slavery reared
its head. There was no evidence for this, but Keir Hardie, the Labour MP,
harassed the Home Secretary, the Pankhursts weighed in, and eventually the
affair was aired in the Commons, that safety-valve for hot air about vice.

The vice industry was changing irrevocably in the century of the
common man: two world wars helped democratise it. For the first time
millions of men were taken away from their homes for long periods, and
this created a sudden surge of demand for commercial sex. The industry
coped by recruiting the many willing women who flocked into London,
drawn by easy money. After the outbreak of the First World War in 1914
the response of the authorities, struggling to control a wave of venereal infections, was a fatuous attempt to suppress immorality. A force of
women morals police, some of them former purity campaigners, was
recruited to patrol parks and other places where young couples who
knew that time was short sought to solace each other. Dance halls were
closed and young people were made uncomfortably aware that even
embracing in public was frowned upon. Having earlier railed against
the flagrancy of commercial sex in London at the outbreak of war, the
journalist Max Pemberton reported in 1917 that snooping was making
it impossible for soldiers on leave to have any fun – 'the prude on the
prowl has ruined London'. Even to kiss a girl in Hyde Park had become

a crime, he pointed out. Yet an army officer suggest~
were of the right class and rank Hogarthian delights w

> At night we used to dine at the Savoy and afterwards have a jolly
> in the rooms off the Palm Court. You can't do that now – it's become
> But I tell you what you can do. You can settle up about midnight and ~
> a house in a by-street not three hundred yards from the Criterion Theat~
> – and if you've got the entree, you can open the door up on the first floor,
> find yourself among a dozen couples who haven't troubled the tailor or the
> costumier; you can dance and drink with them until the cows come home,
> and see an orgy which would make Cleopatra blush. And that's the only kind
> of amusement you seem able to provide for us.

This was not going to curb the spread of VD, nor was official policy over
condoms. Instead of issuing them to soldiers going to France in 1914 the
army gave them a sanctimonious leaflet signed by the Secretary of War,
Lord Kitchener, a bachelor:

> Your duty cannot be done unless your health is sound. So keep constantly on
> your guard against any excesses. In this new experience you may find tempta-
> tions both in wine and women. You must entirely resist both temptations,
> and while treating all women with perfect courtesy, you should avoid any
> intimacy. Do your duty bravely. Fear God, honour the King.

The war ended on Monday 11 November 1918, and that night people
reeled through the streets shouting, singing, kissing and copulating in
doorways, alleys, parks, taxis, many of them with total strangers. That
night brothels were busy.

Between the wars women could make a good living working the
streets and taking men back to their rooms or to small brothels. Inspector
Fred 'Nutty' Sharpe, who in the mid-1930s was head of the Flying Squad,
estimated that in a four-hour day or night a woman could earn between
£15 and £20: at the time, a girl working in a shop would earn about
£2 a week. Street-walkers were still a prominent feature of commercial
sex but there was a degree of technological innovation. A few women

ised the streets in cars looking for pick-ups. The major change, how-
ver, was the use of the telephone by call-girls and their clients.

There were organised vice rings, but their rule was fairly benign.
Victorian London had chains of brothels, but the sex industry consisted mostly of small-scale enterprises, pimps controlling a few women.
Around the time of the First World War there were the first signs of
violent organised criminals attempting to control prostitution. Arthur
Harding, an East End gangster who left an invaluable account of organised crime in the early years of the twentieth century, offers intriguing
glimpses of criminals trying to control sections of the East End vice
trade, for instance the Jewish prostitutes (Samuel, 1981). Recalling the
prostitution of those days, Harding said:

> The brides [prostitutes] were mostly down the other end of Brick Lane where
> the lodging houses were in Flowery Dean Street [the notorious Flower and
> Dean Street]. The Seven Stars next to Christ Church School was mostly used
> by the ladies of the town, and the Frying Pan on the corner of Thrawl Street
> and Brick Lane was famous for being the centre of the red light district.

Because of large-scale Jewish immigration around the turn of the century there were many Jewish prostitutes in the East End, and a fifth of
convictions for keeping brothels involved Jews. But it was not really until
the 1920s that the business threw up some major criminals.

From the end of the First World War until the outbreak of the Second
organised crime in London was dominated by a combination of Italians
and Jews led by Darby Sabini, an Anglo-Italian who grew up in the Little
Italy area around Saffron Hill. Like later gangsters he despised but tolerated organised vice. Inevitably, however, from time to time the worlds of
vice and organised crime collided. On one occasion Sabini was asked for
help by the father of a young Italian woman, Anna Monti, who had been
lured into prostitution by a vice king named Juan Antonio Castanar.
Castanar used a dancing school in Archer Street, Soho to lure young
women into so-called white slavery abroad.

Sabini paid Castanar a visit and Anna, who had been sent to the Middle
East, was restored to her family. Later gang warfare broke out between

Castanar and his main rival, a Frenchman named Casimir Micheletti. After a series of stabbings and shootings there were the inevitable questions in the House of Commons. Finally the two gang leaders were arrested and deported. Castanar tracked Micheletti to Montmartre and shot him dead. He was sent to France's penal colony on Devil's Island. It was believed in the underworld that Sabini had had a secret hand in causing trouble between the two vice kings.

The vice racketeers of the 1920s were a phenomenon of the Jazz Age, that hedonistic era of drugs and drink and heedless pleasure. Vice had the same kind of louche glamour, as though it were part of a theatrical world best suited to the crazy camera angles of Expressionist film makers. With the arrival of the Messina brothers in London the world of commercial vice entered a phase of stark realism and brutal exploitation, a darker world of which Frenchwoman Marthe Watts, the Messina whore and bawd, was a true representative. Nothing better illustrates the squalor of the sex industry at the time than an American soldier's description of her spartan bed as 'a workbench'. Gone for ever was the chandeliered splendour of the great Georgian and Victorian brothels, gone too the superficial fragrance and allure of the girls. Sex had now been stripped to its essentials. The gangsters and their bawds had 'rationalised' the process of selling sex back to its medieval condition – a room, a bed, a whore and a maid to knock on the door after ten minutes, a signal that time was up. In the background lurked the threat of a sharp-suited young thug with a razor to make sure the customer got the message. The girls were terrorised and forced to work in shifts more or less round the clock. Mother Needham would have been in her element.

The five Messina brothers – Carmelo, Alfredo, Salvatore, Attilio and Eugenio – came from a brothel-owning dynasty. Their father Giuseppe, a Sicilian, ran brothels in Malta, then moved with his family to Egypt, where he developed a chain of brothels in several cities, a business that later spread across North Africa. Their operations were so flagrant they were expelled from Egypt in 1932. In 1934 Eugenio arrived in London, followed later by his brothers. They quickly dominated vice in the West End and under their menacing grip prostitution became big business for the first time since the eighteenth century, but without the sense of style and fun.

The campaigning journalist Duncan Webb, who launched a crusade against the Messinas in the pages of the *People* newspaper, wrote: 'By bribery and corruption they organized marriages of convenience both in Britain and abroad to enable their harlots to assume British nationality. They ruled their women by persuasion, threat or blackmail and the use of the knife and the razor. They ruled the streets of the West End by similar methods. Indeed, so terror-stricken did the underworld become at the mention of the word "Messina" that in the end they found little difficulty in building up their vast empire of vice.' By 1945 the girls were bringing in many thousands of pounds a week for the Messina family.

One of the women the Messinas recruited was Watts, who eventually ran the empire when the brothers fled abroad. We probably know more about her than most other bawds in history because she left frank memoirs, *The Men in My Life* (1960). Watts came to England in 1937 and worked as a streetwalker. She was no beauty, as the portrait photograph in her memoirs makes clear, but she had a kind of sultry allure, and was never short of customers. At first she found the climate and the long hours spent on her feet streetwalking difficult, but after she got a regular 'beat' on Bond Street she made a good living. Some of the Englishman's sexual preferences surprised her: she wrote that she was 'astonished' at the number of men who wanted her to tie them up and beat them. She was arrested and fined on more than four hundred occasions for soliciting, something she and the other street women accepted as a kind of business expense. Until the Street Offences Act of 1959 the penalty was invariably a small fine.

Marthe first met the Messinas at the beginning of the Second World War at the Palm Beach Club in Wardour Street, where the brothers went specifically to pick up girls they could seduce and put to work on the streets. The war was, says Watts, 'the biggest godsend on earth to the Messinas. London became filled with British and American troops and with war workers away from home. Time was short, money was loose, morals were out: and this, of course, is where I came in.'

She became a Messina prostitute and the mistress of Eugenio, or Gino. Soon she had painful evidence of their enforcement methods. After they returned to their hotel one evening Gino began to question her about an American soldier she had been talking to. She was sitting dressed only in a nightdress. Gino was holding the flex he had taken from a standard lamp. 'Gino started asking me questions about the sergeant. What had he wanted? . . . When I refused to reply he started to beat me in the most terrible fashion with the electric flex. I was so surprised and taken aback that I allowed him to carry on beating me without saying a word, or without even giving a cry. Gino acted like a man possessed and by the time he had finished I was in the most deplorable state and was black and blue all over with weals from the simple, but horrible instrument.'

There was trouble, too, over Gino's insistence on the ten-minute rule. 'I soon found to my distress and amazement that Gino's strictest instructions were that I could not spend more than ten minutes with a client at a session, even if the latter spent a great deal of money. This was a rigid time limit. It brought me many slaps and blows for, if I stayed with a client even eleven or twelve minutes, it led to scenes. . . .' She also soon discovered that Gino was jealous of his girls and would not let them look at male pin-ups in magazines. 'The reason was, I imagine, that Gino was afflicted with an inferiority complex and was evidently afraid of us comparing these wonderful people with him. It was probably for a similar reason that he would not let us stay too long with a client, for fear that we might find someone with more prowess than his own in bed.' However, prostitutes all over London were introducing similar time limits, although not quite so strict, as the streets were full of potential customers and every minute off the streets was money lost. Women would no longer agree to spend the night with a client – they could make far more by picking up as many men as possible.

Watts claims that at least three-quarters of the Messina girls' clients were left unsatisfied as a result of the ten-minute rule. Usually the girls refused to refund their money, and some of the customers became violent. She recalls the occasion when an American officer refused to leave. She went out to find a policeman and they returned just in time to stop the officer setting fire to the furniture in her flat, which he had piled up. Another American soldier pulled out a revolver, and was immediately repaid. Yet another client, a Chinese, threw Watts down a flight of stairs. He 'stepped over my prostrate body at the bottom of the stairs and went quietly out, leaving me black and blue for several days afterwards'. On another occasion a dissatisfied client took Watts's mattress. They found it outside St James's Palace. Incidentally, many of the flats where the girls entertained their clients were in the old elite brothel district around what had been King's Place. Yet another frustrated client, a paratroop officer, tried to attack one of the Messina girls. Watts got in the way and he struck her in the face with his stick. Although she had a black eye for two weeks, Gino would not allow her a day off. They had only two days off a year, were not allowed to smoke and after Gino heard them laughing with a Belgian soldier who made jokes in French, they were forbidden to laugh. While out on their beats they were also forbidden to lean against a wall for a rest. In case they dared to deviate from his rules, Gino followed them around either on foot or in his yellow Rolls-Royce.

Marthe Watts's most heroic effort was, appropriately enough, on the night of VE (Victory in Europe) Day, when she succeeded in taking home forty-nine clients, working through the night until six o'clock the following morning. She wanted to round up the figure to fifty but could not find another customer.

Some vestige of gentility survived elsewhere. In February 2001 the Marquess of Aberdeen and Temair, by then in his eighties, described in the *Independent* a wartime establishment, Mrs Fetherstonhaugh's 'private hotel' in Elvaston Place, Kensington. The bawd had an interesting way of recruiting staff. She would invite likely women – out-of-work actresses and wives whose husbands were serving abroad – to a party. 'If they then showed signs of enjoying themselves, it would be suggested that they continue to do so for money.' Such brothels were 'illegal, but superbly appointed, well run and discreet, and the girls were of the highest quality'. There was an apocryphal story of a Guards officer being shown into a bedroom where the girl assigned to him turned out to be his sister.

By the end of the war the Messinas were very wealthy. In 1946 Gino bought his first Rolls-Royce. They had terrorised most rivals into quiescence but occasionally there was a challenge from the wilder fringes of the capital. A gang led by a Maltese, Carmelo Vassallo, started demanding protection money from the Messina girls. Their demands were modest enough: £1 per girl per day. The girls could easily have paid, as they were earning £100 a night each for the Messinas, who paid them £50 a week. But in the underworld any compromise is seen as a sign of weakness. To warn him and his henchmen off Eugenio Messina cut off two of Vassallo's fingertips. After Eugenio had been jailed for three years for this assault, during which time Watts says the semi-literate Gino concentrated on improving his reading and writing skills, his girls decided justice had not been done and told the police about the Vassallo gang's protection racket. Police were watching as the Vassallos drove up to some of the girls near Piccadilly and one of them shouted: 'It's better for you to give us the money, otherwise I will cut your face.' Police searched the car and found a hammer wrapped in newspaper, a knife and a cosh. Four of the Vassallo gang were prosecuted and given up to four years' penal servitude. After that rival vice racketeers either formed partnerships with the Messinas or stayed away from the West End. Among the former was the man who would eventually succeed the Messinas as the overlord of West End vice, the East End gangster Bernie Silver.

The scale and wealth of the West End vice rackets were notorious, mainly because of the exposés of the journalist Duncan Webb. Questions were of course asked in Parliament, but the Home Secretary, Chuter Ede, refused to order a special inquiry into vice in London. He said: 'Any inquiry would not help the police because their difficulties arise from the fact that, although they may have good reason to suspect such activities, they are sometimes unable to obtain evidence upon which criminal proceedings could be based.' He was told that the Messinas were making £500,000 a year from prostitution and had twenty girls working for them. In fact for years the family were never prosecuted for organising vice. Eventually, says Watts, the Messinas considered themselves invulnerable. 'They were laughing at the Home Secretary's answers in Parliament, and chuckling when one Member of Parliament suggested that the gang had coined millions from the proceeds from prostitution.'

Instead of using the strong-arm methods that got Gino imprisoned the Messinas began to frame their rivals, perhaps with the connivance of the police. 'They framed false charges against them, usually with some success. There was a succession of court cases in which the accused persons pleaded that they had been framed by the Messina Gang. Magistrates expressed their annoyance with this, what they thought to be an empty plea, and only increased the sentence.'

Duncan Webb acted where the police couldn't, or wouldn't. According to Watts, he began to follow the Messina girls as they worked the streets. Gino, who until then had enjoyed newspaper reports about his activities, began to fear an exposé. He told Watts that if he were to meet Webb on the continent he would know how to deal with him. In the meantime he told her to 'beat him up' whenever possible. 'Obedient to Gino's will as ever, I am ashamed to say that this is what I did on more than one occasion. My poor friend Duncan, whom later I came to know so well, describes in his book [*Crime is My Business*, 1953] the occasion when he was in one of the bars in Stafford Street with another man when I spotted him. I had to wait almost two hours before at last he came out at closing time. I then cornered him against the door of the bar. He said nothing at all to me, but I began to insult him and slap his face, so that his pipe and glasses fell on the pavement. Then I walked away without giving Duncan the chance to say a word.'

In the course of his campaign against the Messinas Webb was threatened and occasionally attacked. A car tried to run him down in Old Compton Street in Soho: 'A streetwalker came up to me. With a sneer on her lips, she said: "That was meant for you, dearie",' he recalled. To Webb the wealth of the Messinas was an affront, and the brothers were certainly flaunting it. Watts said that she alone earned £150,000 for Gino Messina between 1940 and 1955. On 3 September 1950 Webb named the 'four debased men with an empire of crime which is a disgrace to London'. At that stage the brothers owned properties that operated as brothels in Shepherd Market, Stafford Street, Bruton Place and New Bond Street, all in the West End. Webb catalogued their connections with prostitutes and exposed their cover addresses before passing his dossier on to Scotland Yard, which later said its detectives had been aware of much of what was happening.

The following week Webb was attacked in the street by a thug. His assailant said: 'The Messinas are pals of mine. It's about time you journalists were done proper.' But it was the Messinas who had been 'done proper' by Webb. Some of them fled abroad, others went into hiding. Effectively their reign was over.

The fall of the Messinas led to a scramble for their territory by vice racketeers from outside the area, mostly the East End. It was won by the Messinas' former satellite Bernie Silver, in league with the Maltese 'Big Frank' Mifsud. Their partnership, known as The Syndicate, had many of the characteristics of the Messinas' operations. If anything, they were more ruthless and by the 1960s they virtually controlled Soho's vice rackets. They charged prostitutes £100 a week for an almost-bare Soho room, used threats and violence to get tenants out of rooms they wanted for their girls, and on one occasion set fire to a building. When the protection gangster Tommy Smithson tried to blackmail them they had him murdered. They got away with it by bribing witnesses to disappear; Smithson's killers were each given £60,000 to start new lives abroad.

Silver, known as the 'Godfather of Soho', was described by Webb as 'one of the two most evil men in London', the other, presumably, being his partner Mifsud. The Syndicate was making £100,000 a week, according to the police. Silver, sleek and well dressed, looked like a Hollywood gangster and eventually became an important figure in the Soho pornography industry. Mifsud, a former traffic policeman from Malta, was described as aggressive, generous, forever buying drinks, always loaded with money but dressed 'like a bum'.

Silver went on trial at the Old Bailey in September 1974. The Syndicate was accused of running what prosecutor Michael Corkery called 'a vicious empire . . . an unsavoury world of prostitutes, ponces and pimps'. After a trial that lasted sixty-three days, Silver was found guilty of living on immoral earnings, given six years in jail and fined £30,000. Six Maltese men were also jailed. The judge, Lord Justice Geoffrey Lane, told them: 'The profits you reaped were enormous' – there had been reports that The Syndicate had salted away £50 million in Swiss bank accounts. Mifsud, who had been in hiding in Austria, was extradited and sentenced to five years' imprisonment, then freed on appeal. He died in Malta in 1999.

Just how violent The Syndicate was prepared to be was suggested by a witness at another trial, Joseph Spiteri, who screamed at Silver: 'He has blood on his hands. He killed the girl I was living with and six other girls. He was the head man. He is a bloodhound. He killed the girl and framed me.' When defence counsel asked why the police had failed to act, Spiteri said: 'They used to run the police.' The Syndicate was now a spent force, and while others moved in on their patch and their business, the great days were over for the gangsters, if not for the old-style vice trade. A prostitute named Anita went to work in a block of flats in Soho in the early 1980s after being told that she could earn £400 a day there. Anita recalled:

> It was ten pounds a time, straight sex, eight minutes. Then the maid would knock on the door and if he wanted to stay longer it was extra money: plus if he wanted you to take your top off it was an extra five pounds, everything was always extra . . . you always had six or seven waiting to come in, the door never stopped, and it was a twelve-hours shift. The insides of my thighs used to *kill* (Roberts, 1992).

Occasionally the industry threw up a colourful character who shone in the general drabness. Janie Jones, a flamboyant 1970s bawd, became enmeshed in scandals involving two-way mirrors, sex orgies for BBC disc jockeys and a teddy-bear-clutching peer with a predilection for prostitutes dressed as schoolgirls. She was jailed and met the Moor's murderer Myra Hindley, who fell in love with her – 'she fancied me rotten'. Jones, now in her fifties, said she was an accidental victim of the sex-and-drugs culture of the time. Like some other bawds, she claimed she disliked sex.

Jones was a cabaret singer with some modest successes as a recording artist when she began to organise parties for minor celebrities and people on the fringes of the pop music world. She had many girls on her books, mostly out-of-work actresses and models, who would appear as hostesses at these events. When called on she could supply girls by the dozen for aristocratic parties but claimed she was not paid a penny. 'A girl would visit a diplomat at Claridge's. If she dropped her drawers or anything kinky, she'd arrange the money.'

A bedroom at her home in Campden Hill Road had a 7-foot bed and a two-way mirror between it and another room. Guests would be invited to watch the antics of some of her girls through the mirror and would then join in. This behaviour, which might be thought to be no one's business but that of those involved, seemed to irritate the police and the courts. In 1966 she faced the first of a series of charges for black-mail. A man referred to as Mr A claimed Jones had threatened to tell his wife about his exploits – he had sex with Jones's girls Tania, Maureen, Nina, Janice, Tessa and Chrystal – unless he paid her £1,200. Jones was acquitted. A month later she was arrested for running a brothel. Police claimed they watched her flat from the balcony of a house opposite. There was no house opposite and the case collapsed (Donaldson, 2002). In June 1971 the *News of the World* exposed a sex scandal at the BBC. The newspaper alleged that Jones was tricking her girls into having sex with producers and disc jockeys, in the belief that they were auditioning for radio and TV – the so-called BBC Payola Scandal. There was a trial but Jones was found not guilty. Two years later she was tried at the Old Bailey on a variety of charges, which included blackmailing a peer referred to as Lord Y, who liked Jones's girls to dress as schoolgirls. Jones was found not guilty of blackmail, but given the astonishingly heavy sentence of seven years in prison for controlling prostitutes. The judge, Alan King-Hamilton, said she was the most evil woman he had ever sentenced. In 1987 the satirical magazine *Private Eye* alleged that King-Hamilton had been a client of the noted dominatrix Lindi St Clair (Donaldson, 2002).

Today Jones is plumper and tougher but still theatrical, described by Caroline Phillips in the *Evening Standard* as 'colourful in appliqué jumper and crushed-velvet skirt, with a rag-doll painted face, Barbara Cartland lashes and peroxided hair'. She says that while others enjoyed the sexual freedom at her parties she never joined in – 'I think sex is all a big pain.'

Cynthia Payne, the so-called 'Luncheon Voucher Madam', was the human face of the profession. When she was sent to prison because of the antics at her south London brothel many people felt that an injustice had been done, that the law was an ass, and that it was time for reform. Nothing was done. Payne's trial in 1978 for 'keeping a disorderly house' gave many readers their first glimpse of the world of the suburban brothel, and of a fascinating character who tried to make sex fun. She gave discounts to old-age pensioners, and charged only half price to men who could no longer perform. Cynthia Payne was born in 1932. Her obsession with sex began early, as did her vocabulary of vulgar words and her mischief-making. After a series of unreliable men, pregnancies, abortions and two children she became a prostitute's maid and then a reluctant prostitute. Finally she began organising sex parties for other people, and found that she was very good at it.

On 6 December 1978 she was giving a Christmas party at her brothel in Ambleside Avenue, Streatham, south London when the premises were raided by the police. They found a queue of men on the stairs. A naked black woman ran down the stairs; another woman, wearing only a red bra and panties, rushed out of the lounge, saw the police and ran back in again. In a room called the Group Sex Room a naked couple were clambering from a large double bed and trying to scramble into their clothes. In the Mirror Room a couple were close to climax. When ordered to stop what he was doing the man said: 'Not until I've come.' Fifty-three men and seventeen women were found in the house. At the subsequent trial the court heard of some of the sex aids found in the house: packets of contraceptives, bottles of baby oil, whips, ropes, leather straps – although the defence said these were brought by the clients for their own use. Many obscene films were also found.

Among the evidence was a box filled with vouchers with face values of 10p and 15p. Asked what they were for, Cynthia told the police: 'These are my luncheon vouchers. They are for my gentlemen to satisfy their appetites' (Bailey, 1982). Most men visiting the house paid Cynthia £25 on arrival. For this they could eat and drink as much as they liked, watch a sex film and a live lesbian display and have the girl of their choice. 'One of the older clients explained why he was charged less: "I only pay £15 because I don't go with a girl because I'm impotent."' When those who were still capable of enjoying the girls had sex they gave them the vouchers. At the end of the party each girl would give Cynthia the vouchers she had collected, and would be paid *pro rata*.

The middle-aged and elderly customers – politicians, barristers, clergymen, businessmen and other professionals – were ferried to Streatham police station for questioning. Sixteen months later – by which time she was a national celebrity referred to in the tabloid newspapers as 'Madam Sin' – Cynthia Payne went on trial at the Inner London Crown Court.

There was only one defendant: the other women involved were not charged, nor, of course, was any of the customers. Because of widespread and sympathetic coverage by most newspapers, perhaps for the first time the public were brought face to face with the hypocrisy of the law, the double standard that punished women for meeting a demand created by men. There was genuine shock when Judge West-Russell sentenced Cynthia to eighteen months' imprisonment for keeping a disorderly house. This was reduced on appeal to six months. She was also heavily fined.

Four days later the *Spectator* published an editorial which pointed out the manifest injustices in the case:

> It is difficult to discern any justice in this very typical case. The punishment itself is altogether excessive: nothing is gained in imprisoning Cynthia Payne and her kind unless they have corrupted the young and innocent. The transactions between Mrs Payne, her male clients and the women in her house were transactions between freely consenting adults. According to the law, the men committed no offence, and if the women did, they were not charged with any. Only Cynthia Payne is regarded as legally culpable, even though she, the men and the women were all engaged in the joint exercise of an improper Christmas party.

The law has been enforced, but justice has manifestly not been done. The quite unnecessarily severe sentence apart, there remains an outrageous indecency in the law as it stands and is enforced. If prostitution be an offence punishable at law, then a law should be written and enacted to this effect; and, if offence it be, then the man and woman, clearly sharing the offence, should be held to be both of them culpable. Commonsense would go further, and say that, of the two, the man – who, after all, is creating the demand and supplying the cash – is the more responsible for the illegal enterprise, the more culpable and the more appropriate to be punished.

> But our legislators have not wished prostitution as such to be an offence, precisely in order to avoid the punishment – and the publication of the names – of the men whose demands create the supply....

In prison, Cynthia thought that one day she would like to run a home for the elderly with special wards for the disabled. She envisaged that those who couldn't afford to pay for sex would get it free on the National Health Service (Bailey, 1982). Instead she went on the after-dinner speaking circuit, sometimes for charity. In 2000 at the age of sixty-seven she reflected on fame without fortune. The two films about her life brought her only £10,000, she said in a *Daily Express* interview, and she never made much money from her sex parties, either. 'I charged only £15 initially and I was being fiddled by some of the girls. I also offered money-back guarantees, £5 discounts for old-age pensioners and free access to the parties for disabled people. I was just too soft – I was not hard and ruthless enough.'

APPENDIX I

MOLLIES' HOUSES

The lusty, rip-roaring world of heterosexual commercial vice had a shadowy doppelgänger, its homosexual counterpart. This was a much more dangerous and furtive world, its participants in constant fear of blackmail or exposure. Under Henry VIII sodomy was made a capital offence. The preamble to his Act of 1533 stated:

> Forasmuch as there is not yet sufficient and condign punishment appointed and limited by the course of the laws of this Realm for the detestable and abominable vice of buggery committed with mankind or beast....

The savagery of the law was often mitigated by juries, who were reluctant to convict. Only if 'penetration' was proved would the death penalty be imposed. Mostly the juries would decide that homosexual acts were common assaults, meriting a fine.

After the opening in 1570 of Sir Thomas Gresham's Bourse, which later became the Royal Exchange, the area soon became the haunt of prostitutes and catamites, both categories soliciting and finding customers among the City's rich merchants. Establishments exclusively for men were known as 'mollies' houses' and one opposite the Old Bailey had been in existence since 1559, the men addressing each other as 'Madam' or 'Ladyship'. In 1661 there was the Three Potters in Cripplegate Without while the Fountain in the Strand was a known haunt of homosexuals throughout the eighteenth century. The manager of a mollies' house in Camomile Street, Bishopsgate, was known as the Countess of Camomile. The writer Ned Ward, whose *London Spy* (1700) is a rich source of information about vice, tells of male prostitutes at another Fountain, a tavern in Russell Square. Dressed as women, they would enact mock childbirths using a doll, which would be

'Christened and the Holy Sacrament of Baptism impudently Prophan'd'. In a later edition he wrote:'There is a curious band of fellows in the town who call themselves "Mollies" (effeminates, weaklings) who are so totally destitute of all masculine attributes that they prefer to behave as women. They adopt all the small vanities natural to the feminine sex to such an extent that they will try to speak, walk, chatter, shriek and scold as women do, aping them as well in other respects.'

In May 1726 the *London Journal* wrote of twenty 'Sodomitical Clubs' where 'they make their execrable Bargains, and then withdraw into some dark Corners to perpetrate their odious Wickedness'. These 'clubs' included Mother Clap's in Holborn, where there were beds in every room with 'commonly thirty to forty Chaps every night – and even more – especially on Sunday Nights'. The Talbot Inn in the Strand was another haunt, as were even the 'Bog-Houses' of Lincoln's Inn.

The moral obloquy could result in tragedy. There was 'a tremendous upsurge in sodomy' around the beginning of the eighteenth century, and in 1707 a raid on a 'Buggerantoes' Club' in the City caused a great scandal. About forty men were arrested, including the respected Cheapside mercer Jacob Ecclestone, who later committed suicide in Newgate. Another respected City figure, the Cheapside draper William Grant, hanged himself there, and the curate of St Dunstan's-in-the-East, a Mr Jermain, cut his throat with his razor, as did another merchant, a Mr Bearden. Several others also committed suicide before the case came to trial. All these men frequented the alleys around the Royal Exchange. The favourite meeting place was Pope's Head Alley. In nearby Sweetings Alley the 'breeches-clad bawds' congregated.

The pillory was particularly dangerous for homosexuals. In October 1764 the *Public Advertiser* reported:'A bugger aged sixty was put in the Cheapside Pillory ... the Mob tore off his clothes, pelted him with Filth, whipt him almost to Death ... he was naked and covered with Dung ... when the Hour was up he was carried almost unconscious back to Newgate.'

In such a moral climate blackmail was inevitable. In September 1724 a young man walking in the streets was accosted by a man who seized him and cried out, 'A sodomite! A sodomite!' The terrified young man was advised by a passing 'gentleman' who was really the blackmailer's accomplice to give his accuser 5 or 6 guineas. When he protested that he did not have the money the two older men followed him to the place where he worked but were driven off by one of the young man's colleagues, who drew his sword. The blackmailers ran off, 'leaving the boy prostrate with shock'. In January 1725 two men were found guilty of a similar attempt at blackmail, and were sentenced to 'two hours on Tower Hill Pillory, two hours on the Cheapside Pillory, a fine of Twenty pounds and six months in Newgate'.

Some men caught *in flagrante* were lucky to escape with their lives. One such was John Dicks, who picked up a young boy and took him to alehouses where he got him drunk. He buggered the boy in the yard behind the Golden Ball in Fetter Lane. When a pot-boy who heard the commotion went to see what was going on Dicks attempted to bugger him as well, and the landlord caught him 'in the very act of buggery'. It was 1722, a year in which there had already been a spate of prosecutions, and fearing the worst Dicks pleaded with the landlord not to report him, 'for if you swear against me you swear away my life'. His entreaties ignored, Dicks was found guilty of attempted sodomy, fined 20 marks, stood in the Temple Bar pillory for an hour and sent to Newgate for two years.

Women streetwalkers, for whom life was hard at the best of times, protested at the unwanted competition:

How Happy were the good old English Faces
'til Mounsieur from France taught PEGO a Dance
to the tune of Old Sodom's Embraces.
But now WE are quite out of Fashion.
Poor whores may be NUNS, since MEN turn their GUNS
And vent on each other their Passion.
But now, we find to our Sorrow we are over-run
By the Parks of the BUM
and Peers of the Land of Gomorrah!

Mother Clap's mollies' house in Holborn was one of the biggest and most notorious. In 1726 the Society for the Reform of Manners targeted her. She was found guilty of keeping a 'sodomitical house' and put in the pillory at Smithfield. Three of her prostitutes were hanged. One of the witnesses for the prosecution was Samuel Stephens:

> *Stephens*: On Sunday night, the 14th November last, I went to the prisoner's house in Field Lane, in Holborn, where I found between 40 and 50 men making love to one another, as they called it. Sometimes they would sit in one another's laps, kissing in a lewd manner and using their hands indecently. Then they would get up, dance and make curtsies, and mimic the voices of women. 'O, Fie, Sir! —— Pray, Sir —— Dear, Sir, —— Lord, how can you serve me so? —— I swear I'll cry out. —— You're a wicked devil, —— and you've a bold face. —— Eh, you dear little toad! Come, buss!' —— Then they'd hug, and play, and toy, and go out by couples into another room on the same floor, to be married, as they called it. The door of that room was kept by —— Eccleston, who used to stand pimp for 'em, to prevent anybody from disturbing them in their diversions. When they came out they used to brag, in plain terms, of what they had been doing. As for the prisoner, she was present all the time, except when she went out to fetch liquors. There was among them William Griffin, who has since been hanged for sodomy; and —— Derwin, who had been carried before Sir George Mertins, for sodomitical practices with a link-boy. . . . I went to the same house on two or three Sunday nights following, and found much the same practices as before. The company talked all manner of gross and vile obscenity in the prisoner's hearing, and she appeared to be wonderfully pleased with it.

The court heard from one of the young catamites, Edward Courteney, about another mollies' house, the Royal Oak in Pall Mall. Courteney described several rooms at the back of the tavern which were used by homosexuals who acted as married couples. The landlord had 'put the bite on him' to go with a country gentleman who promised to pay him handsomely. He 'stayed all night but in the morning he gave me no more than a sixpence'.

The fury of the mob was vented even on those found innocent. After a 'club of paederasts' was raided at the Bunch of Grapes in Clare Market eighteen members appeared in court wearing women's clothes. They were found not guilty for lack of evidence, but as they left the court they had to run the gauntlet of a large crowd which had gathered outside. Handcuffed together, they could do little to protect themselves from a storm of stones and filth hurled by these vindictive spectators.

In 1814 Robert Holloway published *The Phoenix of Sodom: or, the Vere Street Coterie* about the notorious male homosexual brothel at the White Swan in the street running north from Oxford Street. Holloway's book gives a description of the interior of the brothel:

> The fatal house in question was furnished in a style most appropriate to the purposes it was intended. Four beds were provided in one room: —— another was fitted up for the ladies' dressing-room, with a toilette and every appendage of rouge, &c. &c.: a third room was called the Chapel, where marriages took place, sometimes between a female grenadier, six feet high, and a *petit maître* not more than half the altitude of his beloved wife! These marriages were solemnised with all the mockery of bride maids and bride men; and the nuptials were frequently consummated by two, three or four couples, in the same room, and in the sight of each other! . . . Men of rank and respectable situations in life might be seen wallowing either in or on the beds with wretches of the lowest description. . . . Sunday was the general, and grand day of rendezvous! and to render their excuse the more entangled and doubtful, some of the parties came from a great distance . . . to join the festivity and elegant amusements of grenadiers, footmen, waiters . . . and all the Catamite Brood. . . .

In July 1810 officers from Bow Street, backed by a unit of troops, raided the premises and twenty-three people were arrested. Seven of them were sentenced to terms ranging from one to three years' imprisonment. They also had to endure a brief spell in the pillory. Here is a contemporary newspaper report of their ordeal, both in the pillory and travelling to and from it.

> The miscreants were then brought out and placed in the caravan; Amos began a laugh, which induced his vile companions to reprove him, and they all sat upright apparently in a composed state, but having cast their eyes upwards, the sight of the spectators on the tops of the houses operated strongly on their fears, and they soon appeared to feel terror and dismay. . . .

MADAMS: BAWDS & BROTHEL-KEEPERS of LONDON

The mob, and particularly the women, had piled up balls of mud to afford the objects of their indignation a warm reception ... when the prisoners passed the old house which once belonged to the notorious Jonathan Wild they resembled beasts dipped in a stagnant pool. The shower of mud continued during their passage to the Haymarket. Before they reached half-way to the scene of their exposure they were not discernible as human beings. ...

At 1 o'clock four of them were exalted on the new pillory made purposely for their accommodation. ... Their faces were completely disfigured by blows and mud; and before they mounted their persons appeared one heap of filth.

Upwards of fifty women were permitted to stand in a ring who assailed them incessantly with mud, dead cats, rotten eggs, potatoes and buckets of grub, offal and dung which were brought by a number of butchers' men from St James's Market. ... When the hour was expired they were again put in the cart and conveyed to Coldbath Fields Prison. ... When they were taken from the pillory the butchers' men and the women who had been so active were plentifully regaled with gin and beer procured from a subscription made on the spot. In a few minutes the remaining two, Cook ... and Amos ... were desired to mount. Cook held his hands to his head and complained of the blows he had already received; and Amos made much the same complaint and showed a large brickbat which had struck him in the face.

Cook said nothing but Amos ... declared in the most solemn manner that he was innocent; but it was vouchsafed from all quarters that he had been convicted before and in one minute they appeared a complete heap of mud and their faces were much more battered than those of the former four. Cook received several hits in his face and had a lump raised upon his eyebrow as large as an egg. Amos's two eyes were completely closed up; and when they were untied Cook appeared almost insensible, and it was necessary to help them both down and into the cart when they were conveyed to Newgate by the same road they had come and in their passage they continued to receive the same salutations the spectators had given them on their way out. As they passed the end of Panton Street, Strand, on their return a coachman stood up in his box and gave Cook five or six cuts with his whip (*Morning Herald*, 28 September 1810).

Some of the women who took such a prominent part in the wretches' torment may have been streetwalkers. Henriques suggests that 'highly placed male homosexuals may possibly have fomented the feelings of the mob' to conceal their own complicity (1962–8, Vol. 3).

A prominent member of the Vere Street coterie was the notorious preacher the Revd John Church. Holloway's book didn't mention him, but he was pictured on the front cover. He officiated at transvestite weddings and at funerals of men executed for sodomy and his sermons were so popular that in 1813 he moved from his Obelisk chapel in Vere Street to larger premises. In 1817 he was jailed for two years for attempting to sodomise an apprentice potter named Adam Foreman. The lad told the Old Bailey that he woke one night after someone took hold of him 'very tight'. When he asked who it was the man replied, 'Don't you know me, Adam? It is your mistress.' A man named Clarke, whose son had been seduced by Church, recognised the picture on the cover of Holloway's book. Clarke armed himself with a brace of pistols and confronted Church. However, the excitement proved too much for Clarke and he fainted before he could fire a shot.

Church had a history of homosexual affairs before arriving in London in the early 1800s. In 1808, after the 25-year-old clergyman had been appointed rector at Banbury in Oxfordshire he was accused of seducing a string of men. He replied: 'If there was anything of which you speak, it must have been when I was asleep and supposing that I was in bed with my wife.'

The subject of homosexuality was virtually taboo among middle-class Victorians, which may account for the muddle and misunderstanding which surrounded a celebrated case, that of Boulton and Park, transvestites who in 1871 were charged with 'conspiring and inciting persons to commit an unnatural offence'. Ernest Boulton worked at a stockbroker's, his friend Frederick Park was articled to a solicitor. Four other men were charged with them: three failed to appear for trial, and the fourth, Lord Arthur Clinton, son of the Duke of Newcastle, committed suicide before it began. For some reason officialdom decided to make an example of Boulton and Park, and the prosecution was led by the Attorney General and the Solicitor General. The court was told that the two defendants had been seen dressed as women in the Alhambra in Leicester Square, in the Surrey Theatre and the Burlington Arcade. A man called Cox had flirted with Boulton in a public house, believing him to be a woman. He told how he had kissed 'him, she or it'. When he discovered the truth he confronted Boulton and Lord Arthur Clinton in Evans's in Covent Garden, saying: 'You damned set of infernal scoundrels, you ought to be kicked out of this place.'

After they were arrested Boulton and Park were examined by a police surgeon. He paid particular attention to their anuses, a fact which incensed the judge, who asked him if he had thought of getting permission from a magistrate first. The surgeon replied: 'No, my lord, I never wait for a magistrate's order in any case.' Summing up, the judge said that if the surgeon had behaved like that with two strong instead of two effeminate men he might have got the beating he deserved. At the same time the judge condemned the behaviour of Boulton and Park as outrageous. In an outburst which suggests the uncertainty of male self-confidence he said: 'When it is done even as a frolic, it ought to be the subject of severe and summary punishment. . . . If the law cannot reach it as it is, it ought to be made the subject of . . . legislation, and a punishment of two or three months' imprisonment, with the treadmill attached to it, with, in the case of a repetition of the offence, a little wholesome corporal discipline, would, I think, be effective, not only in such cases, but in all cases of outrage against public decency.' The jury took a less extreme view of the affair, and found Boulton and Park not guilty after considering their verdicts for less than an hour.

The attitude of the Establishment to the foibles of Boulton and Park did not bode well for Oscar Wilde when he faced trial for gross indecency in 1895. Wilde's homosexuality was commonly known, but his plays and children's stories were so loved that he would probably have been safe had he not provoked the authorities with his contempt for conventional morality. His intimate relationship with Lord Alfred Douglas, who was fifteen years his junior, infuriated Douglas's father, the violent and unstable Marquess of Queensberry. When the Marquess left his card at Wilde's club accusing him of being a sodomite Wilde sued for libel. Unfortunately, his wit and flippancy worked against him, he lost the case and was arrested and tried for homosexuality. The court heard revelations about a homosexual brothel in

Little College Street, Westminster, with rooms 'with their heavily draped windows, their candles burning on through the day, and their languorous atmosphere heavy with perfume'. Wilde got two years' hard labour, and W.T. Stead commented: 'Should everyone found guilty of Oscar Wilde's crime be in prison, there would be a very surprising immigration from Eton, Harrow, Rugby and Winchester to the jails. . . .'

The Criminal Law Amendment Act of 1885 had made almost any sexual contact between males a serious criminal offence, and made blackmail easier. It was called a 'blackmailer's charter' at the time, and men who could face prison if convicted of what had hitherto been overlooked were now in real danger of falling victim to extortion.

The Wolfenden Report of 1957 led to changes in the law ten years later, making homosexual acts between consenting adult men legal if they took place in private. (Homosexual acts between women have never been illegal.) This ended the scandal of police officers hanging around public toilets in the hope of catching homosexuals in the act, or even enticing them.

APPENDIX II

THE ENGLISH VICE

Foreigners have long been amused and amazed by the English addiction to flagellation. After she came to work in London in the 1930s, Marthe Watts, accustomed to continental habits, was astonished at the number of Englishmen who wanted her to thrash them. It has often been suggested that the *vice anglais* owes much to the prevalence of caning in public schools. In Thomas Shadwell's 1676 play *The Virtuoso* one character explains his addiction to the habit: 'I was so us'd to't at Westminster School I could never leave it off since.' Swinburne was thrashed at Eton, and emerged uninterested in normal sexual relations. London was the world capital for flagellation, and so popular were houses specialising in the practice in the nineteenth century that one madam, Mrs Theresa Berkely, was reputed to have made £10,000 in eight years.

The book *Venus School Mistress*, published in 1830 with a preface by another madam, Mary Wilson, and devoted wholly to flagellation, gives an account of Mrs Berkely and her establishment at 28 Charlotte Street. Wilson says that she is giving up her own whipping establishment in St Pancras, and suggests that her patrons could do worse than try the delights of Mrs Berkely's. Interestingly, she indicates that flagellation has psycho-therapeutic value. 'She [Mrs Berkely] is a clever, pleasing, and trustworthy woman, in the prime of life, and perfectly mistress of her business. She is an excellent *ontologist*, and therefore quite *au fait* in treating the *aberrations* of the human mind. Her museum of natural and artificial curiosities and her collection of "*Illustrations de arcanis Veneris et amoris*" are by far the most extensive to be found in any similar institution.' *Venus School Mistress* lists Mrs Berkely's extraordinary equipment:

Her instruments of torture were more numerous than those of any other governess. Her supply of birch was extensive, and kept in water so that it was always green and pliant; she had shafts with a dozen whip thongs on each of them; a dozen different sizes of thin bending canes; leather straps like coach trades; battledoors, made of thick sole-leather, with inch-nails run through to docket and curry-comb tough hides rendered callous by many years' flagellation. Holly brushes, furze brushes, a prickly evergreen called butcher's brush; and during the summer, glass and china vases, filled with a constant supply of green nettles, with which she often restored the dead to life. Thus, at her shop, whoever went with plenty of money could be birched, whipped, fustigated, scourged, needle-pricked, half-hung, holly-brushed, furze-brushed, butcher-brushed, stinging-nettled, curry-combed, phlebotomised and tortured. . . .

Sadists who preferred to scourge rather than be scourged could whip Mrs Berkely, as long as they paid a large fee and were not too violent. For those who wanted to inflict serious pain she kept a number of strong women to play victim.

Mrs Berkely's greatest claim to fame was the Berkely Horse. This remarkable contraption on which she could flog her clients was invented in 1828. The *Venus School Mistress* says:

It is capable of being opened to a considerable extent, so as to bring the body to any angle that might be desirable. There is a print in Mrs Berkely's memoirs, representing a man upon it quite naked. A woman is sitting in a chair exactly under it, with her bosom, belly and bush exposed she is manualizing his embolon, while Mrs Berkely is birching his posteriors. . . . When the new flogging machine was invented the designer told her that it would bring her into notice, and go by her name after her death; and it did cause her to be talked about, and brought her a great deal of business. . . . Mrs Berkely also had in her second floor, a hook and pulley attached to the ceiling by which she could draw a man up by the hands. . . .

Mrs Berkely died in 1836 and her brother, who had been a missionary in Australia for thirty years, returned to claim her fortune as his inheritance. When he learned how she had earned it, however, he renounced his claim and returned to Australia. Mrs Berkely's executor, a Dr Vance, refused to administer the estate and the wages of sin became the property of the Crown. The Berkely Horse was given to the Royal Society of Arts.

Another famous whipping establishment was Mrs Colet's in Covent Garden, established about 1766, among whose clients was said to be the Prince Regent. 'It is not known whether the Royal Wrist wielded the whip or whether the Royal Buttocks submitted to it!' Nicky Roberts writes in *Whores in History*. 'Such was the fever for scourging during this period that "Chace Pine [a roué] devised a machine which could whip forty persons at a time."' Other women who kept whipping establishments included Mrs Colett's niece Mrs Mitchell, whose place of business was first in Waterloo Road and later in Kennington. According to Henriques (1962–8, Vol. 2), Mrs James of Carlisle Street, Soho made enough money to retire to 'jewelled splendour' in Notting Hill.

Mary Wilson, proprietor of the Eleusinian Institution, wrote extensively about men's addiction to flagellation, and classified the different types drawn to this form of masochism:

1. Those who like to receive a fustigation, more or less severe from the hands of a fine woman, who is sufficiently robust to wield the rod with vigour and effect.

2. Those who desire to administer birch discipline on the white and plump buttocks of a female.

3. Those who neither wish to be passive recipients nor active administrators of birch discipline, but derive sufficient excitement as mere spectators of the sport.

Miss Wilson makes it clear that the taste for flagellation is not confined to the elderly debauchee or worn-out roué.

Many persons not sufficiently acquainted with human nature, and the ways of the world, are apt to imagine that the *lech* for Flagellation must be confined either to the aged, or those who are exhausted through too great devotion to venery: but such is not the fact, for there are quite as many young men and men in the prime and vigour of life, who are influenced by this passion as there are amongst the aged and the debilitated.

It is very true that there are innumerable old generals, admirals, colonels and captains, as well as bishops, judges, barristers, lords, commoners and physicians, who periodically go to be whipped, merely because it warms their blood, and keeps up a little agreeable excitement in their systems long after the power of enjoying the opposite sex has failed them; but it is equally true, that hundreds of young men through having been educated at institutions where the masters are fond of administering birch discipline, and recollecting certain sensations produced by it, have imbibed a passion for it, and have longed to receive the same chastisement from the hands of a fine woman. . . .

Miss Wilson goes on to say that the expert flagellant or governess would have learned her skills from some older practitioner of the art. 'It is not merely keeping a rod, and being willing to flog, that would cause a woman to be visited by the worshippers of birch.' She mentions some of the teachers, including 'the late Mrs Jones, of Hertford Street and London Street, Fitzroy Square; such was the late Mrs Berkely, such is Betty Burgess of York Square, and such is Mrs Pryce, of Burton Crescent . . .'.

One of Mrs Berkely's most famous successors was Sarah Potter, alias Stewart. At various times she had establishments, including brothels specialising in flagellation, in Castle Street off Leicester Square, Wardour Street, Albion Terrace off the King's Road, Howland Street off Tottenham Court Road, the Old Kent Road and eventually, before her death in 1873, in Lavinia Grove, King's Cross. She was arrested in 1873 and a pamphlet gave the following account of her business:

Under the auspices of the Society for the Protection of Females, seizure was made at the then notorious 'Academy' of Sarah Potter, alias Stewart, in Wardour Street, and a rare collection of Flagellation appurtenances taken to the Westminster Police Court when the general public for the first time became aware that young females were decoyed into Stewart's School of Flogging, to undergo the ordeal of the birch from old and young Flagellists, for the benefit of the woman Stewart. These curious specimens of her stock-in-trade consisted of a folding ladder, with straps, birch rods, furze brooms and secret implements, for the use of male and female.

Her method of conducting business was to get hold of young girls, board, lodge and clothe them, and in return they were obliged to administer to the lusts of the patrons of the boarding-house. They were flogged in different ways. Sometimes strapped to the ladder, at others they were flogged round the room – at times they were laid on the bed. Every device or variation which perverted ingenuity could devise was resorted to to give variety to the orgies, in return for which the mistress of the house was paid sums varying from £5 to £15. The profits of this school enabled Stewart to keep a country house and a fancy man, to the great scandal of the community.

The case against Mrs Potter/Stewart was brought by a girl of 'about fifteen', Agnes Thompson, at the instigation of the Society for the Protection of Females and Young Women. Agnes said that a year previously she had gone with a man to a house where he had 'effected her ruin'. Since then she had worked for Mrs Potter at the Albion Terrace address. She said: 'I was flogged by gentlemen with birch rods. I was beaten on my naked flesh.' She described an occasion when she was whipped by a man called 'Sealskin' and another known as 'The Count'. During this ordeal she had been tied to the ladder which was produced in court. Two other girls, Catherine Kennedy, who was seventeen, and Alice Smith, described in a report in *Lloyd's Weekly London Gazette* as 'a young woman of considerable personal attractions', told of similar floggings. Smith said she was not paid for her services. Mrs Potter was found guilty and sent to prison. However, she cannot have been a bad mistress, for Agnes Thompson returned to her when she was released and worked for her for some time. Mrs Potter died in 1873 'and is commemorated by an imposing tombstone in Kensal Green Cemetery' (Thomas, 1998).

Flogging in schools has often been blamed for the Englishman's addiction to flagellation, but girls were also whipped. The London magazine *Society* had a long correspondence on the subject. 'Your correspondents often ask whether corporal punishment is still in force in the better class girls' schools. I can assure you that it does still exist. . . . Others of our better class girls' schools use the old-fashioned canes, sticks and scourges, sometimes on the upper and sometimes on the lower parts of the body' (Henriques, 1962–8, Vol. 3). This magazine also carried correspondence on the merits of chastisement in marriage. 'With my whole heart I endorse the opinion of your correspondent with regard to the reciprocal punishment of man and wife; family discords of many sorts can easily be avoided thereby. . . . There is a unique attraction in whipping one's wife or being whipped by her hand. I hope a time will come when all quarrels will be settled by the hand.'

The fact that girl apprentices in trades such as bonnet-making and millinery were whipped and that the public whipping of women was not abolished until 1817 leads Henriques to conclude that 'a definite tradition of flagellation existed in Britain over a long period, and this tradition helps to explain the addiction which characterised so many of the prostitutes' clients in the nineteenth century.' The poet Algernon Charles Swinburne was addicted to flagellation. He would go to 7 Circus Road, St John's Wood, to be flogged by two matronly dames, rouged and golden-haired. He was also a secret pornographer with an obsession with Queen Victoria, about whom he wrote obscene fantasies and verses. His *La Soeur de la Reine*, about Queen Victoria's twin sister, a Haymarket prostitute, is splendidly subversive. The Queen herself is subject to ungovernable passion and copulates with William Wordsworth and 'Peel'. Pearsall (*Worm in the Bud*) quotes one of Swinburne's obscene verses:

This is a dildo the Queen used
Once in a pinch in an office,
Quite unaware it had *been* used
First, by a housemaid erratic.
Soon, though obese and lymphatic,
Symptoms she felt all that month as it went on
What sort of parties had used it and spent on.

APPENDIX III

PROSTITUTES' PRICES

What prostitutes charged tended to fluctuate widely, and depended on supply and demand. When young women were flooding into the capital in a vain search for work many swelled the flocks of street-walkers and the increase in availability depressed rates. It also seems clear that prices rose and fell according to the state of the economy. They were probably never higher than in the middle years of the eighteenth century, when some London courtesans charged the equivalent of thousands of pounds for a night's pleasure. Further down the scale they were almost arbitrary. The going rate for what Pepys called a 'bout' was 6d in the country and up to 20d in the city. In *The Road to Tyburn* (1957) Christopher Hibbert writes that eighteenth-century street prostitutes, many of them little more than children, would hire out their bodies for 6d. James Boswell (1740–95) wrote of 'the splendid Madam at fifty guineas a night down to the civil nymph with white thread stockings who tramps along the Strand and will resign her engaging person for a pint of wine and a shilling'. On several occasions he found the latter best suited to his pocket. A better guide to average prices in the mid-eighteenth century is Harris's *List of Covent Garden Ladies*, where the eighty or so women who advertised in one edition charged an average of 2 guineas – about two weeks' wages for a working man. Again, it must be remembered that the women in Harris's *List* were either at the top of the profession, or near it. Casanova wrote of 'a magnificent debauch' in a Covent Garden bagnio costing him 6 guineas, but the average price may have been more than 10 guineas. On the other hand, the wretched sailors' women of the Ratcliffe Highway brothels might have to settle for a few pence, or even a glass of wine.

A Victorian prostitute called Swindling Sal, interviewed by Henry Mayhew for his *London Labour and the London Poor*, got as much as £5 or as little as a few shillings, depending on what the customer could afford. The author known as Walter, who left an account of his encounters with hundreds of prostitutes (*My Secret Life*) would pay widely different rates according to the state of his finances. When they were low he often paid 5s. When he could afford it he would pay a guinea, although he said 10s would get 'as nice a one as was needed' from among the streetwalkers. Some high-class streetwalkers earned between £20 and £30 a week (Pearsall, 1969). According to the historian Judith Walkowitz, in Victorian times West End streetwalkers could expect a pound and upwards 'from well-heeled customers'.

Prices declined in the twentieth century. The gangster Arthur Harding described in *East End Underworld* the rates charged by local girls in about 1900:

> There were two kinds of girl. Those who went up West and mixed with the toffs. They would get as much as ten shillings a time or even £1 and they would ride home in hansom cabs . . . the girls who stayed at Spitalfields were very poor. That was what you called a 'fourpenny touch' or a 'knee trembler' — they wouldn't stay with you all night. . . . Even if you stayed all night with girls like that it was only a couple of shillings.

After the First World War wages fell rapidly and many of the women who had been attracted to prostitution during the conflict could no longer find customers. In the 1930s when the average wage was about £3 5s street prostitutes in the better areas of the West End were charging 10s or £1, which was more than most men could afford. During the Second World War girls in London were charging servicemen up to £5 for ten minutes, which was thought high.

In the 1950s police who arrested a Soho prostitute's pimp found a notebook kept by the woman's maid. In it were day-by-day records of the prostitute's earnings. These showed that in a six-hour period each night she would have about thirty customers. Her income over twenty days was nearly £1,000 – amounting to an enormous tax-free annual income of around £18,000. The prostitute Edna Kallman giving evidence in the Attilio Messina trial in 1959 informed the court that over a period of eight years she had earned about £40,000 working her beat in New Bond Street.

By the 1960s, when the Street Offences Act had come into force and prostitutes faced higher fines by the courts, streetwalkers in Mayfair were charging between £5 and £10 for brief sex, in Soho the range was between £4 and £6 and the girls in South Kensington, Maida Vale and Bayswater were said to be charging from £3 to £5. Girls in Hyde Park charged £1 for sex standing up, and £2 for it lying down. The Hyde Park women also used taxis for sex, and charged between £2 and £3. Call-girls at the top of the profession were said to charge up to £50 for the night, and girls further down the scale up to £30. In 2001, women working at and around King's Cross charged around £30, roughly the equivalent of 33p at 1720 prices. A high proportion of the women on the streets in 2001 were drug addicts. In 2004 a court was told of a business-man who paid a call-girl £1,000 a night for her services.

NOTE ON SOURCES

The annals of bawdry are sparse, particularly for the Victorian period. The first biography we have of a noted bawd is that of Elizabeth Holland. *Holland's Leaguer*, published anonymously in 1632, has the intriguing subtitle, *An Historical Discourse of the Life and Actions of Dona Britannica Hollandia, the Arch Mistris of the Wicked Women of Eutopia, wherein is detected the notorious Sinne of Panderisme, and the Execrable Life of the luxurious Impudent.* Whether it delivers on this promise is hard to tell, as the style is so affected and dense the work is in parts almost unreadable, but it is the only source we have for her early life. There are other biographies of early bawds, including Anodyne Tanner's *Life of the Late Celebrated Elizabeth Wisebourn, Vulgarly called Mother Wybourn*. Margaret Leeson, a bawd with a sense of humour and a heart, left the immensely entertaining *Memoirs of Mrs Leeson, Madam*, a kiss-and-tell account of the Dublin sex industry in the middle of the eighteenth century. Much more common are lives of courtesans, of which the anonymous *Memoirs of the Celebrated Miss Fanny Murray* of 1759 is typical, that is to say informative and inaccurate. The *Nocturnal Revels*, of 1779, gives a useful if satirical overview of the sex industry. It is from the *Revels* that I have taken the list of prices at Charlotte Hayes's King's Place brothel, which is believed to reflect accurately the charges in a high-class establishment at the time. Guides to whores' charges and attractions long predate the cards now plastered all over phone boxes in central London. Around the turn of the sixteenth century, the astrologer and quack Simon Foreman (1552–1611) circulated a *Register of the Ladies of Love*, and between 1660 and 1663 John Garfield's *The Wand'ring Whore* informed the town of the doings of whores and bawds, among the latter Priss Fotheringham, Mother Cresswell and Mother Cunny. The most comprehensive and amusing of these guides is Jack Harris's *List of Covent Garden Ladies*. It first appeared in 1746, and Horace Walpole noted that it was 'an Exact Description of the Person, Temper and Accomplishments of the several Ladies of Pleasure who frequent Covent Garden and other Parts of the Metropolis'. The *List* was published regularly until Harris's death in 1766. Afterwards hack writers were employed to continue it, but it had lost its sparkle.

The diaries and memoirs of Pepys, Boswell and William Hickey are in their different ways invaluable guides either to the underworlds of vice or to the moral tone of their age, or to both. Hickey visited some of the best-known brothels, including Charlotte Hayes's. Ned Ward's *The London Spy* (1698–1700) describes the moral squalor of the city, and the cruel flogging of prostitutes in Bridewell. The now-forgotten Commodore Edward Thompson contributed the *Meretriciad*, a kind of verse gossip column on the doings of Lucy Cooper, Kitty Fisher and other women of pleasure, in about 1760. He later enlarged it and it went through at least eight editions. Thompson was a war hero and man of parts and his rough verse is amusing, if sometimes hard to follow. It would be interesting to know how he acquired his detailed knowledge of the demi-monde in a busy career which included preparing an edition of Marvell's works.

The Regency courtesan Harriette Wilson's dazzling memoirs are still worth reading. The mysterious Walter, whose *My Secret Life* chronicles his encounters with hundreds of women of pleasure, is an invaluable guide to various aspects of Victorian vice. Walter has never been satisfactorily identified. Shaw's *London in the Sixties* describes many of the high-class haunts of such women, including Mott's, Kate Hamilton's and the Argyll Rooms. It catches something of the dangerous glamour of upper-class gallantry in the mid-nineteenth century. The modern age is poorly served. The memoirs of the Messina whore and bawd Marthe Watts cover the war and postwar years. Fernando Henriques's three-volume *Prostitution and Society*, a comprehensive survey of vice through the ages, is still useful, as are, in their various ways, the books listed below. E.J. Burford's works on London vice from the Cromwellian period until the end of the Regency are a starting point for all writers on the subject, but are sometimes inaccurate in detail. I.M. Davis's *The Harlot and the*

Statesman is good on the upper reaches of the sex industry in the late eighteenth century, and Katie Hickman's recent *Courtesans*, a study of five women including Sophia Baddeley and Catherine Walters, is masterly. Horace Bleackley's *Ladies Fair and Frail* of 1909, a series of brief sketches of famous harlots including Fanny Murray, Kitty Fisher and Nancy Parsons, is useful, in particular for the bibliographies attached to each portrait. He lists newspaper references, and often specifies edition and page.

The most amusing and atmospheric, if unreliable, guides to vice in Hanoverian London are popular newspapers and journals. Before the blight of Victorian hypocrisy drove such topics underground there was great interest in upper-class gallantry, and the press fed it, often maliciously. Gossip columns were less accurate then than now – evidently libel was less of a problem. Newspapers would accept and print items sent in by readers without checking them. They would later print responses, also without checking them. The *Town and Country Magazine*, which ran from 1769 to 1797, carried erotic engravings and gossip of amatory and sexual adventures in high places. A very popular feature, said to have pushed the journal's circulation to an unlikely 14,000 copies per issue, was the 'Tête-à-Tête' series. This consisted of side-by-side engravings of a well-known woman, usually a courtesan, and a man, usually an important public figure. The accompanying text was sometimes well informed, sometimes out of date or even made up. Among those to feature in the 'Tête-à-Tête' series were the future Duke of Queensberry and his mistress the 'Contessa' della Rena, whose affair had in fact recently ended. Courtesans featured included Sophia Baddeley and Elizabeth Armistead. In Goldsmith's *She Stoops to Conquer* the absurd Mrs Hardcastle reads the 'Tête-à-Tête' series avidly to keep abreast of events in the capital. Anxiety about disclosures meant there were calls for its suppression, to which the magazine presciently replied that 'the suppressing of this publication would be depriving posterity of a very curious piece of biography'. Horace Walpole figured in it, and his friend the Revd William Cole wrote: 'Should such practices be allowed in any civilised country? It is carrying the liberty of the press to such an excess that it disquiets private families, and turns the head of the people.' Questions still very much alive today. The issue of February 1769 contains a description of Charlotte Hayes's brothel. The *Covent Garden Magazine* (1772–5) is interesting on sexual manners in high and low society. Its formula was copied, among others, by the *Rambler's Magazine, or the Annals of Gallantry, Glee, Pleasure and the Bon Ton* (1783–90). Daily newspapers were also a rich source of gossip about courtesans and their lovers. The *Public Advertiser*, *Morning Post* and, above all, the *Morning Herald* recorded their triumphs and disasters, their rise and fall, with sometimes a touching humanity you might not find in the popular press today. *Private Eye* was the twentieth century's equivalent, and a trawl through its archives shows that recent generations have been as scandal-prone as their forebears. The *News of the World* is proverbially the paper of record for sexual tittle-tattle.

BIBLIOGRAPHY

Anon., *A Genuine History of Sally Salisbury alias Mrs S. Prydden*, 1668

Anon., *The Genuine History of Mrs Sarah Pridden, usually called Sally Salisbury*

Anon., *The History of the Remarkable Lives and Action of Jonathan Wild, Thief-Taker, Joseph Blake alias Blueskin, Footpad, and John Sheppard, Housebreaker*, 1725

Anon., *The Life and Character of Moll King . . .*, 1747

Anon., LOW LIFE, *or, One half of the World knows not how the Other Half Lives, being a critical account of what is transacted by People of almost all Religions, Nations, Circumstances, and Sizes of Understanding, in the Twenty-four hours between Saturday-Night and Monday-Morning . . .*, 1752

Anon., *Memoirs of the Celebrated Miss Fanny Murray*, 1759

Anon., *Nocturnal Revels – The History of King's Place and other Modern Nunneries, by a Monk of the Order of St Francis*, 1779

Anon., *The Poor Whores' Complaint to the Apprentices of London*

Anon., *Some Authentic Memoirs of the Life of Colonel C——s, Rape Master of Great Britain*, 1730

Ackroyd, Peter, *Dickens' London*, Headline, 1987

—— *London the Biography*, Chatto & Windus, 2000

Acton, William, *Prostitution Considered in its Moral, Social and Sanitary Aspects . . .*, 1857

Archenholz, J. W. Von, *A Picture of England*, 1789

Bailey, Paul, *An English Madam: The Life and Work of Cynthia Payne*, Cape, 1982

Bartley, Paula, *Prostitution: Prevention and Reform in England, 1860–1914*, Routledge, 2000

Bleackley, Horace, *Ladies Fair and Frail*, Allen Lane, 1909

Bloch, Iwan, *Sexual Life in England Past and Present*, London, Francis Aldo, 1938

Booth, Charles, *Life and Labour of the People in London*, Macmillan & Co., 1902–3

Boswell, James, *London Journal*, 1763, ed. Frederick Pottle, Edinburgh University Press, 1991

Bristow, Edward J., *Vice and Vigilance: Purity Movements in Britain Since 1700*, Gill and Macmillan, Dublin, 1977

Brome, Vincent, *Havelock Ellis, Philosopher of Sex*, Routledge, 1979

Burford, E.J., *Wits, Wenchers and Wantons, London's Low Life: Covent Garden in the Eighteenth Century*, Robert Hale, 1986

—— *The Orrible Synne*, Calder & Boyars, 1973

—— *Royal St James's*, Robert Hale, 1988

—— *The Synfulle City*, 1990

—— and Wotton, Joy, *Private Vices, Public Virtues*, Robert Hale, 1995

Butler, Josephine, *Personal Reminiscences of a Great Crusade*, 1896

Cameron, David Kerr, *London's Pleasures*, Stroud, Sutton, 2001

Casanova, Giacomo, *History of My Life*, Baltimore, MD, Johns Hopkins University, 1997

Champly, Henri, *The Road to Shanghai*, 1934

Chancellor, E. Beresford, *The Lives of the Rakes*, Philip Allan, 1924

Chesney, Kellow, *The Victorian Underworld*, Penguin, 1991

Childs, J. Rives, *Casanova, A New Perspective*, Constable, 1989

Cleland, John, *Fanny Hill or Memoirs of a Woman of Pleasure*, Penguin reprint, 1985

Colquhoun, Patrick, *Treatise on the Police of the Metropolis*, 1796

Cunningham, Peter, *The Story of Nell Gwyn*, L. Owen, 1903

Davis, Godfrey, *The Early Stuarts*, Oxford, Clarendon Press, 1959

Davis, I.M., *The Harlot and the Statesman*, Kensal Press, 1986

Dawson, Nancy, *Authentic Memoirs of the Celebrated Miss Nancy Dawson*, 1762

Donaldson, William, *Brewer's Rogues, Villains and Eccentrics*, Cassell, 2002

Dormer, Joseph, *The Female Rake or a Modern Fine Lady*, 1763

Dryden, John, *Satire on the Players*, 1691

Dunton, John, *The HE-Strumpet, A Satyre on Sodomites*, 1707

Evelyn, John, *Diary*, ed. William Bray, 1951

Finch, B.E. and Green, Hugh, *Contraception through the Ages*, Owen, 1963

Fraser, Antonia, *The Weaker Vessel*, Mandarin, 1993

Garfield, John, *The Wand'ring Whore*, 1660–3

Geijer, Erik, *Impressions of England 1809–10*, trans. by Elizabeth Sprigge and C. Napier, 1932

Gramont, Comte de, *Memoirs*, ed. Horace Walpole, tr. 1714, rev. Sir W. Scott, 1814

Greenwood, James, *The Seven Curses of London*, 1869

—— *In Strange Company: The Notebook of a Roving Correspondent*, 1873

Hardman, Sir William, *A Mid-Victorian Pepys: The Letters and Memoirs of Sir William Hardman*, Cecil Palmer, 1923

Harris, Jack, *List of Covent Garden Ladies or the New Atlantis*, 1764

Harrison, Michael, *Fanfare of Strumpets*, W.H. Allen, 1971

Hazzlewood, Charlotte, *True and Entertaining History of Charlotte Lorraine, Afterwards Mrs Hazzlewood*, 1790

—— *Secret History of the Green Room*, 1795

Head, Richard, and Kirkman, Francis, *The English Rogue*, 1665

Henderson, Tony, *Disorderly Women in Eighteenth-century London*, Longman, 1999

Henriques, Fernando, *Prostitution and Society*, 3 vols, MacGibbon & Kee, 1962–8

Hibbert, Christopher, *The Road to Tyburn*, Longmans Green, 1957

—— *The Roots of Evil: A Social History of Crime and Punishment*, Weidenfeld & Nicolson, 1963

—— *George IV, Prince of Wales*, Longman, 1972

Hickey, William, *Memoirs*, reprinted 1948

Hickman, Katie, *Courtesans*, HarperCollins, 2003

Hickman, Tom, *The Sexual Century*, Carlton Books, 1999

Higgs, Mary, *Glimpse into the Abyss*, 1906

Holloway, Robert, *The Phoenix of Sodom: or, the Vere Street Coterie*, 1814

Huish, Robert, *Memoirs of George IV*, 1831

Inwood, Stephen, *A History of London*, Macmillan, 1998

Jesse, J.H., *Literary and Historical Memorials of London*, 1847

Johnstone, Julia, *Confessions of Julia Johnstone: written by herself in contradiction to the fables of Harriette Wilson*, 1825

Kelland, Gilbert, *Crime in London*, Bodley Head, 1986
Leeson, Margaret, *The Memoirs of Mrs Leeson, Madam*, ed. Mary Lyons, Dublin, Lilliput Press, 1995
Leslie, Anita, *Edwardians in Love*, Hutchinson, 1972
Low, Donald A., *The Regency Underworld*, Stroud, Sutton, 1999
Macauley, Thomas Babington, *History of England*, Heron Books, 1967
McCall, Andrew, *The Medieval Underworld*, 1977
McLynn, Frank, *Crime and Punishment in Eighteenth-century England*, Routledge, 1989
McMullan, John L., *The Canting Crew*, Rutgers University Press, 1984
Masters, Brian, *The Mistresses of Charles II*, Blond & Briggs, 1979
Matthews, R., *Prostitution in London: An Audit*, Middlesex University Press, 1997
May, Tiggey, Harocopos, Alex, and Turnbull, Paul J., *Selling Sex in the City*, South Bank University Faculty of Humanities and Social Study, 2001
Mayhew, Henry, Hemyng, Bracebridge, Binney John and Halliday, Andrew, *London Labour and the London Poor*, 1861–2
—— and Binney, John, *The Criminal Prisons of London . . .*, 1862
Meyrick, Kate, *Secrets of the 43*, John Long, 1933
Misson, H., *Memoirs and Observations of his Travels over England*, 1719
Moreton, Maria, *Memoirs of the Life of the Duke of Queensberry*
Murray, Venetia, *High Society in the Regency Period*, Penguin, 1998
Nead, Lynda, 'The Girl of the Period', *National Art Collections Fund Quarterly*, autumn 2001
O'Connell, Sheila, *London 1753*, British Museum Press, 2003
Pearsall, Ronald, *Worm in the Bud*, Weidenfeld & Nicolson, 1969
Pepys, Samuel, *Diary, 1660–8* ed. Robert Latham and William Matthews, HarperCollins, 1995
Picard, L., *Dr Johnson's London*, Weidenfeld & Nicolson, 2000
Playfair, Giles, *Six Studies in Hypocrisy*, Secker & Warburg, 1969
Porter, Roy, *English Society in the Eighteenth Century*, Pelican, 1990
—— *The Greatest Benefit to Mankind: A Medical History of Humanity from Antiquity to the Present*, Fontana Press, 1997
—— *London, A Social History*, Hamish Hamilton, 1994
Rees, Sian, *The Floating Brothel*, Headline, 2001

Roberts, Nickie, *Whores in History*, HarperCollins, 1992

Salgado, Gamini, *The Elizabethan Underworld*, Sutton, 1992

Samuel, Raphael, *East End Underworld. Chapters in the Life of Arthur Harding*, Routledge & Kegan Paul, 1981

Sanger, William, *A History of Prostitution*, New York, 1859

Saussure, César de, *A Foreign View of England in the Reigns of George I and George II*, London, 1902

Shaw, D., *London in the Sixties*, 1908

Shell, George, *The Whore's Rhetorick: Mrs Cresswell's Last Legacy*

Smithies, Edward, *Crime in Wartime*, George Allen, 1982

Stevens, George Alexander, *Adventures of a Speculist*, 1788

Stow, John, *The Survey of London*, 1598

Tanner, Anodyne, *Life of the Late Celebrated Elizabeth Wisebourn, Vulgarly called Mother Wybourn*, 1721

Thomas, Donald, *The Victorian Underworld*, John Murray, 1998

Thompson, Edward, *The Meretriciad, A Satire*, 1765 and 1770

Tobias, J.J., *Crime and Industrial Society in the Nineteenth Century*, Pelican, 1972

Tomkinson, Martin, *The Pornbrokers*, Virgin Books, 1982

Tristan, Flora, *Promenades dans Londres*, 1840

Uglow, Jenny, *Hogarth, A Life and a World*, Faber & Faber, 1997

Wagner, Peter, *Sexuality in Eighteenth-century Britain*, Manchester University Press, 1982

Walker, Captain C., *Authentic Memoirs of the Life, Intrigues and Adventures of the Celebrated Sally Salisbury*, 1723

Walkowitz, Judith R., *Prostitution and Victorian Society: Women, Class and the State*, Cambridge University Press, 1980

Waller, Maureen, *1700: Scenes from London Life*, Hodder & Stoughton, 2000

Ward, Edward, *The London Spy*, 1698–1709 (various edns)

Watts, Marthe, *The Men in My Life*, Christopher Johnson, 1960

Webb, Duncan, *Crime is My Business*, Frederick Muller, 1953

Weinreb, Ben and Hibbert, Christopher, *The London Encyclopaedia*, Papermac, 1993

Wilmot, John, Earl of Rochester, *A Panegyrick Upon Cumdums*, 1674

Wilson, A.N., *The Faber Book of London*, Faber & Faber, 1993

Wilson, Harriette, *Memoirs*, Folio Society, 1964
Wilson, J.H., *All The King's Ladies*, Chicago University Press, 1958
Wilson, Mary, *Exhibition of Female Flagellants*, 1777
Ziegler, Philip, *London at War*, Mandarin, 1996

INDEX

Gage, Viscount 99
Gainsborough, Thomas 131
Gambarini, Elizabeth 81
Garfield, John 29, 37, 40, 237
Garrick, David 104, 140
Gay, John 47, 55
George I 47, 168
George II 64, 99, 118, 136–8
George III 82, 83, 106, 133, 140
George IV 154, 156
  Prince of Wales/Regent 64, 76, 84,
  85–6, 147–150
Gerald, Queenie 202
Gideon, Sampson 66
Gladstone, William Ewart 163
Goadby, Jane 59, 78
Gonson, Sir John 53, 57, 61, 98, 175
Gordon, Lord William 70
Gould, Elizabeth 58, 61–2
Gower, Lord Granville Leveson 148, 150,
  152
Grafton, Duke of 131–2, 146
Gray, Mabel 196
Greenwood, James 193
Grey, Charles 150
Grosvenor, Lady Henrietta 70, 77, 143
Grosvenor, Lord 64, 77, 143
Gunning, Maria 134

Haddock, Elizabeth 48–9, 90
Haddock, Richard 48
Hamilton, Duke of 107
Hamilton, Emma, Lady 103, 169
Hamilton, Kate 188, 238
Hanger, John 139
Hanger, Sir William 72
Hansford, Phillis 176
Harding, Arthur 204
Harington, Sir John 26
Harrington, Countess of 75–6, 108
Harrington, Earl of 74–7, 141
Harris, Jack 57, 109–16, 129
  List of Covent Garden Ladies 71, 126, 139,
  233, 238
Hartington, Marquess of 160, 161–3
Hastings, Lord 189

Hayes, Charlotte 58, 62, 62–74, 78, 81, 91,
  126, 144, 170, 237–40
Haymarket 131–7, 157, 177, 187–191, 202,
  232
Hayward, Elizabeth 47, 48, 176
Hayward, Richard 37, 176
Head, Richard 41
Heidegger, John Jacob 46
Hellfire Club 68–9, 80
Hemyng, Bracebridge 187, 194
Henley, Robert (Lord Northington) 119,
  122
Henry VIII 217
Hervey, Lt Augustus 107
Hesketh, Elizabeth 79
Hickey, William 66, 79, 102, 104, 106, 125,
  144, 145, 238
Hinton, Moll 40
Hogarth, William 49, 51, 52, 56, 97–8,
  102–3, 116, 121–2, 166, 203
Holland, Elizabeth 17–30, 41, 63
Holland, Mary 40
Holloway, Robert 221
homosexual brothels 41, 217–27
Hunt, Leigh and John 150

introducing houses 152
Ireland/Irish 52–3, 78, 88–9, 110, 178, 183

Jack the Ripper 178–9
James I 23, 25, 27
James II (Duke of York) 35
Jarrett, Barbara 175
Jeffries, Mary 195–201
Jersey, Lady 150
Johnstone, Julia 153
Jones, Janie 212–3
Jones, Nancy 63
Jordan, Dorothea 83
Junius 131–3

Keep, Elizabeth 83
Kennedy, Kate 197
King, Moll 48, 49, 92–106, 176
King, Tom 95–7
King-Hamilton, Alan 213